Pursuing Human Strengths

A POSITIVE PSYCHOLOGY GUIDE

Pursuing Human Strengths

A POSITIVE PSYCHOLOGY GUIDE

Martin Bolt
Calvin College

■

Worth Publishers

Pursuing Human Strengths: A Positive Psychology Guide
© 2004 by Worth Publishers

Printed in the United States of America.
ISBN-13: 978-0-7167-0112-5
ISBN-10: 0-7167-0112-X

Fifth Printing

Acquisitions Editor: Marjorie Byers
Development Editor: Christine Brune
Project Editor: Kerry O'Shaughnessy
Associate Managing Editor: Tracey Kuehn
Marketing Manager: Katherine Nurre
Art Director: Babs Reingold
Cover and Text Design: Lissi Sigillo
Cover Illustration: Nicholas Wilton
Production Manager: Sarah Segal
Composition: Northeastern Graphic, Inc.
Printing and Binding: R.R. Donnelley

Library of Congress Control Number: 2004090094

Worth Publishers
41 Madison Avenue
New York, NY 10010
www.worthpublishers.com

To Nancy, a person of strength.

contents

preface

For more than a century, psychology's attention to human weaknesses outstripped its interest in human strengths. Research on anxiety and depression, hostility and conflict overshadowed studies of hope and joy, love and peace. But times change. In 1998, Martin Seligman, president of the American Psychological Association, called for a more positive psychology that would balance the investigation of weakness and damage with a study of strength and virtue. Positive psychology uses the scientific method in its efforts to assess, understand, and then build the human strengths. It aims to measure, understand, and foster the characteristics that make life most worth living (Seligman, 2002).

With this book I hope to provide a means for instructors and students to learn more about this exciting and relevant approach to psychology and, in the process, to learn more about themselves. In addition to providing an overview of the research related to each strength, I've interspersed numerous self-assessment exercises throughout the book so that students can gauge their own progress in building these characteristics. Each chapter concludes with a compilation of research-based suggestions for building one of the strengths. Positive psychologists assume that we are all capable of some change, and this assumption underlies my motivation in writing this book.

Where Does This Book Fit into the Introductory Psychology Course?

In utilizing the discipline's scientific methodology and diverse theoretical perspectives to study all dimensions of optimal human functioning, one could argue that positive psychology is simply psychology (Sheldon & King, 2001). Indeed, the nine human strengths covered in this brief book map well onto the organization of general psychology texts. For both teachers and students the topic of human flourishing provides an integrating theme for what sometimes seems to be a loosely connected collection of topics in the psychology course.

Here's an overview of how this book's specific chapters connect to psychology's key concepts, along with a summary of each chapter. You will see, for example, that Chapter 1, Love, reinforces important themes typically covered in developmental psychology, and Chapter 4, Wisdom, extends traditional coverage of thought and intelligence. Note that there are many other possible ways to connect this material to the psychology course, but this outline provides one valid way to begin. The Introduction presents positive psychology's central themes and provides a basis for working through the entire book, so you will want to read it first. Otherwise the chapters are self-contained units that may be read in any order and do not depend on one another for comprehension.

Introduction

This first chapter provides an overview of the themes of positive psychology and is a prelude to the rest of the book. This is the place to start regardless of how or where the rest of this book is being used. In this chapter we are reminded that psychology's major theoretical perspectives suggest that we are both creatures and creators of our world. The Introduction focuses on the many different factors that affect our thinking and behavior, but it emphasizes that those who think they can influence and control their world are more likely to initiate action, persist in pursuing goals, and attain more in virtually every area of life. This chapter introduces the core strength of responsibility, which is central to developing other strengths.

Chapter 1, Love

Both nature and nurture contribute to **human development.** This chapter specifically recognizes the interaction of heredity and environment in the formation of social bonds. Infant attachment styles carry over to adult relationships. Secure attachment in early life predicts social competence in adulthood. People not fortunate enough to have developed secure attachment styles can still change, and there are many ways to foster the closeness, care, and commitment common to all intimate bonds.

Chapter 2, Empathy

The organization and interpretation inherent in **perception** are evident in our social judgments. We tend to see people's behavior as reflecting their traits, and thus we often overlook their life situations. By assuming the perspective of others, we come to see what they see and to feel what they feel. This chapter reminds us that empathy enables us to live with greater purpose, and research suggests that empathy may promote genuine altruism. Positive psychologists recognize that assuming the perspective of those who have injured us represents a special challenge. Nonetheless, forgiveness is linked to well-being.

Chapter 3, Self-Control

The study of **learning** highlights the power of immediate rewards and helps us to understand the difficulties of self-control. Psychologists have examined the evolutionary, developmental, and cultural factors that are involved in resisting small, immediate rewards in favor of choosing more rewarding delayed outcomes. Contemporary cognitive theory emphasizes the importance of goal setting. Once a goal has been set, self-regulation reflects a process of feedback control. Recent research contributes to both the understanding of and possible solutions for a wide range of self-control problems.

Chapter 4, Wisdom

Research on **intelligence** shows that productive living requires more than academic aptitude. Recent studies of emotional and successful intelligence have expanded to a consideration of wisdom. People with wisdom have good judgment and offer sound advice in important but uncertain life situations. Wisdom researchers therefore ask people to reason about difficult life dilemmas. We see how wise people carefully balance their short- and long-term interests with those of others, are committed to values of truth and justice, and are keenly aware of the human capacity for self-deception.

Chapter 5, Commitment

Psychologists make an important distinction between intrinsic and extrinsic **motivation.** When important human strivings bring little immediate joy or satisfaction, commitment enables us to persevere in meeting basic needs for competence, relatedness, and autonomy. We will see how obligation merges with enthusiasm when our goals have lasting meaning or value. For example, when our work is a vocation, life is purposeful and satisfying.

Chapter 6, Happiness

After decades of focusing on negative **emotions,** psychologists are now also examining the positive emotions of joy, life satisfaction, and happiness. In considering important predictors of happiness, we learn how people's perceptions of their life situation often prove more important to their sense of well-being than objective circumstances. For example, the desire to maximize all of life's outcomes may foster feelings of regret. Savoring life's best moments facilitates a sense of well-being, and those who live gratefully are happier as well.

Chapter 7, Self-Respect

Personality theorists show how our self-understandings organize our thoughts and feelings. They debate the merits of high self-esteem. We see that examining where people find their self-worth helps us to understand the paradoxical links between self-esteem and behavior. Humble people have an awareness of their inherent value and are able to "forget themselves." They view their weaknesses and strengths realistically. By admitting pride, by seeking accurate feedback, and by taking a cosmic perspective, we cultivate healthy self-respect.

Chapter 8, Hope

Psychological disorders such as depression are often marked by a sense of hopelessness. **Therapy** works, in part, by restoring optimism and hope to demoralized people. Optimists seem to cope better with stressful life events and actually live longer than pessimists. Hopeful people have the motivation to keep moving toward their goals and the ability to generate routes to achieve them. This chapter reminds us that hope survives best in community. Hopeful people have a strong support network and join with others in the pursuit of collective well-being.

Chapter 9, Friendship

The study of friendship is central to **social psychology.** By providing social support, friends foster both our psychological and physical well-being. We see how people regard trust, honesty, and understanding as important features of their closest relationships. One careful analysis of friendship regards intimacy and caring as its core ingredients. Friends share a communal relationship in which they are mutually responsive to each other's needs.

Acknowledgments

All books, even those with one name on the cover, are cooperative efforts. First, my thanks go out to the community of scholars whose research instruments provide a significant portion of this book's content. By graciously permitting their work to be reproduced, they provide readers the opportunity to reflect on their own strengths and to engage in more active learning. Several instructors reviewed and pretested an early portion of the manuscript in their classrooms and provided helpful feedback and direction. For this special contribution, I am grateful to Charlie Blair-Broeker, Don Kober, Terry Lindenberg, Barbara Loverich, Scott Stehouwer, and Rick Straub. Special thanks are due to Jason Brune for skillfully collecting and analyzing the students' input.

My gratitude extends to the talented people at Worth Publishers for their central role in the creation and production of this book. Christine Brune, Development Editor, exemplified the strengths of wisdom, empathy, and commitment to excellence in helping me formulate the vision for this book. Her creativity, insight, and meticulous attention to detail vastly improved both my thinking and my writing. Every author should be as fortunate. Certain people were particularly instrumental in the early stages. Publisher Catherine Woods and Acquisitions Editor Marjorie Byers provided important encouragement and guidance in shaping the plan for the book. Associate Managing Editor Tracey Kuehn and Project Editor Kerry O'Shaughnessy efficiently coordinated editorial input and skillfully directed an outstanding production team. Penny Hull and Anna Paganelli's sensitive and timely copyediting polished the finished work. I am also grateful to others at Worth who made important contributions to this project. Art Director Babs Reingold and Designer Lissi Sigillo together crafted the book's unique cover and layout. Senior Production Manager Sarah Segal maintained a timely schedule. With patient persistence, Diane Kraut secured all permissions, and Alexandra Nickerson prepared the helpful index. The Worth team is truly superlative.

Several individuals read different portions of the manuscript and provided helpful feedback and support. My heartfelt thanks go out to John Brink, Nancy Bolt, Janet Sheeres, and Becky Shingledecker. Calvin College's granting of a sabbatical leave allowed me time to work on this project. Finally, Dave Myers first provided me with the opportunity to reach students beyond my own classroom. To him, I express my deep gratitude for his enduring friendship, strong encouragement, and constant support.

Calvin College
Grand Rapids, MI
bolm@calvin.edu

introduction

The stream of causation from past to future runs through our present choices.
—DAVID G. MYERS, 2002

Sometimes the worst times elicit the best from people. Consider a few remarkable displays of strength.

In 1940, Adolph Hitler ruled most of Europe. The Final Solution appeared on course. Sempo Sugihara, Japan's Consul General in Lithuania, seemed an unlikely roadblock. For 16 years he had provided loyal, obedient service in a variety of government posts. Sempo loved life's luxuries and was ambitious. His career goal? To become the Japanese ambassador to Russia. Nonetheless, when 200 Polish Jews gathered outside his door for help in fleeing the country, he responded. Twice he wired his home government to authorize travel visas. Rejected each time, he decided to prepare them anyway—knowingly throwing away his diplomatic career. And once started, Sempo didn't stop. Even after the consulate was shut down, he continued to write escape papers for the innocent—still frantically preparing travel visas on the train that was to take him back to Berlin. He saved thousands. For his insubordination, Sempo Sugihara lost his position. In fact, he was reduced to selling light bulbs after the war. Interviewed 45 years later about his rescue efforts, he simply said, "They were *human*, and they needed help." (Kenrick, Neuberg, & Cialdini, 2002, p. 304)

Two months after World War II ended, Margie Cooper, a 26-year-old mother of two young sons, was stricken with polio. Except for one resilient toe, she was paralyzed from the neck down. For four decades she lived without bitterness—even joyfully—in an iron lung. Her husband, John, accompanied her on this long journey with equal equanimity. For the first four years that his wife resided in polio wards, John projected home movies on the hospital room ceilings so she could watch her two sons grow up. When he moved Margie home in the iron lung, John became the operator of the life-sustaining bellows. Son Dale remembers his father's daily routine: "He'd fix her breakfast. He'd fluff up her hair. He'd turn the pages of a book. He'd turn on the TV, and he'd turn it off. His wife was his vocation." Telephoning on the couple's thirtieth wedding anniversary, a Chicago television producer was puzzled: "I can't imagine a guy sticking with his wife when she's got nothing to offer." John immediately replied, "I'm just keeping a promise." (Snapper, 2003, p. A6)

In spring 2003, hiker Aron Ralston found himself hopelessly pinned by a boulder that had rolled onto his arm in a remote Utah canyon. For three days he survived on some water, two burritos, and a few crumbs left in candy bar wrappers. On the fourth day he prepared his surgical table. He went through the motions of applying a tourniquet, laid out his hiking shorts to absorb blood, and in his mind worked out how to cut through his arm with a small pocket knife made dull by attempts to chip away at the rock. The next morning the operation began. "I was able to first snap the radius," he remembers, "and then within another few minutes snap the ulna at the wrist and from there, I had the knife out and applied the tourniquet and went to task. It was a process that took about an hour." Having finally freed himself, he crawled through the narrow winding canyon, rappelled down a 60-foot cliff, and walked some 6 miles before finally receiving help. Reflecting on his ordeal at a news conference a few days later, he reported, "I'm not sure how I handled it. I felt pain and I coped with it. I moved on." (Slevin, 2003, pp. A1, A11)

Compassion, commitment, self-control. What are the roots and fruits of human strengths such as these? And how do we foster them in ourselves and others?

After a century of studying human weakness and psychological disorder, psychology is refocusing its attention on the brighter side of human life—on the habits and motivations that underlie human flourishing. An increasing number of psychology researchers aim to create a more positive discipline by exploring optimal human functioning. "The main purpose of a positive psychology," suggests Martin Seligman (2002), "is to measure, understand, and then build the human strengths and the civic virtues." This book is not intended to be an exhaustive survey of this rapidly developing field. Rather, we will explore key directions in positive psychology research so that you may gain a broad understanding of this new approach and perhaps develop some more effective life skills as well. This chapter introduces central themes in the scientific pursuit of human strengths.

■

The Why of Human Behavior

Whether observing human vitality or vulnerability, virtue or vice, all of us are amateur psychologists who try to figure out others (Heider, 1958). Everyone forms a theory of human nature. Are people basically kind and compassionate, or are they selfish and pleasure seeking? Are they rational or irrational? Is each person unique, or are people easily categorized? Different answers to these questions create different psychological worlds that affect how we think, feel, and act.

Most important, like professional psychologists, we want to know the "why" of human behavior. We search for its underlying causes. Are the roots of human strengths such as self-control, commitment, and joy found in our genetic blueprint? Childhood environment? Current situation? Personal values and choices?

Searching for the "why" leads to the most important issue of all: How much control do we have over our thoughts, feelings, and behaviors? If people were shaped solely by heredity and past experience, it would be futile to try to develop strengths. If our motivations and behaviors were determined by forces beyond our control, it would make little sense to pursue "virtue" or "character." We regard people as acting responsibly only if they could have chosen to act differently.

Genetics and past experience are major contributors to human flourishing, but almost all of us have at least some capacity to choose, to change, and to control the direction of our lives. This book reflects the assumptions of most researchers in positive psychology—that people have the ability to build strengths such as wisdom, love, and hope in a self-directed manner.

IN REVIEW

Positive psychology aims to understand and build the human strengths in an effort to help people thrive. People tend to be curious about the underlying causes of both good and bad behaviors, and to wonder about how much control we really have over our behavior. Positive psychologists assume that people can choose, change, and control their life's direction, which validates efforts to build human strengths and foster civic virtues.

■

Human Freedom

We are not billiard balls. We value our sense of freedom and strive to be self-determining. But what does it mean to be "free"? Consider three key components: _choice_ (deciding life's direction), _change_ (altering one's typical behavior patterns), and _control_ (affecting life's outcomes).

1. Choice

Our experience tells us that we make choices. Indeed, decision making is life's wellspring. Consider Steven Pinker's (2002) thought experiment. Imagine for a moment not deliberating over your actions. After all, it's a waste of time; they have already all been determined anyway. Shoot from the hip, live for the moment, do what feels good. A moment's reflection on what would happen if you did try to give up decision making is illuminating: the experience of choosing is real, regardless of how the brain works or experience shapes us. You cannot step outside of choosing or let it continue without you because it _is_ you.

Here's a simple example from visual perception. Different sets of arrows move across the page in opposite directions. You can choose to see the arrows move to the right or you can choose to see them moving to the left. Try it. Make a choice. Does it work? *Right*

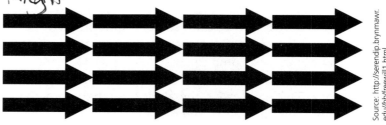

Source: http://serendip.brynmawr.edu/bb/freewill1.html.

We tend to value very highly a sense of freedom and we work hard to protect our capacity to choose. In fact, had I tried to dictate your choice by saying, "Now you must only see the arrows going to the left," you might well have decided, "No, I don't think so. I don't like being manipulated. I choose to see right-pointing arrows."

Imagine that someone stops you on the street and asks you to sign a petition advocating something you mildly support. As you reflect for a moment, you are told that someone else believes that "people absolutely should not be allowed to distribute or sign such petitions." How do you think you would respond? Might this blatant attempt to restrict your freedom actually increase the likelihood of your signing the petition? That is precisely what Madeline Heilman (1976) found when she staged this experiment on the streets of New York City.

Among dating couples, researchers have sometimes observed the *Romeo and Juliet effect*: the more the parents discourage the romance, the more love the partners feel for each other. Although the pattern is not inevitable, it does suggest that parents should think twice before they forbid teenagers to see each other (Brehm, Miller, Perlman, & Campbell, 2002).

This principle works in reverse as well. Try to coerce love and it's lost. Tell a child he *must* eat his favorite dessert, and the preferred food suddenly loses its flavor. Pressure to do what we already enjoy doing makes the activity less satisfying very quickly.

Consider Phil Zimbardo's amusing story of Nunzi, a shoemaker and an Italian immigrant (Middlebrook, 1974).

Every day after school, a gang of young American boys came to Nunzi's shop to taunt and to tease. After attempting a variety of strategies to get the boys to stop, Nunzi came upon a solution.

When the boys arrived the next day after school, Nunzi was in front of his store waving a fistful of dollar bills. "Don't ask me why," said Nunzi, "but I'll give each of you a new dollar bill if you will shout at the top of your lungs ten times: 'Nunzi is a dirty Italian swine. No greaseballs in our neighborhood.'" Taking the money, the boys shouted the chants in unison. The next afternoon Nunzi successfully enticed the gang to repeat their taunts for a mere half dollar. On the third day, however, he stood with a handful of dimes: "Business has not been good and I can only give you each ten cents to repeat your marvelous performance of yesterday."

"You must be crazy," said the ringleader, "to think we would knock ourselves out screaming and cursing for a lousy dime."

"Yeah," joined another, "we got better things to do with our time than to do favors for dumb guineas for only a dime." Away the boys went, never to bother Nunzi again.

Of course, when people *consistently* comply or defy—that is, conform to orders or do just the opposite—they are hardly free. *Autonomy* means acting with a sense of true choice. When autonomous, people embrace what they are doing with interest and commitment. They express their true selves (Deci, 1995). Autonomy, suggests Deci, is a fundamental human need. Is this need currently satisfied in your own life?

Total: 40

SELF-ASSESSMENT ■

Autonomy

Read each of the following statements carefully, thinking about how it relates to your life, and then indicate how true it is for you. Use the following scale to respond:

1	2	3	4	5	6	7
Not at all true			Somewhat true			Very true

7   **1.** I feel like I am free to decide for myself how to live my life.

3   **2.** I feel pressured in my life. 5

4   **3.** I generally feel free to express my ideas and opinions.

2   **4.** In my daily life, I frequently have to do what I am told. 6

6   **5.** People I interact with on a daily basis tend to take my feelings into consideration.

5   **6.** I feel like I can pretty much be myself in my daily situations.

1   **7.** There is not much opportunity for me to decide for myself how to do things in my daily life. 7

To score your responses for this and other self-assessment activities throughout this book, you will need to learn to use a simple reversal method that may seem odd at first. For this autonomy activity, you need to reverse the numbers you gave in answer to statements 2, 4, and 7. That is, if you answered with 1, change it to 7. If you responded with 2, change it to 6. Similarly, change 3 to 5, 4 remains 4, 5 becomes 3, 6 changes to 2, and 7 becomes 1. Make these changes only for statements 2, 4, and 7. Keep the numbers in front of statements 1, 3, 5, and 6 the same. Finally, add up the numbers in front of all seven items. Scores can range from 7 to 49, with higher scores indicating that you experience a greater sense of autonomy in everyday life. Scores above the midpoint of 28 suggest that you tend to feel that you are freely making choices; scores below that midpoint indicate that you do not.

Source: From the Basic Need Satisfaction in General Scale at http://psych.rochester.edu/SDT/measures/needs_scl.html. Currently being developed and researched by Dr. Richard M. Ryan, Department of Clinical and Social Sciences in Psychology, University of Rochester, Rochester, NY.

Just as restricting choice seems to undermine people's enjoyment of a task, so increasing alternatives often enhances it. Deci (1995) reports how, in one laboratory experiment, he and his colleagues varied their research participants' experience of freedom. In one group, subjects were offered a choice about which puzzles to work. In the other group, subjects were assigned puzzles. Subjects offered the simple choice spent more time playing with the puzzles and reported liking them more than participants not offered a choice.

Satisfying our need for autonomy, research suggests, is important to well-being and to personal achievement. It's a need we will come back to later in this book when we look at the factors that foster commitment.

2. Change

Can people change? Are they set, like plaster, or are they more pliable, like clay? Are our characteristics basically fixed, or are they malleable? What do you think? The following scale assesses the degree to which you believe people can change. _Entity theorists_ tend to think that human characteristics are fixed. *Incremental theorists* are inclined to believe that characteristics are malleable.

Total: 24 Entity Theory

SELF-ASSESSMENT ■

Entity Versus Incremental Theory

Using the scale, indicate the extent to which you agree or disagree with each statement by noting the number that corresponds to your opinion.

1 = strongly agree   2 = agree   3 = mostly agree   4 = mostly disagree
5 = disagree   6 = strongly disagree

2 **1.** The kind of person someone is, is something very basic and can't be changed very much.

4 **2.** People can do things differently, but the important parts of who they are can't really be changed.

3 **3.** Everyone, no matter who the person is, can significantly change his or her basic characteristics. **4**

_2_ **4.** As much as I hate to admit it, you can't teach an old dog new tricks. People can't really change their deepest attributes.

_4_ **5.** People can substantially change who they are. _3_

_3_ **6.** Everyone is a certain kind of person, and there is not much that can be done to really change that.

_4_ **7.** No matter what kind of person someone is, he or she can always change significantly. _3_

_4_ **8.** All people can change their most basic qualities. _3_

Source: Adapted from Dweck, 1999, pp. 179–180.

To obtain a total score, first reverse the numbers you placed in front of statements 3, 5, 7, and 8. (Change 1 to 6, 2 to 5, 3 to 4, 4 to 3, 5 to 2, and 6 to 1.) Then add up the numbers in front of all eight statements. Scores can range from 8 to 48. Scores below the midpoint of 28 reflect the belief that traits are fixed (entity theory); scores above 28 indicate the belief that traits are malleable (incremental theory).

Although people at all levels of education and from all walks of life advocate each perspective, our choice of theories does make a difference. It impacts how we think about and evaluate our own behavior, as well as how we perceive, judge, and relate to others. Most importantly, it affects our efforts at change.

In contrast to incremental theorists, entity theorists are more likely to think that a person's underlying character can be revealed by a single behavior or performance. This holds true for both good and bad behaviors. Entity theorists tend to believe that what they see on the outside reflects what people are like on the inside. What you see is what you get.

Taken to an extreme, this belief in a more stable social world seems to offer advantages. We could know others quickly and predict behavior more easily. If people were not mysterious, life would be simpler and more secure. Of course, in reality the world is not so simple. People are complex and don't fall neatly into the categories of those who have intelligence, self-control, and wisdom, and those who don't.

Perhaps most important, the two theories profoundly affect motivation and felt responsibility. If my traits are fixed, then there's not much I can do to change. I'm stuck with who I am. The best I can do is to validate what strengths I already have and hope that they will help me win approval and avoid rejection. There is no sense in trying to promote growth in others, either. They will remain who they are in spite of my best efforts.

On the other hand, incremental beliefs that portray a dynamic self and world see the potential and even the responsibility for improvement. This mindset encourages us to look for ways to grow, to solve our problems, and to remedy our weaknesses. It also encourages us to look for potential in others and help them to grow.

Consider how these two belief systems play out in a specific domain—intelligence—the one most studied by Carol Dweck.

The Nature of Intelligence

Complete the following equation (Mueller & Dweck, 1997):

Intelligence = __40__ % effort + __60__ % ability

Now imagine that you see a puzzle labeled "Test Your IQ!" in a science magazine. You work on it for a very long time, get confused, and start over. You make very slow progress but finally solve it. How do you feel? Do you feel sort of stupid because it required so much effort? Or do you feel smart because you worked hard and mastered it?

Source: Dweck, 1999, pp. 39, 62.

Finally, imagine a child who keeps getting lots and lots wrong on his or her schoolwork and asks you for help. What would you say or do?

Obviously if they keep getting the problems wrong, it wasn't taught right or they didn't comprehend the information correctly or effectively enough. I'd reteach them and try to make them understand in a simpler way... Just break down the process so their minds can understand more effectively.

Source: Dweck, 1999, p. 84.

Entity and incremental theorists respond to these questions and challenges differently. Entity theorists tend to attach greater weight to ability. They might fill out the equation this way:

Intelligence = __35__ % effort + __65__ % ability

For incremental theorists, things are reversed. Effort tends to be weighed more heavily than ability:

Intelligence = __65__ % effort + __35__ % ability

Theorists from the two camps think about effort differently. Entity theorists view a large effort in solving the science magazine's IQ puzzle as evidence of low intelligence. They agree with the statements "If you have to work hard on some problems, you're probably not very good at them" and "Things come easily to people who are true geniuses." Incrementalists, on the other hand, see effort as something that activates people's intelligence and allows them to use it to full advantage. They are more likely to believe "When you are good at something, working hard allows you to really understand it" and "Even geniuses have to work hard for their discoveries."

As you might imagine by now, entity and incremental theorists also respond differently to the child who is doing poorly on his or her schoolwork. Entity theorists tend to be stumped. They often have little advice because "it either comes naturally or it doesn't come." At best, they express sympathy.

However, those who believe that achievement comes only after a long, effortful process have lots of advice. One incremental theorist responded: "Do you quit a lot? Do you think for a minute and then stop? If you do, you should think for a long time— two minutes, maybe, and if you can't get it you should read the problem again. If you can't get it then, you should raise your hand and ask the teacher" (Dweck, 1999, p. 84).

People who see intelligence as fixed see their poor performance on a task as meaning that they are stupid. In fact, many indicate that whenever they fail they feel "worthless" or "like a complete loser." They also conclude, "If I didn't do as well in school as I hoped, I'd think less of myself as a person." In short, they generalize from academic performance to intelligence to personal worth. Those with a malleable view of intelligence see failure as indicating that they have to do something different in the future to succeed. Most important, they intend to do it. For these people, a specific performance may reflect something about skill level at the moment, but it says nothing about broader intellectual abilities. And it certainly suggests nothing about a person's worth.

Entity theorists who are afraid that they may make errors or reveal their ignorance sometimes pass up important learning opportunities. Strange, isn't it? The very notion of learning assumes that there is something you don't know. Most of life's important accomplishments require a heavy investment of effort regardless of how bright you are.

In fact, most famous geniuses worked extraordinarily hard (Dweck, 1999), and many of them had very ordinary beginnings. Charles Darwin, Leo Tolstoy, William James, John Stuart Mill, and Norbert Weiner were not exceptional children. Brilliant musicians, too, are more often made than born. Researchers find that, as kids, these musicians put in thousands of hours of practice. Researchers who study creativity have proposed the "ten-year" rule: no truly great creative contributions come without at least ten years of intense effort and preparation. Mozart's earliest compositions were neither original nor particularly noteworthy.

None of this means that people only pull themselves up by their own bootstraps. Social support is important. It can be foolish, cautions Dweck, to believe that a person continuing in the same environment will change without any educational or psychological help. Our personal strivings are vital, but so are external supports. Parents and teachers play a particularly important role. When students do well, adults should praise their efforts, not their ability. In dealing with failure, parents and teachers should avoid any global statements and should instead give specific feedback on what the student did wrong and what he or she might try next.

Parents and teachers can also teach students to relish a challenge. Doing easy tasks is often a waste of time. The fun comes in confronting something difficult and finding strategies that work. Finally, advises Dweck, adults should help children value learning more than grades. Too often kids rely on grades to prove their worth. Sure, grades are important. But they are not as significant as learning.

3. Control

Now that we've considered the importance of making our own choices and believing we can change, let's focus on how our sense of personal control affects our feelings of freedom.

Hostages and prisoners of war often say that the worst part of their experience was the unpredictability of their fate. They report making every effort to maintain some sense of personal control. Among the Americans held captive by Iranians in the early 1980s, one hostage saved a bit of food from breakfast and later offered it to anyone who came to his cell. The strategy, he said, had the effect of turning his cell into a living room and he, a hostage, into a host welcoming guests.

Feelings of personal control contribute to a sense of responsibility for behavior and its consequences. We feel accountable for pursuing important objectives only if we feel competent to achieve them. Delroy Paulhus designed the following scale to measure one's sense of control in personal achievement situations.

Total: 56 High Sense of Personal Control **SELF-ASSESSMENT ■**

Personal Efficacy

Indicate the extent to which you agree with each statement using the response scale.

1 = strongly disagree   2 = disagree   3 = slightly disagree   4 = neither agree nor disagree   5 = slightly agree   6 = agree   7 = strongly agree

_5_ **1.** When I get what I want, it's usually because I worked hard for it.

_7_ **2.** When I make plans, I am almost certain I can make them work.

_5_ **3.** I prefer games involving some luck over games requiring pure skill. 3

_7_ **4.** I can learn almost anything if I set my mind to it.

_7_ **5.** My major accomplishments are entirely due to my hard work and ability.

__3__ **6.** I usually don't set goals because I have a hard time following through on them. 5

__1__ **7.** Competition discourages excellence. 7

__2__ **8.** Often people get ahead just by being lucky. 6

__5__ **9.** On any sort of exam or competition I like to know how well I do relative to everyone else.

__4__ **10.** It's pointless to keep working on something that's too difficult for me.

Source: Paulhus, 1983.

To score your responses, reverse the numbers you wrote before statements 3, 6, 7, 8, and 10 (that is, change 1 to 7, 2 to 6, 3 to 5, 5 to 3, 6 to 2, and 7 to 1). Then add up the numbers in front of all ten items. Scores range from 10 to 70, with higher scores reflecting a greater sense of personal control. Among one sample of college students (Burger, 2004), males and females obtained mean scores of 51.8 and 52.2, respectively.

Psychological research suggests that some people tend to have an internal locus of control—they believe that they control their own destiny. Others are inclined toward external control—they believe that their fate is determined by chance or powerful others. For example, in terms of academic achievement, students with an internal locus of control believe that their grades depend on their study habits. Those with an external locus of control believe that their grades depend on luck or perhaps their teachers' moods.

People with an internal locus of control not only do well in school, they also exercise greater control over many other aspects of their life. (Self-control is a strength we will examine more carefully in Chapter 3.) Research (Burger, 2004, Myers, 2004) suggests that people who see themselves as more internally controlled are more likely to do the following:

- Successfully stop smoking
- Wear seat belts
- Practice birth control (rather than rely on fate)
- Be happy
- Experience higher levels of job satisfaction
- Cope better with stress
- Delay gratification in order to achieve long-term goals

People with an internal locus of control not only show more control over their internal world, they also exercise more influence in their social worlds. They achieve more in school, are more independent, deal with marital problems more directly, and are more successful in changing other people's opinions. They are also more likely to be involved in working toward social and political change (Levenson, 1981). They take charge in many areas of life and assume more responsibility for the outcomes (Larsen & Buss, 2002).

In contrast, those who feel they have little personal control tend to avoid challenges and abandon activities when faced with setbacks, and they often suffer anxiety or depression. But if you scored low on the Personal Efficacy Self-Assessment, fear not. As we will see throughout this book, we all have potential for change.

IN REVIEW

We value our freedom and resist others' efforts to restrict it. Choice, change, and control are three factors that powerfully affect our sense of personal freedom. Decision making is central to human experience. Autonomy seems to be a fundamental human need that is important to well-being and personal achievement. The belief that human nature can be changed affects motivation and felt responsibility. Entity theorists, who see traits as fixed, exert less effort than incremental theorists, who believe traits can be modified. People vary in their sense of personal control. People with an internal locus of control believe they shape their own destiny. People with an external locus of control believe that chance or powerful others control their outcomes. Compared to externals, internals achieve more in school, act more independently, and enjoy greater physical and psychological well-being.

■

Human Limits

Experiencing choice, change, and control is clearly important to human flourishing and personal development—to living both joyfully and responsibly. Yet this introduction to our study of the human strengths and virtues would be incomplete without flipping the coin over. Do we have unlimited choice? Can we change and control anything? Surely not. Let's briefly revisit choice, change, and control to understand human responsibility more fully.

Unlimited Choice and Illusory Control

Our range of choices seems to multiply daily. We have countless options for colleges, careers, vacation spots, and even the places we call home. Even for relatively inconsequential matters, observes Barry Schwartz (2000), decision making is challenging.

Take the simple task of grocery shopping. In the breakfast food aisle, should we buy hot or cold cereal? Sugar-coated or relatively unsweetened? With or without bran? Or should we opt for the breakfast bars instead? Shopping for a car is more mind-boggling. Should the car be new or used? Foreign or domestic? Automatic or manual? Coupe, sedan, or minivan? Two-door or four-door? Six-cylinder or four-cylinder? Black, white, green, blue, beige, or yellow?

It's overwhelming to have so many alternatives. With all these choices, how does one ever gather enough information to make the right decision? And when the selection is finally made, how can anyone be sure that a different choice would not have produced a better outcome? "Unconstrained freedom," concludes Barry Schwartz (2000), "leads to paralysis and becomes a kind of self-defeating tyranny" (p. 81).

Manufacturers are finally learning the wisdom of limiting alternatives. Some commercial giants have streamlined the number of options they offer. Proctor & Gamble reduced the varieties of their very popular Head & Shoulders shampoo from a staggering 26 to 15. The impact? Sales climbed 10 percent (Schwartz, 2000).

So many choices may also fuel an illusion of control. When coupled with our strong desire to shape our own destiny, we may come to perceive that even chance events are under our personal control. Do you, as I do, sometimes press the elevator call button even though it's already lit, thinking that somehow you will make the car arrive faster? Do you, as I do, twist and turn your body *after* throwing the bowling ball, convinced your gyrations will make the ball knock down more pins?

Gambling establishments thrive on illusory control, and people waste time and money because of it. A perception of control can be self-defeating. Here's a vivid example (McQuaid, 1971):

> One gambler in Las Vegas blew a deep breath against the dice before every roll.
>
> "Do you think that brings you luck?" the man standing next to him at the crap table asked.
>
> "I know it does," the shooter replied with conviction. "Las Vegas has a very dry climate, right?"
>
> "Right," his neighbor nodded.
>
> "So the dice are usually very dry. I have very damp breath, and I always exhale against a six and an ace. That not only gives the six and ace a little extra weight but makes them adhere to the table when they roll across it. The opposite sides come up—the opposite sides of a six and an ace are an ace and a six."
>
> "Does it really work?" his neighboring partner asked.
>
> "Well, not all the time," the shooter admitted. "The load of condensation isn't quite heavy enough. But I've been on a hot liquid diet all day, and tonight ought to be the time I break the bank" (p. 289).

Ellen Langer's (1977) experiments with gambling demonstrate people's ready susceptibility to the illusion of control. For example, in a game of chance, research participants bet significantly more money when playing against an awkward, uncertain opponent than one who appeared confident and smooth. And compared to people assigned a lottery number, people who chose their own number demanded four times as much money if someone asked to buy it. But in such chance tasks, what difference could confidence or personal choice make? Indeed, the perception of control can be illusory.

Biological and Environmental Constraints

Not only chance events but natural, biological constraints limit the range of human choice and control. Look again at the two sets of arrows you viewed earlier in this chapter. Try to see the two sets of arrows simultaneously moving in opposite directions. Can you do it? Not easy, is it? Can you choose to jump a 30-foot wall? Decide to run a 3-minute mile? Commit to memorizing the Encyclopædia Britannica? These would be pointless pursuits—a waste of time. Of course, such constraints are obvious. Decades of careful and productive psychological research define other, less obvious limits.

For example, neuroscientists have made enormous advances in understanding how the body and brain create positive and negative emotions, memories, and sensory experiences. Evolutionary psychologists show how nature selects traits that promote the perpetuation of our genes. Behavior geneticists demonstrate how our unique genetic blueprint contributes to individual differences in intelligence, personality, sexual orientation, and vulnerability to psychological disorder. For example, about 50 percent of most personality traits may be attributable to genetic inheritance (Seligman, 2002). The human strengths are not exempt. Consider happiness. Martin Seligman has suggested that we may inherit a genetic "steersman" urging us toward a specific level of happiness or sadness.

In his book *What You Can Change and What You Can't,* Seligman (1994) shows how the biological underpinnings of behavior make certain psychological conditions harder to change than others. Partly because of biology, a phobia is easier to change than being overweight. Depression is more modifiable than one's sexual orientation. Similarly, genes may make it easier for some to master certain adaptive skills and strengths than it is for others. Seligman's conclusion? Choose your areas of change carefully. Invest in changing traits or behaviors that are more readily modified.

The environment also matters. In important respects we are products of our environment. We typically learn to repeat acts that our environment rewards and avoid acts that it does not. Modeling in the home, culture, and peer groups leaves a lasting imprint. Culture profoundly affects our belief systems and value orientations. And behavioral and social-cultural psychologists have demonstrated the dramatic power of individual situations.

We have already seen the power of the environment in Carol Dweck's analysis of how parents and teachers shape children's self-understandings and subsequent levels of achievement. Other lines of research indicate that our current environment—where and with whom we live—impacts our level of happiness. Those who live in wealthy democracies are happier than those in impoverished dictatorships (Seligman, 2002). Similarly, those who enjoy a rich social network experience a greater sense of well-being than those who live more isolated lives. It's no wonder that one of the important goals of positive psychology is to build a positive ecology including healthy families, communal neighborhoods, and effective schools.

So, is "trying to be happier like trying to be taller," as researcher David Lykken (1999) once concluded and then strongly recanted? No. Although the study of biological and environmental influences on behavior helps define our limits, neither biology nor environment is destiny. Seligman argues that although a genetic steersman impacts our sense of well-being, our actions still make a difference. Similarly, Lykken (1999) now acknowledges that within the broad limits set by genetic inheritance, we steer our own boat: "I can proceed to do some of the positive wave-making things that I might miss out on if I let my four grandparents collectively do the steering" (p. 66).

Research on biological and environmental influences provides specific direction for our efforts at fostering strengths in ourselves and others. The new understandings help us to make wiser choices in pursuing control and change. For example, when findings indicate that those who eat a balanced breakfast are, by midday, more alert and less fatigued, we have a new responsibility to eat accordingly. When research shows that those who regularly exercise are more successful in quitting smoking, losing weight, and maintaining general well-being, we'd better get moving. When studies tell us that social connections are vital to both physical and psychological welfare, wisdom requires that we give priority to close relationships. We choose our environment and then it shapes us. Ironically, knowledge of the internal and external determinants of human behavior can, in important ways, increase rather than decrease our responsibility.

More than a half-century ago, Dorothy Sayers, in *Begin Here: A Statement of Faith* (cited by Yancey, 1989) used a helpful metaphor to capture the relationship between psychological determinism and human freedom. It summarizes our discussion well.

> It is true that man is dominated by his psychological make-up, but only in the sense that an artist is dominated by his material. It is not possible for a sculptor to carve a filigree brooch out of granite; to that extent he is the servant of the stone he works in. His craftsmanship is good in precisely so far as he uses granite to express his artistic intentions in a manner conformable to the stone's own nature. This is no slavery, but the freedom of the sculptor and the freedom of the stone working together in harmony.

The better the sculptor understands the true nature of his raw material, the greater is his freedom in using it; and so it is with every man, when he uses his own mind and emotions to express his conscious intention (p. 30).

IN REVIEW

Although people value their freedom, the availability of too many choices can be paralyzing. It can also fuel an illusion of control. Freedom within constraint fosters optimal functioning. Natural physical constraints limit the range of human choice. Research identifying the biological and environmental determinants of behavior not only define our limits but give direction to efforts for successful change and control.

Initiative and Human Values

Christine Robitschek's (1998) Personal Growth Initiative Scale (PGIS) captures the importance of choice, change, and control to personal development. But there's another key ingredient to flourishing that her scale incorporates: having clear direction. Personal growth, suggests Robitschek, is a person's active, intentional involvement in changing and developing as a person. Growth, she suggests, must be an intentional process. What do you choose, what do you change, what do you seek to control? Try it for yourself.

Total: 37

SELF-ASSESSMENT ■

Personal Growth Initiative Scale

Using the scale, indicate the extent to which you agree or disagree with each statement.

1 = definitely disagree   2 = mostly disagree   3 = somewhat disagree
4 = somewhat agree   5 = mostly agree   6 = definitely agree

5 **1.** I know how to change specific things that I want to change in my life.

4 **2.** I have a good sense of where I am headed in my life.

4 **3.** If I want to change something in my life, I know how to initiate the transition process.

5 **4.** I can choose the role I want to have in a group.

_4_ **5.** I know what I need to do to get started toward reaching my goals.

_3_ **6.** I have a specific action plan to help me reach my goals.

_6_ **7.** I take charge of my life.

_2_ **8.** I know what my unique contribution to the world might be.

_4_ **9.** I have a plan for making my life more balanced.

Source: Robitschek, 1998.

To score your responses, simply add the numbers you circled to obtain a total score. PGIS scores range from 9 to 54. People who score higher (31.5 is the midpoint) recognize and capitalize on opportunities for personal change. More than that, they search out and create situations that will foster their growth. In contrast, people with low scores actively avoid situations that challenge them to grow.

PGIS scores seem to be strongly positively related to psychological well-being and negatively related to psychological distress (Robitschek & Cook, 1999). So as PGIS scores go up, psychological distress tends to go down. Robitschek and her colleagues (Snyder & Lopez, 2002) are currently examining whether PGI might also defend against distress by leading people to seek help earlier—when they first experience negative events—thus reducing the extent and effects of stress. PGIS scores are positively linked to assertiveness, internal locus of control, and instrumentality (knowing how to reach important goals). No differences in scores are found between men and women or between ethnic minority and majority groups.

Although a sense of freedom is important to personal development, the PGIS suggests that it is not enough. It is also a matter of making wise choices, making the right changes, and in the process, exercising appropriate control. And finally, human values are at the core of our personal development. Values, writes Bert Hodges (2001), "provide distant but real guides that help us to find our way, that help us in the journey of life. Values provide not only place but prospective; they indicate where we have come from and where we are going" (p. 478).

But what values? What is life's "game"? More specifically, asks Barry Schwartz (2000), "What kind of game is being a student? Is it to prepare for a career that will be financially rewarding . . . one that is intellectually challenging . . . one that provides public service?" (p. 80). What kind of game is being a businessperson? Are there limits to serving corporate interests? Should businesspeople market whatever people buy, tell people whatever they think people will believe? Should they be concerned about ethics and fairness? Should they demonstrate care for the environment? What kind of game is being a spouse or lover? Ought lovers submerge their own interests or desires to serve those of their partners? When does devotion turn into subjugation? At what point does self-actualization turn into selfishness? Even the notion of responsibility itself is a matter of values. Responsibility for what and to whom?

Most of us would agree that we have responsibility for ourselves, for others, and for our environment and future generations. Most of us, regardless of vocational or family role, aim to live joyfully and responsibly. We want fulfilling and productive lives, but we also want to demonstrate compassion, commitment, and self-control in our interpersonal relationships. Living fully demands the ability to be oneself and at the same time to be intimately connected with others.

A meaningful, productive life, argues Mihaly Csikszentmihalyi (2003) involves two processes. *Differentiation* reflects a strong sense of personal responsibility for developing and using our unique talents—for enjoying the expression of our being in action. *Integration* is the realization that, however unique we are, we are "also completely enmeshed in networks of relationships with other human beings, with cultural symbols and artifacts, and with the surrounding environment" (p. 29). In short, to be happy, people must enjoy doing their best while at the same time contributing to something beyond themselves, ideally with actions that have effects reaching far into the future. "Responsibility," writes Robert Sternberg (2003), "includes the wisdom to be responsible for others . . . as well as for oneself" (p. 5).

We will revisit these responsibilities in the course of this book. For now, we can summarize that autonomy does not refer to being detached, selfish, or even "independent" but rather to the experience of choice. Freedom to choose is linked to responsibility when we acknowledge and meet our obligations to others as well as to ourselves. Fortunately, we not only want to be free, we also have a need to feel connected with others. We have a motive for relatedness (Deci, 1995; Ryan & Deci, 2000), a fundamental need to belong. We are naturally inclined to form bonds with others on whom we then rely and for whom we care—something we will explore more fully in Chapter 1.

Research suggests that, contrary to conventional wisdom, needs for autonomy and relatedness can fit together quite well. For example, cross-cultural research with Korean and U.S. samples has found autonomy to be more strongly linked with collectivistic attitudes than individualistic ones (Kim, Butzel, & Ryan, 1998). Even more interesting are the positive links between autonomy and relatedness that researchers have discovered in American teens. High school is a time when adolescents struggle for independence from their families. Some people have wrongly suggested that relinquishing connections with parents is an important step to maturity. But newer research suggests that a chosen dependence on parents rather than strong independence from them is more positively linked to teenagers' integrity and well-being (Ryan, Stiller, & Lynch, 1994). Teens who have strong connections with their parents are happy and tend to perform well in school.

Edward Deci (1995) uses Garth Fagan's modern dance troupe to illustrate the beauty of freedom with responsibility. In a routine called "Prelude: Discipline in Freedom," the dancers soar to unbelievable heights in elegantly creative postures.

They show truly amazing energy and force. Still, there is no chaos or disorder in their performance. In fact, everyone is in precisely the right place at the right time. There is freedom and flexibility, but also discipline and responsibility to others.

IN REVIEW

Personal growth is more than a matter of exercising freedom. Wise choices, the right changes, and appropriate control are also key. Our own values are at the core of our personal development. Most people would agree that we have responsibilities to ourselves, to others, to our environment, and to future generations. A productive, meaningful life requires the development of our unique talents and a commitment to something beyond ourselves. We have both a need for autonomy and a need to belong.

■

Overview of Positive Psychology

In carefully applying the scientific method, positive psychology aims to assess, understand, and then build the human strengths. With this book I hope to convey some of the field's most important findings and help you explore ways to apply them to your own personal growth. Here is a summary of the book's central themes and strategies:

1. We are creators of our personal and social worlds. We benefit from experiences of freedom and from being able to view ourselves as agents rather than pawns of external forces. The belief in a dynamic self capable of choice, change, and control influences the goals we choose and the energy with which we pursue them. High-functioning people are responsible—they own their actions and answer for them.

2. We are also creatures of our worlds. Biological factors, past experience, and the present situation powerfully shape our behavior. Understanding the impact of external factors enables us to make wise choices and exercise more effective control in fostering change that promotes our well-being. To build human strengths and civic virtues, we must build healthier families, communal neighborhoods, more effective schools, and socially responsive media.

3. In carefully applying the scientific method, psychology can help us sort fact from fiction. This is especially important in understanding subjective well-being and civic virtue. The methods of science that have helped us understand

psychological disorder can also illuminate our understanding of the roots and fruits of the human strengths. Sometimes these methods confirm conventional wisdom and commonsense ideas. In other cases these methods challenge popular assumptions. For example, we will see that research strongly supports the familiar adage "Money does not buy happiness." More surprising are findings that people of different ages, genders, races, and educational levels have roughly equivalent levels of happiness. In considering research on self-respect, we will discover, as we might expect, that people with high self-esteem persist in the face of failure. On the other hand, fostering self-esteem is not an effective vaccine, as many have proposed, for social problems such as aggression.

4. Although recently given renewed emphasis, positive psychology actually has a long and rich history in the discipline. For decades investigators have sought to understand the roots and fruits of such human strengths as love, empathy, and self-control. Most of the important theoretical perspectives contribute to the understanding of positive emotions, positive character, and positive institutions. Working from different points of view, psychologists help us understand the important biological, environmental, and cognitive components of human flourishing. These perspectives complement each other just as psychology's study complements that of other disciplines that study the human strengths and civic virtues.

5. One of psychology's unique contributions to the study of the human strengths is its measurement of individual differences. Scales that assess the strengths are included in every chapter of this book. They are important research tools that you can complete for yourself. Learning proceeds best when we are actively engaged, especially when we relate the new material to ourselves. The scales will help you appreciate how researchers have defined and studied specific human strengths. Remember that the scales are research instruments, not diagnostic tools. Still, if you answer honestly—not merely as you think you should or how others might want you to—the scales will give you some idea of where you fall in the pursuit of a specific strength.

6. For each chapter we will consider the implications and applications of basic research. We will ask, "What does the research suggest we do to foster the strengths and virtues in ourselves and in others? How do we promote human well-being and civic responsibility? How can we build a healthy social environment?" You are invited to participate in this process, to exercise your critical judgment in anticipating and interpreting the research results as well as their appropriate applications.

7. Values penetrate psychologists' work, including what they study, how they study it, the interpretation they give the results, and the applications they make. For example, positive psychology's call to attend to human strength

itself reflects a value judgment. Conclusions of what constitutes a strength or a weakness, a virtue or a vice are also value judgments. The values need to be stated openly so that they can be discussed and debated. One of the important assumptions of this chapter (and of this book) is that we not only have a need to be our own person, we also need to belong. We have a need for relatedness as well as autonomy. Thus, any prescription for human well-being needs to recognize both.

We will revisit these important themes as we pursue specific human strengths in the rest of this book.

IN REVIEW

Positive psychologists acknowledge that we are both creatures and creators of our personal and social worlds. In applying the scientific method to the study of human strengths and civic virtues, investigators from different theoretical perspectives contribute to our understanding of human flourishing. The assessment of specific strengths is one of positive psychology's significant contributions to the scientific study of well being. Positive psychologists recognize the importance of autonomy and relatedness as well as the effects of our values in human flourishing.

love

The supreme happiness of life is the conviction that we are loved.
—VICTOR HUGO, 1862

Learning to love is really about learning to live.
—HARRY HARLOW, 1970

When asked "What missing element would bring you happiness?" most people in one study said "love" (Freedman, 1978). In fact, four in five adults rate love as important to their happiness. Similarly, when they are asked to describe "the last bad thing that happened to you," the majority of American respondents describe a breakup or loss of a significant relationship (Veroff, Douvan, & Kulka, 1981).

Evolutionary psychologists argue that social bonds not only predict happiness, they also are the single most important factor responsible for the survival of our species (Berscheid, 2003). Our ancestors gained strength from numbers. Whether hunting game, erecting shelters, or defending themselves from predators, twelve hands were better than two. Because people living in small, cooperative groups were more likely to survive and reproduce, we today carry genes that predispose social connections.

Attachment

As infants we survive only if an adult is willing to meet our basic needs. Early in life we form bonds with our caregivers. "Love begins at the beginning," suggests Deborah Blum (2002); "perhaps no one does it better, or needs it more, than a child" (p. 170).

Our most important first question is: Can I count on my caregiver to be available and responsive when needed? There are three possible responses to the question: yes, no, and maybe (Hazan & Shaver, 1994). Thinking back to your own childhood, how would you answer?

Nature vs. Nurture (handwritten)

First Attachments

Read the following three paragraphs and select the one that best describes your relationship with your mother when you were a child growing up. Then select the one that best describes your relationship with your father.

F X 1. Warm/Responsive—She/he was generally warm and responsive. She/he was good at knowing when to be supportive and when to let me operate on my own. Our relationship was always comfortable, and I have no major reservations or complaints about it.

X X 2. Cold/Rejecting—She/he was fairly cold and distant or rejecting, not very responsive. I wasn't her/his highest priority; her/his concerns were often elsewhere. It's possible that she/he would just as soon not have had me.

M F 3. Ambivalent/Inconsistent—She/he was noticeably inconsistent in her/his reactions to me, sometimes warm and sometimes not. She/he had her/his own agenda, which sometimes got in the way of her/his receptiveness and responsiveness to my needs. She/he definitely loved me but didn't always show it in the best way.

Source: Hazan & Shaver, 1986.

Answers to the exercise demonstrate how nature—our inherent tendency to bond—and nurture—the responsiveness of our caregivers—shape social ties. Early in life their interaction yields three different attachment styles: secure, avoidant, and anxious.

Infants who experience warm, responsive parents show *secure attachment.* When they are placed in a laboratory playroom with their mother, they happily explore their unfamiliar environment. If she leaves, they become distressed, and when she returns, they run to hold her, then relax and return to playing. About 60 percent of North American infants show this pattern (Hazan & Shaver, 1994).

Babies with cold, rejecting caregivers show *avoidant attachment.* In the unfamiliar playroom, they show little distress during separation or clinging upon reunion. They react to a stranger in the same unresponsive way that they do to the parent and keep their attention focused on the toys. About 25 percent of North American infants demonstrate this type of attachment.

Infants who experience inconsistent parenting show *anxious attachment.* In the unfamiliar setting, they cling anxiously to their mother and cry when she leaves, but then are indifferent or hostile when she returns. These infants tend not to explore their environment. Many continue to cry after being picked up and are not easily comforted. This style, the rarest of the three, averages about 15 percent in North American samples.

From Cradle to Grave

Understandably, early care-receiving experiences affect our view of our social world. Are people trustworthy? Can they be counted on to provide protection and support? Am I a lovable person, someone worth caring for? The answers we give to these questions shape how we approach close relationships. Most important, they affect (1) our level of comfort with closeness and (2) our degree of anxiety over abandonment.

How do the emotional bonds we form with caregivers early in life lay the foundation for our adult love relationships?

SELF-ASSESSMENT ■

Romantic Relationships

Which of the following best describes your current feelings, particularly as they might apply to present or potential romantic love relationships?

1. Secure—I find it relatively easy to get close to others and am comfortable depending on them. I don't often worry about being abandoned or about someone getting too close to me.

2. Avoidant—I am somewhat uncomfortable being close to others; I find it difficult to trust them completely, difficult to allow myself to depend on them. I am nervous when anyone gets too close, and often love partners want me to be more intimate than I feel comfortable being.

3. Anxious—I find that others are reluctant to get as close as I would like. I often worry that my partner doesn't really love me or won't want to stay with me. I want to get very close to my partner and this sometimes scares people away.

Source: Hazan & Shaver, 1990.

How closely did your self-assessment match your earlier ratings of your parents? Adult love relationships do tend to mirror early infant attachments (Myers, 2002).

- Secure adults find it easy to get close to others and are unconcerned about becoming too dependent or being abandoned. Their relationships are characterized by happiness, trust, and friendship. They seem able to accept and support their partner in spite of faults, and their relationships endure longer.

- Avoidant adults tend to be less invested in relationships and more likely to leave them. Some seem to be fearful ("I am uncomfortable getting close to others"), while others are dismissing ("It is very important for me to feel independent and self-sufficient"). Their relationships are marked by emotional highs and lows. They are also more likely to have brief sexual encounters without love.

- For anxious adults, love is obsession; these adults are less trusting, demand reciprocation, and are generally more possessive and jealous. They may break up repeatedly with the same person. When discussing differences, they often get emotional and angry.

In comparison to their secure counterparts, avoidantly attached men and anxiously attached individuals of both sexes report lower relationship satisfaction (Tucker & Anders, 1999). In addition, anxiously attached men are more likely to misread their partner's feelings about the relationship.

Development of Attachment

Both nature—the infant's inherent need to bond and belong—and nurture—parental responsiveness—contribute to attachment. Although many psychologists once assumed that the parent's personality shaped caregiving style, more recent research indicates that the infant's genetically based temperament can elicit different parental responses that in turn affect attachment style. Clearly, nature and nurture interact.

Three components contribute to attachment: closeness, care, and commitment. *Close physical proximity* is the context in which infant and adult attachments unfold. The motives differ—for infants it's security, for adults, sexual attraction is added to the mix. In both types of relationships, close physical contact fosters an emotional bond. Infants and adults generally welcome physical touch, feel distress when separated, and express strong affection when reunited. We tend to judge the relationships between parents and children, and between adult lovers as the "closest," and only in those relationships is prolonged bodily contact considered normal. The intensity of our need for close contact gradually diminishes—a finding that still awaits full explanation (Hazan & Shaver, 1994).

From closeness emerges the second important characteristic of attachment: a safe haven. Proximity brings us together, and the degree to which attachment provides *care,* including both comfort and emotional support, grows over time. How our parents and partners regard us is very important to us. Research (Kotler, 1985) suggests that sensitive and responsive care, not passionate attraction, is the better predictor of the strength of relationships over the long term.

Over time, *commitment* makes the safe haven a base of security. With a consistently available, supportive, and reassuring caregiver, one can confidently confront life's everyday challenges. Free of relationship concerns, the child eagerly explores a new world, the adult enthusiastically engages in work and community opportunities. Commitment, suggest Cindy Hazan and Philip Shaver (1994), is the glue that holds relationships together and ensures safety and security over the long haul. Most parents are naturally committed to their children. On the other hand, adult relationships are chosen, and we must develop commitment to our life partners.

Closeness, care, and commitment make up the stuff of which attachment and, as we will see, love are made.

Can Attachment Style Change?

Before turning to more specific research on adult love relationships, let's consider an important question you may be wondering about: Can early attachment style, with all the implications for the quality of our interpersonal relationships, change? Can avoidant or anxious attachment become secure? Yes! Attachment patterns provide a dramatic example of how both nature and nurture shape the course of one's life. Yet these patterns are not fixed. Researchers suggest several routes to change. Simply reflecting, as you have in this chapter, on how beliefs about yourself and others have their roots in early experience is an important first step in altering an avoidant or anxious attachment.

"Corrective" relationship experiences, argues John Bowlby (1988), also foster more secure attachments. Given that the function of attachment is to attain security, change is more likely to occur in the direction of secure than insecure attachment. We are more likely to enter relationships that promise more, rather than less, security than we have experienced in the past. And research indicates that secure bonds are more stable than either avoidant or anxious attachments. We will revisit this concern later in the chapter as we examine more specific strategies for fostering loving relationships.

IN REVIEW

Social attachments are important to our personal happiness and have enabled our survival as a species. Our interactions with our first caregivers yield different attachment styles: secure, avoidant, or anxious. The emotional bonds formed early in life lay the foundation for later love relationships. Childhood attachments and adult romantic attachments are marked by physical closeness, caring, and long-term commitment. Both nature and nurture are crucial factors in shaping attachment style, and our patterns of relating can change.

■

Exploring Love

We will first review love's important features and see how they have been incorporated in an influential model of love. Then we will explore two types of love that psychologists have researched extensively.

Love's Features

Some researchers have studied human traits, including the strengths, by asking respondents to identify the important features *or characteristics* of those traits. For *example, if you were to list the characteristics of the concept* EXTRAVERSION, *you might write "liveliness," "vivaciousness," "sociability," and so on. What are the important features or characteristics of the concept* LOVE? *List up to ten features as they come to mind. Take only a minute or two.*

1. Caring
2. Honesty
3. Spontaneous
4. Creative
5. Energetic
6. Good Physique
7. Adventurous
8. Humorous
9. Crazy
10. Generous

How do other respondents view love's crucial features? Beverly Fehr (1988) asked 141 men and women and found that the characteristics most often mentioned were caring (by 44 percent of respondents), happiness (29 percent), wanting to be with the other (28 percent), friendship (23 percent), feeling free to talk about anything (20 percent), warm feelings (17 percent), accepting the way the other is (16 percent), trust (15 percent), commitment (14 percent), sharing (14 percent), thinking about the other all the time (14 percent), and sacrifice (14 percent). A total of 68 features were listed by more than one respondent.

When a second group was asked to rate how central each of these 68 features was to the concept of love by using a scale from 1 (extremely poor feature of love) to 8 (extremely good feature of love), the features regarded as <u>most central</u> were trust (7.50), caring (7.28), honesty (7.18), friendship (7.08), respect (7.01), concern for the other's well-being (7.00), loyalty (7.00), commitment (6.92), accepting the way the other is (6.82), supportiveness (6.78), and wanting to be with the other (6.82). Among those receiving somewhat <u>lower ratings</u> were warm feelings (6.04), touching (5.82), sexual passion (5.81), and energy (4.29).

Love's Triangle

By using the sophisticated statistical tool of factor analysis, Arthur Aron and Lori Westbay (1996) found that the 68 prototypical features of love could be organized into three categories: passion, intimacy, and commitment. Robert Sternberg's (1988) triangular theory of love recognizes these three dimensions as the major components of love. *Passion* is the motivational component of love and reflects attraction, romance, and sexual desire. *Intimacy* involves feelings of closeness, trust, and the sharing of one's innermost thoughts. *Commitment* is the decision to maintain a long-term caring relationship.

Completing Sternberg's love scale takes a bit longer than most exercises in this book, but it will be well worth the effort. Taking and scoring it will help you better understand the research on love and will provide insight into the nature of your own close relationships.

Sternberg's Triangular Love Scale

In responding to the statements, think of one person you love or care about deeply. Then rate your agreement with each of the items by using the nine-point scale. Use intermediate points on the scale to indicate intermediate levels of feelings.

1	2	3	4	5	6	7	8	9
Do not agree at all				Moderately agree				Extremely agree

7   **1.** I actively support my partner's well-being.

8   **2.** I have a warm relationship with my partner.

8   ③ Just seeing my partner excites me.

9   **4.** I know that I care about my partner.

7   ⑤ I find myself thinking about my partner frequently throughout the day.

6   **6.** I am able to count on my partner in times of need.

9   **7.** I am committed to maintaining my relationship with my partner.

3   **8.** I have confidence in the stability of my relationship with my partner.

7   ⑨ My relationship with my partner is very romantic.

9   **10.** My partner is able to count on me in times of need.

6   ⑪ I find my partner to be personally attractive.

5   **12.** Because of my commitment to my partner I would not let other people come between us.

2   **13.** I expect my love for my partner to last the rest of my life.

4   ⑭ I idealize my partner.

9   **15.** I am willing to share myself and my possessions with my partner.

___1___ (16.) I cannot imagine another person making me as happy as my partner does.

___1___ (17.) I would rather be with my partner than with anyone else.

___5___ 18. I could not let anything get in the way of my commitment to my partner.

___6___ 19. I receive considerable emotional support from my partner.

___7___ 20. I will always feel a strong responsibility for my partner.

___6___ 21. I give considerable emotional support to my partner.

___4___ (22.) There is nothing more important to me than my relationship with my partner.

___9___ (23.) I especially like physical contact with my partner.

___5___ 24. I communicate well with my partner.

___8___ 25. I value my partner greatly in my life.

___9___ 26. I feel close to my partner.

___3___ 27. I view my commitment to my partner as a solid one.

___1___ 28. I cannot imagine ending my relationship with my partner.

___7___ (29.) There is something almost magical about my relationship with my partner.

___9___ 30. I have a comfortable relationship with my partner.

___9___ (31.) I adore my partner.

___6___ 32. I am certain of my love for my partner.

___1___ 33. I view my relationship with my partner as permanent.

___1___ (34.) I cannot imagine life without my partner.

___5___ 35. I view my relationship with my partner as a good decision.

___7___ 36. I feel that I really understand my partner.

___9___ (37.) My relationship with my partner is passionate.

___4___ 38. I feel that my partner really understands me.

___7___ 39. I feel a sense of responsibility toward my partner.

___2___ 40. I feel that I can really trust my partner.

___4___ (41.) When I see romantic movies or read romantic books, I think about my partner.

_9_ **42.** I share deep personal information about myself with my partner.

_5_ **43.** I plan to continue in my relationship with my partner.

_7_ **44.** Even when my partner is hard to deal with, I remain committed to our relationship.

_8_ **45.** I fantasize about my partner.

Source: Sternberg & Whitney, 1991, pp. 82–84.

To score yourself, first add up the numbers on the passion *subscale (statements 3, 5, 9, 11, 14, 16, 17, 22, 23, 29, 31, 34, 37, 41, 45). Then add up the numbers on the* intimacy *subscale (1, 2, 6, 10, 15, 19, 21, 24, 25, 26, 30, 36, 38, 40, 42). Add up the numbers on the* commitment *subscale (4, 7, 8, 12, 13, 18, 20, 27, 28, 32, 33, 35, 39, 43, 44). Divide each of the three totals by 15 to obtain an average rating for each of the three components:*

Passion = __85__   *Intimacy =* __104__   *Commitment =* __75__

5.67   6.93

An average rating of 5 on a subscale indicates a moderate level of the component represented by the subscale; for example, an average rating of 5 on the intimacy subscale indicates a moderate amount of intimacy in the relationship you chose to measure. A higher average rating would indicate more intimacy, and a lower average rating would indicate less intimacy. Examining your ratings for each of the three subscales will give you an idea of how you perceive your love relationship in terms of these important dimensions.

According to Sternberg's model of love (1988), the three components—passion, intimacy, and commitment—form the vertices of a triangle. Their various combinations create seven basic subtypes of love.

Types of Love Relationships	Passion	Intimacy	Commitment
Liking	Low	High	Low
Infatuated love	High	Low	Low
Romantic love	High	High	Low
Empty love	Low	Low	High
Companionate love	Low	High	High
Fatuous love	High	Low	High
Consummate love	High	High	High

Sternberg's love triangle follows. Looking back at your scores, can you locate your specific love relationship on it?

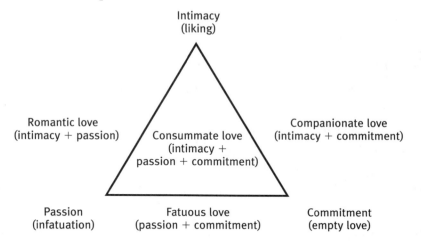

Sternberg's description of the development of consummate love parallels the unfolding of secure attachment. The passion associated with physical closeness grows very quickly and initially dominates a relationship. Over time it declines. Proximity and passion prompt reciprocal sharing and caring, and a healthy love relationship shows a slow but steady increase in intimacy. Commitment involves both a short-term decision to love someone and a longer-term decision to maintain the love. In enduring relationships, the increase in commitment is gradual at first, accelerates, and then remains at a high level.

In practical terms, the triangular theory of love can give both couples and therapists a better sense of how partners view a relationship. Differences on the triangular love scale indicate where change may be necessary to preserve and strengthen the relationship.

Romantic Love

Of the love types Sternberg identifies, psychologists have studied romantic and companionate love the most extensively. In considering the components of romantic love, let's begin by looking at mate preferences.

SELF-ASSESSMENT ■

Mate Preferences

When you think of the ideal romantic partner, what image comes to mind? The following list of 18 traits has been used in research investigating mate preferences over several decades. Rate each of the traits in terms of their importance in choosing a mate, using the following scale:

3 = indispensable   2 = important but not indispensable   1 = desirable but not important   0 = irrelevant

_3_   **1.** Ambition and industriousness
_0_   **2.** Chastity (no prior intercourse)
_3_   **3.** Dependable character
_1_   **4.** Desire for home and children
_3_   **5.** Education and intelligence
_2_   **6.** Emotional stability and maturity
_2_   **7.** Favorable social status or rating
_1_   **8.** Good cook and housekeeper
_3_   **9.** Good financial prospect
_3_   **10.** Good health
_3_   **11.** Good looks
_3_   **12.** Mutual attraction–love
_0_   **13.** Pleasing disposition
_0_   **14.** Refinement, neatness
_0_   **15.** Similar education
_0_   **16.** Similar religious background
_0_   **17.** Similar political background
_2_   **18.** Sociability

Source: Buss, 1989.

David Buss (1989) reports outcomes for this trait list in a comprehensive study of hundreds of people in 37 cultures. For these international samples, both sexes rated mutual attraction–love (12), dependable character (3), emotional stability and maturity (6), and pleasing disposition (13), as most important. Chastity (2), similar religious background (16), and similar political background (17) were least important. How do your ratings compare?

Buss also found important gender differences in mate preferences. Good looks (11) and chastity (2) were more important to males; a good financial prospect (9) and ambition and industriousness (1) were more important to females. Do your scores support Buss's findings?

Evolutionary psychologists provide an intriguing explanation for these findings. They argue that nature selects behavioral tendencies that increase the likelihood of sending one's genes into the future. Obviously, mate selection becomes important. Gene survival is more likely if one has a mate who is committed to the relationship and is reliable, cooperative, and unselfish. No wonder both sexes regard mutual attraction, dependability, stability, and a pleasing disposition to be essential qualities in a mate!

Sex differences in reproductive biology may also lead to some important sex differences in mating preferences. Evolutionary psychologists point out that, compared to eggs, sperms are cheap. While a woman incubates and nurses one child, a male can spread his genes by impregnating many other females. In our ancestral history, women most often sent their genes into the future by pairing wisely, men by pairing widely (Myers, 2002). Women look for features in a mate that communicate protection and support for offspring. Thus, a good financial prospect (9) as well as ambition and industriousness (1) become important. In contrast, men desire features that communicate fertility and assure paternity. Good looks (11), especially youthful features, suggest reproductive capacity, and chastity (2) helps assure paternity. Why assure paternity? Evolutionary psychologists explain that while women are always certain that they are mothers of their children, men are never certain that they are the fathers. Interestingly, research shows that men feel most jealous over their mate's having sex with someone else, while women tend to feel greater jealousy over their mate's becoming emotionally attached to someone else (Larsen & Buss, 2002).

Passion

For both sexes, mutual attraction–love (12) tops the list of important traits for choosing a mate. What does such attraction involve? Clearly "being in love" is different from "love." Ellen Berscheid and Sarah Meyers (1996) asked college undergraduates to compose three lists: people they "loved," people they were "in love with," and people they were "sexually attracted to." Only 2 percent of those in the "love" category also appeared in the "sex" list. However, the overlap of the "in love" with the "sex" list was 85 percent. Similarly, when Pamela Regan and her colleagues (1998) asked people to list the characteristics of romantic love, two-thirds mentioned sexual desire—well ahead of happiness, loyalty, sharing, or commitment. Yes, passion is a key component of romantic love.

Now answer this question: If a man or woman had all the other qualities you desired in a mate, would you marry this person if you were *not* in love? In 1967, a whopping 76 percent of American women and 35 percent of American men said yes. Just two decades later, only 20 percent of women and 14 percent of men indicated that they would marry someone with whom they were not in love (Simpson, Campbell, & Berscheid, 1986). After spontaneously enumerating all the sparkling qualities of her close male friend, one of my recent students matter-of-factly concluded, "But there's no chemistry, no spark—we could never marry." No fire, no future.

Consider Robert Epstein's (2002) recent proposal. As editor of the popular magazine *Psychology Today* and holder of a Harvard Ph.D. in psychology, he published a request for a woman who would, over 6 months to a year, learn to love him and cowrite a book about intentionally falling in love. Epstein proposed that together they would read extensively about love, receive counseling, and engage in various bonding exercises. All this would be done with the goal of falling deeply in love by the end of the contract period. More than 300 expressed interest. How have things turned out? Stay tuned. Epstein and Venezuelan Gabriela Castillo are currently working on their relationship (Peterson, 2003).

In making his proposal, Epstein (2002) noted that 60 percent of the world's marriages are not for love. Divorce rates for these arranged marriages are very low, and even more surprising, in about half of them the spouses fall in love with each other. Epstein writes:

> We teach our children, especially our little girls, that a knight in shining Porsche is going to drive up one day, awaken perfect passion with a magical kiss and then drive the blessed couple down the road to Happily Ever After, a special place where no one ever changes. Hollywood tells us that the One is out there for everyone, so no one is willing to settle for Mr. or Ms. Two-Thirds. We want our relationships to be like our antidepressants—perfect and effortless—and if they don't look as perfect today as they did yesterday, unskilled and gutless, we abandon them (p. 5).

Is Epstein right? Is passionate love something we control? Do you think we *fall* in love or do we *learn* to love?

Passionate love, writes Elaine Hatfield (1988), is a "state of intense longing for union with another." If the love is returned, one is fulfilled, even ecstatic. If not, one is despairing and anxious. To explain passionate love, Hatfield suggests that any state of physiological arousal can be experienced as one of several emotions, depending on how we interpret and label the emotion. A pounding heart and sweating palms can be interpreted as fear, anger, or surprise, depending on the environmental context. If the situation is interpreted as potentially romantic, for example with an attractive person present, we may experience the arousal as passion.

Several research findings support Hatfield's theory. In a clever field study (Dutton & Aron, 1974), young men crossed one of two bridges in North Vancouver—a solid, safe structure or a narrow, wobbly suspension walkway that was 230 feet above rocks and rapids below. As each man crossed the bridge, an attractive college woman approached to ask if he would fill out a questionnaire for her. Offering to explain her "class project" further, she left him her phone number. Far more of the men who crossed the suspension bridge than those who used the safe structure called the woman. Similarly, laboratory studies have found that men who have been aroused by exercise, humorous tapes, or an alarming situation feel more attracted to a girlfriend or even to a woman just introduced to them. A pounding heart makes the heart grow fonder.

Many action movies follow a story line that involves a man and a woman who are initially strangers. A series of harrowing experiences elicit fear, anger, and then euphoria. By the end of the movie they have fallen madly in love. At the end of the feature film *Speed,* Los Angeles SWAT cop Jack Traven disposes of bomb expert Howard Payne on the top of a racing train and then descends into the railcar to rescue Annie, padlocked to a handrail. Although the train is out of control, Jack risks his life to save Annie. Unable to stop the conductorless train, he finally accelerates it with the hope that it will leap the track at an upcoming curve. Excitement (in both actors and audience) builds as the train finally jumps the rails and crashes. The last scene finds Jack and Annie in each other's arms. "You didn't leave," cries Annie gratefully. "I didn't have anywhere to go just then," responds Jack. Then he adds, "I have heard relationships based on intense experiences never work." Annie answers, "Then we'll just have to base it on sex." The couple embraces passionately as the film ends.

Intimacy

But romantic love, according to Sternberg's triangular theory of love, is not only passionate. It is also intimate.

Intimacy, suggests Hatfield (1988) is a process in which a person attempts to get close to another—exploring similarities and differences in the way they think, feel, and behave. What most clearly fosters intimacy? A critical element seems to be self-disclosure. Designed by Lynn Miller, John Berg, and Richard Archer (1983), the Opener Scale assesses the capacity to elicit intimate disclosure from others.

Total: 37

SELF-ASSESSMENT ■

Openers

Respond to each statement using the following scale:

1	2	3	4	5
Strongly disagree				Strongly agree

3 **1.** People frequently tell me about themselves.

5 **2.** I've been told that I'm a good listener.

4 **3.** I'm very accepting of others.

5 **4.** People trust me with their secrets.

4 **5.** I easily get people to "open up."

4 **6.** People feel relaxed around me.

3 **7.** I enjoy listening to people.

3 **8.** I'm sympathetic to people's problems.

2 **9.** I encourage people to tell me about how they are feeling.

4 **10.** I can keep people talking about themselves.

```
10
16
 9
+2
___
37
```

Source: Miller, Berg, & Archer, 1983.

To score, simply add up the numbers you placed in response to the ten items. Scores can range from 10 to 50, with higher scores reflecting a greater tendency to elicit revelations from others. Mean scores for a sample of 487 undergraduate women and 253 undergraduate men were 40.68 and 38.01, respectively.

Some people, especially women, are skilled "openers." They tend to be what Carl Rogers (1980) called "growth-promoting" listeners: *genuine* in revealing their own feelings, *accepting* of others' feelings, and *empathic*—readily assuming the other's perspective. We are especially likely to disclose when distressed—when angry or anxious. Having an intimate partner with whom we can share threats to our self-image helps us survive such stresses. Research confirms that dating and married couples who reveal themselves most to one another express greatest satisfaction with their relationship and are more likely to remain committed to it.

Intimacy is an essential element of a loving relationship. Typically it grows gradually as partners reveal more and more of themselves to each other. Disclosure tends to elicit disclosure, a process appropriately dubbed the *disclosure reciprocity effect*. As one person reveals a little, the other reciprocates, and the process spirals. Over time their knowledge of each other penetrates to deeper and deeper levels. Trust builds and partners feel accepted. Dropping our masks and letting ourselves be known as we truly are, suggested Sidney Jourard (1964), nurtures love.

Companionate Love

Typically the passion of romantic love cools. Its intimacy, however, can foster a companionate love—an affection for those with whom our lives are intertwined. We may even begin to incorporate a partner into our view of ourselves.

SELF-ASSESSMENT ■

Self and Other

Think of the person with whom you have the closest relationship. Which of the following diagrams best describes the relationship?

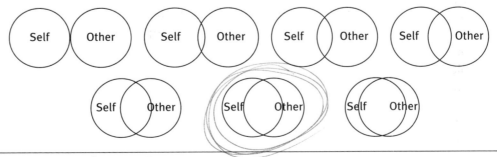

Source: Aron, Aron, & Smollan, 1992, p. 597.

Arthur Aron and his colleagues (1992) found that the longevity of a romantic relationship can be predicted by how people choose to portray their partnership. The more overlap, that is, the more one incorporates a partner into the self, the more enduring the relationship. The more overlap, the stronger is the commitment to maintaining the relationship. "Love is the expansion of two natures in such a fashion that each includes the other," claimed eighteenth-century European philosopher Felix Adler, "and each is enriched by the other."

In companionate love, commitment accompanies intimacy. Commitment, the intention to maintain a relationship, springs from different sources. Three quite different types of commitment are reflected in the following sample items from Jeffrey Adams's and Warren Jones's (1997) Dimensions of Commitment Inventory.

Commitment

Pause for a moment to think of commitment in the context of marriage. Whether you are now married or not, consider how the following statements reflect your beliefs about the nature of the marital relationship.

Ⓣ F **1.** I'm dedicated to making my marriage as fulfilling as it can be.

T Ⓕ **2.** I am completely devoted to my spouse.

T Ⓕ **3.** I believe that marriage is for life regardless of what happens.

Ⓣ F **4.** A marriage should be protected at all costs.

T Ⓕ **5.** It would be particularly hard on my family and friends if my spouse and I divorced.

T Ⓕ **6.** A divorce would ruin my reputation.

Source: Adams & Jones, 1997.

Agreement with the first two statements suggests *personal commitment*—people desire to continue a relationship because the relationship is satisfying and they are attracted to their partners. Statements 3 and 4 reflect *moral commitment* or obligation—people feel they ought to continue the relationship because marriage is an important social or religious institution and it would be improper to break one's promises or vows. Statements 5 and 6 suggest *constraint commitment*, in which people feel they have to continue a relationship because they fear the social, financial, and emotional costs of ending the relationship.

The three types of commitment not only feel different, they also have different consequences (Brehm, Miller, Perlman, & Campbell, 2002). Normally, personal commitments are more satisfying. For people in a long-distance romantic relationship, moral commitment better predicts its longevity than does personal commitment.

It can keep a relationship intact even though the partners' level of satisfaction wanes.

Commitment in the context of a loving relationship can serve several important functions, including the following:

- Like intimacy, commitment leads partners to think of themselves as "us" instead of "me" and "him" or "her." Events that please one's partner produce indirect benefits for oneself. Sacrifices for one's partner become less costly.

- When people know they are in a relationship for the long term, they may be better able to tolerate times of high cost and low reward, much like long-term investors in stock tolerate periods of low earnings.

- Commitment motivates people to take more deliberate action to protect and maintain a relationship even when it is costly for them to do so. Committed people seem to respond with greater self-restraint when provoked by their partner and to show greater willingness to sacrifice self-interest for the good of the relationship.

When you think of your closest peer relationship—friend or romantic partner—how would you describe it? Does your partner contribute more to it than you do? Less? Or would you say that you each contribute equally?

Often casual acquaintances maintain their connections through tit-for-tat exchanges. From coworkers in a carpool taking turns driving, to neighbors rotating responsibility for hosting the annual block party, people trade similar benefits. As you reflect on your closest friendship or love relationship, is that how things go? Probably not. As relationships form, we are less concerned with instant repayment. Lovers respond to each other's needs without expecting immediate repayment. Mother Teresa stated this much more strongly: "If you really love one another you will not be able to avoid making sacrifices."

Only when the benefits are voluntary, when partners freely give and receive, do we view the relationship as true friendship or love. In fact, Margaret Clark and Judson Mills (1993) reported that tit-for-tat exchanges increased people's liking when the relationship was relatively formal, but the same social economics decreased liking when the two sought a close relationship.

Nonetheless, one important key to an enduring relationship is *equity*—the outcomes people receive from a relationship are proportional to what they contribute to it. Commitment is likely to be fostered if, over the long term, the relationship is perceived as fair as well as intimate. Those who perceive the other as receiving a better deal experience distress and irritation, sometimes even depression. Those who believe they are receiving a better deal may feel guilty. As you might expect, however, being overbenefitted is less troubling to most than being underbenefitted (Brehm et al., 2002).

Robert Sternberg's triangular theory identifies passion, intimacy, and commitment as the key components of love. Various combinations of these factors may yield different types of love. The key ingredients of romantic love are passion and intimacy. Although men and women express somewhat different mate preferences, they identify mutual attraction to be the most important factor in choosing a romantic partner. Hatfield's two-factor theory suggests that we are likely to interpret physiological arousal that occurs in a romantic context as passion. Intimacy is fostered by mutual self-disclosure.

Companionate love, the affection we feel for those with whom our lives are intertwined, combines intimacy with commitment. Such commitment leads partners to think of themselves as "we" and enables people to endure times of high cost and low rewards in a relationship. Long-term commitment is fueled by equity in which outcomes are proportional to investments.

Building Close Relationships

What factors promote enduring, satisfying love relationships? What can partners do to maintain and enhance their relationship connection? John Harvey and Julia Omarzu (1997, 1999) provide one answer in their minding theory of relationships. First complete their minding scale.

SELF-ASSESSMENT ■

Minding Scale

Respond to each of the statements using the following scale:

1 = strongly agree   2 = moderately agree   3 = slightly agree   4 = slightly disagree   5 = moderately disagree   6 = strongly disagree

_____ **1.** Successful romantic partners have the same opinions about things.

_____ **2.** You should avoid telling a loved one too much personal detail about your past.

_____ **3.** It is irritating when people ask you to do favors.

_____ **4.** Partners should be as much alike as possible.

_____ **5.** People will take advantage of you if they can.

_____ **6.** There is no reason to discuss your past relationships with a new love.

_____ **7.** Partners who have different opinions will have a poor relationship.

_____ **8.** It is difficult to be close to someone whose past is different from your own.

_____ **9.** Partners should spend lots of time talking together.

_____ **10.** People mainly look out for their own welfare even in close relationships.

_____ **11.** You should find out as much as you can about a new love.

_____ **12.** Even when people love you they think mainly about themselves.

_____ **13.** It is important to keep some mystery about yourself in a relationship.

_____ **14.** Romantic partners should agree about all things.

_____ **15.** The people we love are really strangers to us.

_____ **16.** Partners should give each other the benefit of the doubt no matter what.

_____ **17.** People who do nice things for you usually want something from you in return.

_____ **18.** Close partners often have different friends and interests.

Source: Omarzu, Whelan, & Harvey, 2001.

The minding theory of relationships suggests that certain types of perceptions and expectations are key to satisfying close relationships. First, a person seeks to build a foundation of knowledge about one's partner. Items 2, 6, 9, 11, 13, and 15 measure the knowledge component of "minding." Reverse the numbers (1 = 6, 2 = 5, 3 = 4, 4 = 3, 5 = 2, 6 = 1) you placed in front of items 9 and 11, and then sum the numbers for all six items. Scores range from 6 to 36, with the mean for 152 students being 27.73 with no gender difference. As a relationship develops, mutual self-disclosure leads partners to feel increasingly comfortable sharing their thoughts and experiences with each other. The focus is less on self-expression and more on eliciting information about the other. Moreover, as circumstances change, partners stay attuned to each other.

Second, partners must be willing and able to accept what they learn about each other. Items 1, 4, 7, 8, 14, and 18 compose the acceptance component of "minding." Reverse the number you placed in response to statement 18 and then sum the numbers for the six items. Scores again range from 6 to 36, with a mean score of 25.07. Again, there is no gender difference. This acceptance includes respect for differences in opinions, values, and habits that inevitably occur. Respect prevents partners from falling into criticism that impairs and can destroy relationships.

Third, minding theory states that the attributions partners make for each other's behaviors can support or handicap intimate relations. Items 3, 5, 10, 12, 16, and 17 assess the attributions that partners make. Reverse the number you chose in response to statement 16 and then add the numbers for the six items. Scores range from 6 to 36 with higher scores reflecting a tendency to provide more favorable attributions. The mean is 24.24, with women scoring slightly higher than men. Partners who give each other the benefit of the doubt are happier in their relationship and are more likely to remain together for longer periods of time.

In their theory, the authors make clear that these behaviors and thinking patterns must be *reciprocal*. That is, both partners must be committed to pursuing knowledge, acceptance, and positive attributions for the relationship to thrive. In addition, these expectations and perceptions must have *continuity*. Over time, partners must continue to find out about each other, respect the other's individuality, and engage in positive attributions.

Specific Strategies

Our overview of the literature on love concluding with the minding theory of relationships suggests several principles for strengthening love. The most important and effective strategies include the following:

1. **Carve out time to talk.** Through his in-depth examination of hundreds of marriages, John Gottman (1994) is able to predict with better than 90 percent accuracy which relationships will last. In comparison to their divorced counterparts, successful couples devote an extra five hours per week to their marriage. What do they do? Most important, they talk. Before these couples part every morning, they find out one thing that each is going to do that day. And at the end of each workday, they have a low-stress reunion conversation.

   One sage suggests that we are born with two ears and one mouth because we need to listen twice as much as we speak. Tuning out distractions, including turning off the TV, is the first step. The second is to listen without interrupting. Of course, conversation is a two-way street. Although we think our partners know us inside and out, they are not mind readers. If we want them to understand us we have to speak up and mean what we say. Choosing the right time to talk about important matters is also a skill to be cultivated. Bringing up a sensitive topic just before bedtime is hardly wise.

2. **Handle conflict constructively.** Minding theory recommends that we strive to accept differences in opinions, values, and habits that inevitably occur. Unquestionably some of the differences will lead to conflict. A marriage lives and dies, suggests Gottman (1994), by how well disagreements and grievances are aired. Or as one popular self-help book states,

   > Marital happiness has little to do with whom you marry and everything to do with how you cope with conflict. . . . Simple truth #2: One zinger will erase twenty acts of kindness. . . . It takes one put-down to undo hours of kindness you give to your partner (Notarius & Markman, 1993, pp. 20, 28).

In dealing with conflict, respect for one's partner needs to override anger. Relationships that fail are typically marked by harsh startups in disagreement, partner criticism and contempt, hair-trigger defensiveness, and stonewalling. Instead, recommends Gottman (1994), remain calm, edit yourself (avoid uttering every angry thought when discussing touchy topics), soften your startup, speak nondefensively, validate your partner (express understanding and acknowledge that his or her perspective may have some validity), and accept influence. Successful couples, continues Gottman, know when to exit and repair by using humor, changing the topic to something unrelated, stroking ("I understand this is hard for you"), and communicating that they are on common ground ("This is our problem; we're in this together").

3. **Express admiration.** Minding theory suggests that we give partners the benefit of the doubt and strive to make relationship-enhancing attributions for each other's behavior. Such explanations attribute negative behaviors to external causes and positive behaviors to personal, internal causes. That is, a partner's negative behaviors are explained in terms of something outside the relationship; the partner's positive behaviors are viewed as reflecting his or her inherent virtues.

   In *The Seven Principles for Making Marriage Work,* Gottman and Nan Silver (1999) suggest that in successful relationships, partners make at least five times as many positive statements about each other and their relationship than they do negative ones. Communicate admiration directly: "I believe you've done a good job, and I'm proud of you." Such genuine praise cements connections and also becomes a powerful source of motivation that extends beyond the relationship.

4. **Show affection.** Compared to their less successful counterparts, couples successful in marriage have three common behaviors.

   - They regularly show physical affection—touching, holding, kissing—that reflects tenderness and forgiveness.
   - They have one weekly date.
   - They show genuine appreciation at least once a day.

   Sometimes nothing needs to be said, just the expression of quiet acts of tenderness—touching or holding hands while watching TV or listening to a concert, intertwining feet while reading the Sunday newspaper, taking an evening walk regularly, a spontaneous kiss while doing household chores.

   Romance fades in the midst of family or household responsibilities. Wise couples step back and step out to stoke their passion. They make a date to do something together on a regular basis (Shepell, 2000). They build in playtime. Taking turns organizing the details of the date adds to the enjoyment. And when they're having a really good time, they express delight. They let their partners know.

5. **Create shared meaning.** The willingness to grow and assume responsibility for life together, suggest Robert Sternberg and Catherine Whitney (1991), is a fundamental quality of a successful relationship. When we are stuck in a negative self-story, he observes, we do not take advantage of the gift of life. People who succeed in close relationships are willing to try new things.

Developing interests and activities that can be shared as a couple strengthens bonds. From the simple sharing of a hobby or spending time with mutual friends to formulating life-altering plans for the future—building a house, raising a family—are strategies for creating shared meaning. Annual family rituals that surround important events such as birthdays and holidays serve to build a shared identity. "The heart of marriage," observes Bill Cosby, "is memories."

Remember Hatfield's two-factor theory of passionate love? Any physical arousal in a romantic context may be interpreted as passion. Perhaps it explains why couples who engage together in novel and arousing activities—outdoor activities, new sports, travel, even card games—report greater relationship satisfaction than those who participate in more mundane activities. Surveys as well as field and laboratory experiments (even the simple 7-minute task of jointly carrying a pillow through an obstacle course without using hands, arms, or teeth) confirm the effect (Aron, Norman, & Aron, 2001).

6. **Model Michelangelo.** Our close relationships powerfully shape our well-being. When they are satisfying, our lives are enriched. In fact, close relationships affect the very core of our existence—our self-identity.

Would both you and your partner say this of each other? "My partner regards me as the person I would most like to become," "My partner thinks I have the traits and dispositions that I believe are most desirable," "I find my partner often creates situations in which my ideal self can shine." And thinking back over your relationship, to what degree have you changed as a result of being involved with your partner? Are you closer to your ideal self than before you met?

The careful minding of a relationship—including reciprocity and continuity in building knowledge, acceptance, and positive attributions—can produce the Michaelangelo effect (Drigotas, 2002), in which partners come closer to the people they most aspire being. Just as Michelangelo released the ideal form buried in a block of marble, so romantic partners can foster each other's realization of their ideal selves. When acted on, positive expectations become self-fulfilling prophecies.

In modeling Michelangelo, be specific. Identify three strengths you know your partner values in himself/herself. Then write down recent events in which he or she displayed the strength and share it.

Consummate Love: A Model Relationship

Is consummate love that includes passion, intimacy, and commitment possible? Yes, but it's a challenge. Observe how the three love components come together in Christine Brune's remarkable reflection on her dear friends Wilbur and Anna Comer of Mechanicsville, Iowa (personal communication, September 22, 2003):

> Wilbur and Anna were married just days before he was drafted into heavy combat in World War II. When he was injured and returned nearly two years later, they were finally able to begin what was to be a beautiful married life of over 50 years together. They were inseparable even in their seventies—always touching while sitting side by side, linking arms while walking, patting each other's arms while gesturing. They talked about anything and everything and were truly the best of friends. In retirement, "Wib," as Anna so affectionately called him, took a job as a security guard at the local college. Wib never went anywhere without Anna, and they often publicly spoke fondly about one another: "Wib was the best driver—that's why he worked such long hours in the war. None of the other men were so reliable." "Anna knows just how to set up those peas. You never saw plants with so many peas on them!" And oh, how they laughed! They joked about each other, the weather, the meal, about those "spoiled college kids" who threw everything away instead of trying to fix it. They loved to laugh almost as much as they loved each other. Unfortunately, the one thing they did not share was equally good health. Wib was spiraling downward, yet Anna was as spry and healthy as ever. When Wib passed on, we thought Anna would follow. She fell into a deep depression and would have died without electroconvulsive therapy used as a last resort. It took her two years to recover enough to want to be around. Now she lives with her daughter and shares her memories, and her love, with her family and friends. Though she still says, "It just isn't the same without Wib."

IN REVIEW

The minding theory of relationships states that building knowledge about our partners, respecting differences in habits and values, and making favorable attributions for their behavior builds lasting bonds. Carving out time to talk, handling conflict constructively, expressing admiration, practicing affection, creating shared meaning, and modeling Michelangelo are additional strategies for fostering a consummate love of passion, intimacy, and commitment.

2 empathy

The adult whose concerns extend beyond family and beyond nation to mankind has become fully human.
—LEON EISENBERG, 1972

Compassion is the keen awareness of the interdependence of all things.
—THOMAS MERTON, 1968

Nearly everyone recognizes the bird in the following figure. Do you?

But what kind of bird? And in what direction is it flying? Is it a dove going east, or a goose heading west?

Source: Block & Yuker, 1989.

Here's an ambiguous figure that's a bit more challenging. What's your first impression?

A Native American face looking left? Or could it be an Eskimo returning home from work? In both cases, the same stimulus elicits different perceptions.

Perspective matters. In fact, it can transform both attitudes and actions. Eric Eckard knows. As Tonya Harding's bodyguard, Eckard engineered a debilitating attack on Nancy Kerrigan, Harding's chief competitor for the 1994 Olympic gold medal in figure skating. With her left knee battered, Kerrigan was sidelined for several months. However, when Eckard saw the image of a sobbing Kerrigan on television, he identified with her plight, experienced remorse, and bared his soul to a friend. The series of events finally led to the arrest of the attackers.

Source: Block & Yuker, 1989.

Or consider the case of Carl Lee Hailey in John Grisham's popular novel *A Time to Kill*. Hailey, a poor black farmer in the deep South, was given little chance of escaping death row. His crime? Hailey shot his daughter's drunken rapists as they departed from a preliminary courtroom hearing. After several brutal assaults, they had left 10-year-old Tonya Hailey for dead. There is little question that their punishment was precisely what they deserved.

Still, with an inexperienced defense attorney, a biased judge, and an unsympathetic jury, Hailey faces an uphill fight—a nearly impossible task. In the middle of jury deliberations, however, Wanda Womack asks her fellow white jurors to engage in a simple role-play. Imagine, she says, that the victim is your daughter, that the two assailants were black, that they repeatedly raped her while cursing her for being white. They kicked her in the mouth, knocked out her teeth, broke both jaws, crushed her nose. "Now be honest with yourself," implores Wanda, "Wouldn't you kill if you got the chance?" By secret ballot, all twelve agree that they would do the killing. Carl Lee Hailey is acquitted.

■

Seeing and Feeling from Another's Perspective

Perceiving another's situation can elicit strong emotions and sometimes even that elusive feeling called *empathy*. Psychologist Edward Bradford Titchener (1909) coined the word to refer to the tendency of observers to project themselves into the scene of a painting.

Ezra Stotland (1969) demonstrated that assuming the perspective of another in need fosters feelings of empathy. His research participants watched someone undergo what they believed was a painful medical treatment. Observers who were instructed to imagine how the victim felt showed greater physiological arousal and reported stronger empathic feelings than those who were merely asked to watch the target person's movements.

Empathy involves the capacity to imagine the way the world looks through another's eyes. As we consider another's world, our heart vibrates with its emotional impact. By putting ourselves in another's shoes, we come not only to see what another sees but to feel what another feels. *Compassion,* a term closely linked to *empathy,* comes from the Latin *cum passio,* meaning "suffer with," or "suffer alongside the other."

The following Self-Test, designed by Mark Davis (1980), captures the "seeing" and "feeling" components of empathy. Taking the test will help you appreciate the nature of empathy as many psychologists have studied it, and it will give you a rough idea of how your current level of empathy compares with others'.

Score: 36

Self-Test

For each item, indicate the degree to which the statement is self-descriptive using the following scale:

0	1	2	3	4
Does not describe me well				Describes me very well

2 **1.** Before criticizing somebody, I try to imagine how I would feel if I were in their place.

3 **2.** If I'm sure I'm right about something, I don't waste much time listening to other people's arguments.

4 **3.** I try to understand my friends better by imagining how things look from their perspective.

3 **4.** I believe there are two sides to every question and try to look at them both.

2 **5.** I sometimes find it difficult to see things from the "other guy's" point of view.

4 **6.** I try to look at everybody's side of a disagreement before I make a decision.

1 **7.** When I'm upset with someone, I usually try to put myself in his or her shoes for a while.

3 **8.** When I see someone being taken advantage of, I feel kind of protective toward him or her.

0 **9.** When I see someone being treated unfairly, I sometimes don't feel very much pity for him or her.

2 **10.** I often have tender, concerned feelings for people less fortunate than I am.

4 **11.** I would describe myself as a pretty soft-hearted person.

0 **12.** Sometimes I don't feel very sorry for other people when they are having problems.

3 **13.** Other people's misfortunes do not usually disturb me a great deal.

3 **14.** I am often quite touched by things that I see happen.

Source: Davis, 1980.

Items 1 through 7 *assess one's ability to* step outside the self and assume another's perspective. *In scoring your responses, first reverse the numbers before statements 2 and 5 (i.e., 0 = 4, 1 = 3, 2 = 2, 3 = 1, 4 = 0). Then add the numbers in front of all seven items to obtain a total score. Average scores are 17 or 18; higher scores indicate a greater capacity for perspective taking.*

47

EMPATHY

Items 8 through 14 assess one's capacity to experience feelings of warmth, compassion, and concern for another. *Reverse the numbers before statements 9, 12, and 13 (i.e., 0 = 4, 1 = 3, 2 = 2, 3 = 1, 4 = 0). Then add the numbers for all seven items to obtain a total score. Average scores are approximately 20; higher scores reflect greater empathic concern.*

Empathy and Social Action

Different streams of evidence suggest that empathy makes a difference. For example, several studies (see Schroeder, Penner, Dovidio, and Piliavin, 1995 for a review) report significant positive relationships between empathy as measured by Davis's questionnaire and social action. People with higher scores were more likely to respond to an unexpected request for help, whether it was assisting in a Special Olympics Track and Field Day for mentally challenged children or volunteering to help a researcher complete her study. Empathy also relates to long-term commitments to help. For example, an analysis of more than 400 adults with significant involvement in a variety of charitable organizations found that they had high scores in both perspective taking and empathic concern (Unger & Thumuluri, 1997).

Among the twentieth century's most courageous altruists (those who help selflessly) were people who risked their lives to save Jews in Nazi-ravaged Europe. In attempting to understand the motives for their extraordinary efforts, Samuel and Pearl Oliner (1988) conducted extensive interviews of more than 400 rescuers. Many interviewees pointed to feelings of empathy as guiding their actions. In some cases, it was simply the awareness of another's peril or misery that evoked compassion. Merely knowing others were suffering was sufficient to arouse them—"I could not stand idly by and observe the daily misery that was occurring." In other cases, empathy was the reaction to a compelling plea for help. In explaining how she cared for a ragged, starving Jewish man who had escaped from a concentration camp, one rescuer said, "How could one not have helped such a man? . . . He was shivering and I was shivering, too, with emotion."

Of course, empathy is not the only response to human suffering. Our gut reactions to human tragedy and the distress of others can include shock, anger, fear, or even apathy. Seeing suffering can lead to considerable personal distress.

Daniel Batson (1991, 2002) believes that both self-serving and selfless considerations motivate helping. Seeing someone suffer causes us distress, which we may seek to relieve by escaping the distressing situation. But suffering also elicits empathy, particularly when we feel attached to the victim. Such "other" orientation lifts us above self-centered need and reflects genuine compassion. We help even if escape is possible.

Controlled laboratory experiments have been especially helpful in sorting out how these different reactions to human suffering impact behavior. In one study Batson and his colleagues (1981) instilled empathy in some research participants by informing them that they were very similar in attitudes and values to "Elaine," a young woman they observe receiving what they believe are electric shocks. In the course of the experiment, Elaine explains that a childhood fall against an electric fence has left her acutely sensitive to shock. In sympathy, the experimenter suggests that the observers might take Elaine's place and receive her remaining shocks. The research team then tells some of the observers that their part in the experiment is completed and they are finished observing Elaine's suffering. They can escape the distressing situation. Others are told that they will continue to see the victim suffer. In short, there is no escape. Results indicated that those who felt empathic concern helped regardless of whether escape was available or not. Those who felt no empathy were more likely to choose escape when it was made available.

IN REVIEW

Individuals may perceive even a simple stimulus quite differently. Judgments of others are very much in the eye of the beholder. By putting ourselves in others' shoes we come to see what they see and to feel what they feel. Research suggests that empathy is an important source of prosocial action. In fact, laboratory studies indicate that it may promote genuine altruism.

Dangers of Snap Judgments

Although our perceptions are almost automatic, they are not always accurate. Try the following puzzles.

Does this shape appear to be a spiral? Now cover half the figure and you'll see that it's really a series of concentric circles.

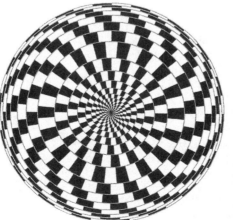

Source: Seckel, 2002.

Are the lines in the following figure straight, or are they distorted? Check them with a ruler.

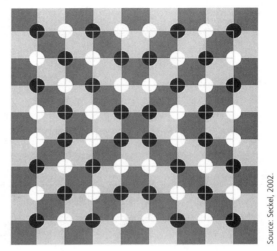

Source: Seckel, 2002.

Finally, are all the lines in this pattern the same length? Measure them.

Source: Seckel, 2002.

Things are not always what they seem.

We make snap judgments quickly and easily. Here are my impressions of a few students I've had in recent classes. Take a look. Do you share my impressions?

1. *Behavior:* For each of the first three days of an introductory psychology class, a female student arrives ten minutes late. *Impression:* This tardy student seems both irresponsible and inconsiderate.

2. *Behavior:* An international student sits near the back of class. Even questions addressed specifically to him need repeating. *Impression:* This unmotivated student has probably never learned to study. He needs to get on track.

3. *Behavior:* In the week before the first test, a student comes to my office several times for help in understanding course material. On the day of the test she arrives late and performs poorly. *Impression:* Although she craves attention, she lacks both the ability and the motivation to succeed.

4. *Behavior:* A student in the front row appears emotionless. Always entering and leaving class alone, she ignores greetings as well as good-byes. *Impression:* This student is aloof and socially inept.

5. *Behavior:* The highest scoring student in class majors in another subject. Often smirking, he rarely makes eye contact and never contributes to class discussion. *Impression:* He is here merely to meet a course requirement. Rather arrogant, he finds the subject matter neither challenging nor interesting.

In each case, the student's life situation proved my snap judgment horribly wrong. The tardy student turned out to be a single mom whose kindergartner climbed on the school bus just as our class started. From the bus stop she rushed to join us. The international student? He had recently learned that his father had terminal cancer and he had no money to return home for a good-bye visit. The privately tutored student was knocked off her bike on the way to class. Although severely shaken and late, she had studied hard and did not want to postpone the test. The "aloof" student's course journal at semester's end movingly described years of childhood sexual abuse she had not previously disclosed. The tragic experience had devastated her emotional and social life. And how about my "arrogant" student? He was painfully shy. He appeared in an elective class the following semester eager to minor in psychology.

People are not always what they seem at first glance. This is not to say that negative judgments are always erroneous or that people never contribute to their own failure, merely that life situations are unique and shape people's actions more than we know.

Snap judgments are the greatest competitor to empathy. We tend to think that people's behavior and their life outcomes necessarily reflect their inner traits. Because the impact of a situation on people's behavior is less apparent, sometimes even buried in the past, this important contributor often is ignored. It takes time and effort to consider the situational context.

"At its simplest, empathy means feeling the same thing that another person's feeling," suggests psychologist Martin Hoffman (cited in Glass, 2001). "At its most sophisticated, it's understanding his entire life situation." Compassion often requires that we look beneath the surface in seeking genuine understanding and insight.

But the demands and pressures of daily living often force snap judgments. We are people with important jobs to do. We intend to do them well and want not to be interrupted. We have classes to meet, appointments to keep, books to read, papers to write, clothes to wash, and rooms to clean. Our calendars are filled, our watch alarms set. Workaholics always have an edge, observes Lewis Smedes (1982, p. 30), "We deserve to be excused because we are so virtuous."

Timothy Miller (1995) suggests that the first step to empathy is overcoming snap judgments. "Most blanket condemnations," he writes, "of a person's character, intelligence, intentions, or social value are non-compassionate. It doesn't matter whether they are spoken or remain private."

Practice empathy with the following Critical Thinking activity, and then consider the effects of your preconceptions and expectations on your empathy levels.

Practicing Empathy

Read the following frustrating situations, allowing yourself first automatic, non-compassionate reactions. Then follow them, suggests Miller, with more empathic reflections that take into account the person's possible life situation.

Frustrating/Annoying Situation	Noncompassionate Thoughts	Compassionate Thoughts
1. Your pizza order gets lost, and you have to call again to get it delivered.		
2. A fellow student always reminds you of his latest accomplishments.		
3. A neighbor's barking dog wakes you early in the morning.		
4. A telemarketer calls to sell you magazine subscriptions.		
5. A friend fails to meet you at the airport as she promised.		

Preconceptions and Expectations: Is It a Just World?

Do you agree with the following statements? True or false?

T   F   **1.** Basically, the world is a just place.

T   F   **2.** By and large, people deserve what they get.

T   F   **3.** People who get "lucky breaks" have usually earned their good fortune.

T   F   **4.** People who meet with misfortune have often brought it on themselves.

T   F   **5.** Students almost always deserve the grades they receive in school.

Source: Selected items from Rubin & Peplau, 1975.

Do you tend to agree or disagree with these statements? Do you believe the world is a just place or not?

Another reason why we rush to judgment, suggests psychologist Melvin Lerner (1980), is a deep-seated belief in a just world. We need to believe that the world is a place where people generally get what they deserve. From early childhood we are taught that good is rewarded and evil is punished. Success comes to those who do what's right and suffering to those who don't. Hard work will pay off; laziness will not.

According to Lerner, people do care about justice for others as well as for themselves. This concern may motivate people to help those in distress, if only to eliminate what they perceive as a threat to their belief in a just world. However, the desire for a just world may also lead them to rationalize injustice. When the British marched German civilians through the Bergen-Belsen concentration camp after World War II, one German responded: "What terrible criminals these prisoners must have been to receive such treatment."

We may come to believe that those who are rewarded must be good, and those who are punished must be evil. Especially when we feel powerless to change things, it's a short step from believing that people get what they deserve to believing that people deserve what they get.

Perceived Dissimilarity

Empathy, and avoiding a rush judgment, seems to flow from the awareness that we are all made of the same basic stuff. Samuel and Pearl Oliner's interviews with the rescuers of Jews in Nazi Europe repeatedly indicated that it was the perception of human kinship that motivated the rescuers. In general, the rescuers experienced feelings of connection to diverse people and groups. They tended to see others as similar to themselves; nonrescuers were more likely to emphasize their distinctiveness. Using "extensivity" ratings to assess the degree to which one's perception of similarity reaches beyond one's immediate family to include acquaintances, unfamiliar groups, and finally all of humanity, the Oliners were able to identify rescuers and nonrescuers 73 percent of the time.

Common Fire: Leading Lives of Commitment in a Complex World (Daloz, Keen, Keen, & Parks, 1997) relates the stories of more than 100 humanitarians. Although a variety of motives contributed to helping, every single person shared one experience in common. Early in life, these future humanitarians came to know someone very well whom they previously thought was very different from themselves. By working or studying or traveling together, they came to understand that the person was more like them than not. The experience transformed their understanding of who is "us" and who is not.

Perceived dissimilarity and, with it, the apparent inability to assume another's perspective, have opposite effects on behavior. Imagining the absence of empathy helps us understand how criminal psychopaths, child molesters, spouse abusers, rapists, and torturers can engage in their horrifying acts.

Snap judgment is a major obstacle to empathy. Our strong tendency to see people's behavior as reflecting their traits often leads us to overlook their life situations. Time pressures, the belief in a just world, and perceived dissimilarity also short-circuit compassion.

Forgiveness

Empathy for suffering victims is one thing. Empathy for the perpetrators of suffering is another matter, especially if we have been their targets. How easy is it to forgive? This Transgression Narrative Test (TNT) by Jack W. Berry and his colleagues (2001) provides a brief measure.

SELF-ASSESSMENT ■

Likeliness to Forgive

Below are a number of situations in which people might find themselves. People respond in different ways to these situations in terms of what things they will forgive. Read each situation and imagine that it has happened to you. Using the scale, indicate how you think you would respond to the situation.

1 = definitely not forgive   2 = not likely to forgive   3 = just as likely to forgive as not   4 = likely to forgive   5 = definitely forgive

_____ **1.** Someone you occasionally see in a class has a paper due at the end of the week. You have already turned this paper in, and your classmate says that he or she is under a lot of time pressure and asks you to lend him or her your paper for some ideas. You agree, and your classmate simply retypes your paper and hands it in. The professor recognizes the paper, calls both of you to her office, scolds you, and says you are lucky she doesn't put you both on academic probation. Imagine yourself in such a situation and rate how likely you are to forgive the person who borrowed your paper.

_____ **2.** A fairly close friend tells you that he or she needs some extra money for an upcoming holiday. You know a married couple who needs a babysitter for their 3-year-old for a couple of nights and you recommend your friend. Your friend is grateful and takes the job. On the first night, the child gets out of bed after your friend has fallen asleep watching television and drinks cleaning fluid from beneath the kitchen sink. The child is taken by ambulance to the hospital and stays there for two days for observation and treatment. The married couple will not speak to you. Imagine yourself in such a situation and rate how likely you are to forgive your friend.

_____ **3.** A friend offers to drop off a job application for you at the post office by the deadline for submission. A week later, you get a letter from the potential employer saying that your application could not be considered because it was postmarked after the deadline and they had a very strict policy about this. Your friend tells you that he or she met an old friend, went to lunch, and lost track of time. When he or she remembered the package it was close to closing time at the post office and he or she would have had to rush frantically to get there. He or she decided that deadlines usually aren't that strictly enforced, so he or she waited until the next morning to mail the package. Imagine yourself in such a situation and rate how likely you are to forgive your friend for not mailing the application on time.

_____ **4.** After high school graduation, you start a new job, and it turns out that a former classmate from high school works there, too. You think this is great; now you don't feel like such a stranger. Even though the classmate wasn't part of your crowd, there's at least a face you recognize. You two hit it off right away and talk about old times. A few weeks later you are having lunch in the cafeteria and you overhear several of your coworkers, who do not realize you are nearby, talking about you and laughing; one even sounds snide and hostile toward you. You discover that your old classmate has told them about something you did back in school that you are deeply ashamed of and did not want anyone to know about. Imagine yourself in such a situation and rate how likely you are to forgive your old classmate for telling others your secret.

_____ **5.** A distant cousin you haven't seen since childhood calls you one day and asks if he can stay with you while he looks for work and an apartment. You say it will be fine. He asks you to pick him up at the bus station that night and you do so. Your cousin is just as you fondly remember him; you reminisce for several hours. The next morning you give him some advice on job and apartment hunting in the area, then you go about your own business. That night you come home and witness an angry argument in front of your residence between your cousin and a neighbor. Your cousin is obviously very drunk, cursing, and out of control. You ask what's happening, and without really taking the time to recognize you, your cousin throws a bottle at you, cutting the side of your head. The police arrive and with some scuffling, take your cousin away and take you to the emergency room where your cut is stitched up. The next afternoon, your cousin calls from the police station. He says he is really sorry about the whole scene and that it was not like him; he was upset about being turned down for three jobs that day. Imagine yourself in such a situation and rate how likely you are to forgive your cousin.

To obtain a total score, add up the numbers you used to respond to the five situations. Scores range from 5 to 25, with higher scores reflecting a greater disposition to forgive. A sample of 88 undergraduate students at an urban, mid-Atlantic state university obtained a mean score of 13.3.

Fostering Forgiveness

The essence of forgiveness, suggests Michael McCullough and his colleagues (2000), is a motivational change. When people forgive, they become less driven to harm their transgressors. In fact, they become more motivated to act in ways that will benefit them.

Forgiveness seems positively linked to mental health and well-being. Forgiving people report less depression, hostility, and anger. They are more hopeful and experience higher self-esteem. Of particular interest is recent research relating forgiveness to physical well-being. Charlotte vanOyen Witvliet and her colleagues (2001) tested the physiological responses of undergraduates as they imagined responding to their real-life offenders in both unforgiving ways and forgiving ways. During forgiving imagery trials (empathizing with the humanity of the offender, granting forgiveness), participants experienced less physiological stress, lower levels of negative emotion, higher levels of positive emotion, and greater perceived control. Those who adopt forgiving responses may reap psychological and physiological benefits, at least in the short run.

Research indicates that people's reports of forgiveness for specific transgressors are highly correlated with the extent to which they experience empathy for them (McCullough, 2001). In fact, when examined experimentally, empathy for the transgressor seems to be a powerful route to forgiveness.

CRITICAL THINKING ■

Forgiveness Journal

Many—perhaps most—of us live with the memory of hurt received from someone. Often that person had been close to us. Should we and can we forgive? In Forgiveness Is a Choice, *Robert D. Enright (2001) suggests that you tell the story of the person who hurt you. In an effort to foster compassion, your journal might address the following questions:*

1. What was life like for the offender when growing up? Because most hurts occur at the hands of people close to us, we usually know something of their life history. Try to enter the offender's world and describe three or four things about his or her past that may have contributed to vulnerability. Be careful not to confuse forgiving with excusing. The person's hardships should not become your own.

2. At the time of the hurtful event, what was life like for the person? Try to imagine what he or she may have been thinking and feeling. Was he or she under considerable pressure? Was vulnerability present, too?

3. Tell the story of your relationship with the person in a broader sense than the offense itself. How long had you know the person? Had you shared good times? Try to think of at least three times the person showed good judgment or strong character.

4. Write down any impressions of how the offender may be worse off now than are you as a result of the painful event. What is life like for him or her because of what happened?

5. What is the person like apart from the offense? Forgiving does not necessarily mean that you must welcome the person back as a spouse, employer, or close friend. Merely try to see the person as a member of the human community with intrinsic value. Review your answers to the previous questions and describe what makes the person human.

6. Has your view of the person changed in any way as a result of answering these questions? Is there anything you must still do to deepen or broaden your story of the person?

IN REVIEW

Empathy for those who have injured us is a special challenge. However, forgiveness is positively linked to well-being. Retelling the story of the person who has harmed us can be an effective route to forgiveness.

■

Cultivating Empathy

Why cultivate empathy? Let's first consider the many benefits that come from developing compassion.

Benefits of Empathy

Both philosophers and psychologists have claimed that empathy is the bedrock of human morality. We might cultivate it for no other reason than as a tool for doing our moral duty. But compassion is more than a rule. In many respects, it is the most natural thing in the world. Most of us come hard-wired for empathy. Newborns cry in response to the sound of another infant's cry. It is no mere echo either, but a vigorous, intense, spontaneous cry. In hospital nurseries, one newborn's distress can evoke a chorus of crying. Rudimentary forms of compassion and helping—for example, offering a toy to a distraught sibling—can be observed in children before their second birthday. Time and again people asked to reflect on their motives for rescuing Jews during the Holocaust refused to see themselves as heroic: "I insist on saying that it was absolutely natural to have done this," or "I did nothing unusual; anyone would have done the same thing in my place," or "Well, where else could they go? I had to take them in."

In shifting our attention to others, compassion keeps us from self-preoccupation and thus enables us to live with greater purpose and freedom. "Nothing makes you happier," suggests Mother Teresa, "than when you really reach out in mercy to someone who is badly hurt" (Myers, 1992, p. 194). Reflecting on what she learned in her work in Calcutta with the Missionaries of Charity, one volunteer wrote: "One lesson is that you become *less* vulnerable when you concern yourself with other people's vulnerability rather than your own. We've found that when we're fully involved with helping others, we haven't really got time to worry about our own fears—and so they fall into perspective."

Neal Plantinga (1987) captures the same simple truth: "The more self-absorbed we are, the less there is to find absorbing. To have no real involvement in others, no identification with them, no interest—in other words, to lack *compassion*—is to shrink one's world down to the cramped precincts within one's own skull. And there is not enough there for one long solo trip in a car without a tape deck, let alone for a lifetime."

CRITICAL THINKING ■

Happiness and Helpfulness

Try a simple test. List ten people you know well, using just their initials or nicknames.

1. _____
2. _____
3. _____
4. _____
5. _____
6. _____
7. _____
8. _____
9. _____
10. _____

*Beside each name write an **H** if that person tends to be happy, an **N** if he or she is not happy.*

*Go through the list again, writing an **S** if that person tends to be selfish, that is, shows a stable tendency to devote time and resources primarily to his or her own interests and welfare and is unwilling to be inconvenienced by others. Write a **U** if the person tends to be unselfish.*

*Examine your list. Is there any pattern between the assignment of **H**'s and **N**'s and the assignment of **S**'s and **U**'s?*

Most people perceive happy people as being unselfish. Likewise, unhappy people are more likely to be characterized as selfish. Bernard Rimland (1982), who first suggested this little exercise, notes that these relationships provide an interesting paradox: selfish people are those who are devoted to bringing themselves happiness. As judged by others, however, these selfish people are far less likely to be happy than those who are devoted to making others happy.

As with forgiveness, empathy-induced altruism also boosts physical and psychological well-being (Batson, 1991, pp. 222–223). One survey of over 1700 women regularly involved in prosocial action found that they experienced a "high" while helping and a sense of "calm" afterward. Similarly, fostering heart patients' interest in the welfare of others, and in doing things for others, not only made them feel better, it actually led to reduced coronary artery blockage. The "helper's high," suggests Robert Cialdini (cited in Elias, 2002) lowers the output of stress hormones and strengthens the immune system.

Indeed, the old adage "It is better to give than to receive" seems true. Compassionate people live longer. Following 423 older couples over a five-year period, University of Michigan psychologist Stephanie Brown and her colleagues (2003) found that giving support and assistance was a better predictor of longevity than receiving it. People who reported giving day-to-day help were half as likely to have died at the study's end. To make sure that "givers" were not healthier at the outset of the study, the researchers controlled for a host of factors linked to longevity, including age, gender, smoking, and drinking.

Fostering Empathy

How do we foster empathy? How do we nurture social compassion in ourselves and in our children? This chapter's brief overview of the relevant psychological research suggests several specific answers:

1. **Put on new glasses.** If indeed we make snap judgments of people's behavior, it helps to practice the opposite, especially when others irritate us. What factors in her situation might contribute to her not calling as she promised? What might be happening in his life that makes it difficult for him to communicate and seem unfriendly? What factors lead her to exaggerate and distort what really happened?

2. **Turn on the receptors.** Practicing compassion requires active listening, not only to those closest to us, but also to distressed people we rarely talk with

in our daily lives. "To spend time talking with street people," writes Alfie Kohn (1990, p. 162), "to learn how they fear falling asleep in the wrong places lest someone steal what little they have, how they drink to blot out the hopelessness, how fiercely loyal friendships blossom in alleys and parks—this is to turn an abstract problem (homelessness) into real human beings."

3. **Learn from stories and films.** Narratives put a human face on social problems and provide a helpful channel of communication for both us and our children. Films that transport us into the experience of specific individuals and families are particularly effective in fostering empathy. Many years ago, two film series—*Roots* and *Holocaust* (both still available on video)—elicited great empathy for African-American and Jewish suffering. More recently, the portrayal of schizophrenia in *A Beautiful Mind* and the coverage of AIDS through victims' eyes in *A Closer Walk* have fostered empathy for those suffering these horrific illnesses.

4. **Broaden the range of our experiences.** "How can you truly know the poor," challenged Mother Teresa (1995, p. xxxi), "unless you live like them?" One of the most encouraging developments on college campuses throughout the country has been the explosion in service learning. Students who participate in the programs subsequently demonstrate greater citizen involvement, social responsibility, cooperation, and leadership (Andersen, 1998; Putnam, 2000). After volunteering in a homeless shelter, one student wrote: "My work in the shelter was emotional learning. I was forced to not-so-gently confront my assumptions, the barriers in my mind between us and them. When a former high school classmate needing a free lunch appeared among the homeless, I realized what a narrow line separated my life from hers. I am recommitted to a career in the helping profession where caring becomes a vocation, not just an avocation" (Mother Teresa, 1995, p. 183).

5. **Role-play.** Assuming the role of those closest to us, if only for a brief time, can enhance mutual understanding. Listen to this heart-warming note to advice columnist Ann Landers (1990):

> I want you to help me say thank you to my wife. We both have full-time jobs, and there's plenty to do to keep this household running. Last night we fell asleep knowing there was one more load of laundry to move from the washer to the dryer. I woke about 12:15. I knew my wife needed those clothes in the washer to wear to her job the next day, so I figured I'd just toss them in the dryer. When I got there, the dryer was full, and so was the clean clothes basket. I started to fold and stack underwear and socks to make room for the next load. Ann, there were at least 100 pieces to handle from just one load, and I'm sure my wife does at least four or five loads every week. Well, 35 minutes later, while standing on that cold cement floor, I had a much deeper appreciation for what my wife does several times a week with never a complaint. I decided not to sign my name,

because there are probably thousands of women out there who would fit this description, and I'd like each one to think this thank-you is from a grateful mate.

—A Lucky Guy, Canton, Ohio

6. **See similarities.** To foster compassion, we need to see that kinship extends beyond our immediate family, group, and country to every member of the human race. As Robert C. Roberts (1982, p.110) notes, vulnerability to suffering, weakness, and death are things we have in common with absolutely every human being. In this respect we have fellowship with anybody who comes along. I, too, am vulnerable to disease and early death. I, too, may suffer unhappiness in my work and perhaps the pain of lost employment. I, too, may experience family discord and rejection by loved ones. Coming to such awareness is hardly easy, but it is essential to the development of empathy as well as self-understanding.

7. **Perform random acts of kindness.** Aristotle observed, "We become just by the practice of just actions, self-controlled by exercising self-control, and courageous by performing acts of courage." And we become compassionate by exercising compassion. Our actions powerfully shape our attitudes.

8. **Raise helpful children.** Several child-rearing practices strengthen compassionate habits, including the following:

   a. Be a responsive parent. Parents who establish warm, nurturing relationships with their children teach them to approach life with trust and the sense that the world is a benevolent, safe place. As a result, the children themselves are more caring. To teach children empathy, one must show children empathy (Borba, 2001).

   b. Build the child's emotional vocabulary. Parents help foster empathy when they tune in to their children's feelings, recognize what's causing the emotion, and label how they are feeling. As children acquire emotional literacy, they become more capable of experiencing and understanding other people's concerns and needs (Borba, 2001).

   c. Let children know how you feel. Children are clearly affected by parents' accounts of their personal reactions to others. Compassion-modeling parents regularly take into account another's perspective ("Boy, I guess that waitress must have had a long, hard day to forget to bring our drinks, huh?") and behave accordingly.

   d. Give reasons. Parents and teachers need to explain the reasons for rules and, more specifically, the impact that hurting and helping have on others. ("When you share your paper dolls with Katie, she gets to have fun, too, and that makes her happy.") Undergraduates raised in homes characterized by a rational rather than a punitive approach to discipline are later more likely to be involved in social service and political activism (Kohn, 1990, p. 90).

e. Provide hands-on experience. Children do not have to leave school to experience a different world. For years, all students, K–5, at Swansfield Elementary School of Columbia, Maryland, have learned compassion firsthand at the school's Disabilities Awareness Day (Peterson, 1992). The entire school spends the day with the disabled, including the blind and their seeing eye dogs, the wheelchair-bound playing basketball, and people with AIDS.

f. Introduce cooperative learning. Research has shown that Elliot Aronson's (Aronson & Bridgeman, 1979) "jigsaw" technique sharpens youngsters' general empathic capacity. Jigsaw is a group learning experience that requires everyone's cooperative effort to achieve success. Students in a history class may be divided into small groups of five or six each. In a unit on France, one student might be assigned to become the expert on France's culture, another on its government, another on its economy. First, the various "experts" meet to research their assignment. Then each expert returns to the home group to teach what has been learned to the class. Students quickly learn that they are dependent on each other: each has a piece of the puzzle. The only way to master the material is to pay attention to what every group member has to say. Students learn to listen attentively as well as to put themselves in each other's shoes in order to ask questions in a clear and nonthreatening manner. Self-confident students have to listen carefully to learn from the more reticent, who in turn learn that they have something important to contribute to their peers. Research findings suggest that the strategy changes "those people" to "we people," and the newly discovered empathy spills over into other relationships.

g. Encourage a compassionate self-image. Hands-on experiences not only promote learning by doing but also encourage children to think of themselves as compassionate, caring people. Thus, a self-fulfilling prophecy is set in motion. Prompting children with enough justification to perform a good deed may increase their pleasure in performing such deeds on their own. Furthermore, when children are generous, an unanticipated compliment—for example, "It's great that you were willing to take an hour out to help your little brother"—is likely to strengthen an empathic self-image and promote continued generosity.

IN REVIEW

Empathy can enable us to live with greater purpose and freedom and with better physical and psychological health. Promoting empathy begins with a conscious effort to surmount its obstacles. Informing ourselves of others' life situations helps cultivate empathy. Active listening is a first step. Sharing others' experiences, even vicariously through role-playing, also helps. Responsive, nurturant parents provide models of empathy. Providing children with hands-on experiences builds bonds with people in need as well as a compassionate self-image.

self-control

3

*I count him braver who overcomes his desires than him who conquers his
enemies, for the hardest victory is over self.*
—ARISTOTLE (384–322 B.C.)

Homer's Odysseus knew the power of human desires and impulses. He recognized
what he should do, yet he questioned his ability to do it. To avoid self-destruction,
Odysseus took preemptive action. To sail past the Sirens, whose sweet melodies
lured men to the rocks and shipwreck, he plugged the ears of his crew with wax and
then tied himself to the mast of his ship.

Consider a contemporary example:

In a cocaine addiction center in Denver, patients are offered an opportunity to submit to
extortion. They may write a self-incriminating letter, preferably a letter confessing their
drug addiction, addressed to an important person. They deposit the letter with the clinic
and submit to a randomized schedule of laboratory tests. If a laboratory test finds evidence
of cocaine use, the clinic sends the letter to the addressee. An example is a physician who
addresses a letter to the State Board of Medical Examiners confessing that he has admin-
istered cocaine to himself in violation of the laws of Colorado and requests that his license
to practice be revoked. Faced with the prospect of losing career, livelihood, and social
standing, the physician has a powerful incentive to stay clean (Schelling, 1992, p. 167).

Power of Immediate Rewards

Sometimes we are our own worst enemies. Many of us have been guilty of the
following:

- Sleeping in rather than going to work
- Partying the night before a test
- Charging purchases to credit cards without having money to pay them off
- Watching television rather than exercising
- Taking an expensive vacation instead of saving for college

- Blowing a diet with a high-calorie dessert
- Consuming excessive alcohol that damages our brain and liver
- Smoking, vastly increasing our vulnerability to cancer, emphysema, and other ills

What do these self-control failures have in common? In each case, small, immediate rewards prove more powerful than large but delayed rewards (Logue, 1995).

Marshmallow Test

Think back to when you were only 4 years old. Imagine that a man takes you into a room and places one of your favorite treats—a marshmallow—on the table in front of you. He then says, "You can have this marshmallow now if you want, but if you don't eat it until after I run an errand, you can have two."

What would you do? Do you think you could wait?

Some years ago Walter Mischel and his colleagues (e.g., Mischel, Ebbesen, & Zeiss, 1972) presented the marshmallow dilemma to preschoolers at Stanford University. The children found the task real and utterly involving. Most, of course, wanted the double treat and decided to wait. However, as the time passed for the experimenter to complete his errand, their patience was tested. The delay became increasingly frustrating. Children showed significant differences in their ability to wait the seemingly endless 15 minutes it took for the experimenter to return.

The importance of kids' ability to delay gratification in the marshmallow test became apparent as the years passed (Goleman, 1995). Researchers who revisited the children as adolescents found important differences. Compared to the impulsive children, those who resisted temptation at age 4 were, as adolescents, more confident, trustworthy, and dependable. They were better at handling stress. They were more likely to welcome challenges and to persevere in the face of difficulty. More than a decade after they had been put to the test, they were still better able to delay gratification in pursuit of larger rewards.

Even more surprising was that when the children were again tested as high school graduates, those who had patiently waited for the extra marshmallow proved to be superior students. Compared to those who had succumbed to temptation, they showed a greater ability to concentrate and were more persistent in pursuing their goals. Most astonishingly, they had dramatically higher college-placement test scores. In fact, those who had waited the longest for the marshmallows scored more than 200 points higher than those who had immediately grabbed for one. Compared to their IQ at age 4, passing the marshmallow test was a much better predictor of college preparation success (Goleman, 1998).

The advantage persisted into adulthood. Followed into their late twenties, those who resisted temptation were more socially competent. Compared to their counterparts, they developed more stable interpersonal relationships and were more dependable in the workplace (Goleman, 1998).

How about you? Are you more prone to favor the here and now rather than what's to come? To what extent do you reflect on the future consequences of your current behavior? The following scale measures our tendency to consider the distant outcomes of our current behaviors.

Consideration of Future Consequences Scale

For each statement, use the scale to indicate whether or not the statement is characteristic of you.

1 = extremely uncharacteristic   2 = somewhat uncharacteristic   3 = uncertain
4 = somewhat characteristic 5 = extremely characteristic

_____ **1.** I consider how things might be in the future and try to influence them with my day-to-day behavior.

_____ **2.** I often engage in a particular behavior to achieve outcomes that may not result for many years.

_____ **3.** I only act to satisfy immediate concerns, figuring the future will take care of itself.

_____ **4.** My behavior is only influenced by the immediate (i.e., a matter of days or weeks) outcomes of my actions.

_____ **5.** My convenience is a big factor in the decisions I make or the actions I take.

_____ **6.** I am willing to sacrifice my immediate happiness or well-being in order to achieve future outcomes.

_____ **7.** I think it is important to take warnings about negative outcomes seriously even if the negative outcome will not occur for many years.

_____ **8.** I think it is more important to perform a behavior with important distant consequences than a behavior with less important immediate consequences.

_____ **9.** I generally ignore warnings about possible future problems because I think the problems will be resolved before they reach crisis level.

_____ **10.** I think that sacrificing now is usually unnecessary since future outcomes can be dealt with at a later time.

_____ **11.** I only act to satisfy immediate concerns, figuring that I will take care of future problems that may occur at a later date.

_____ **12.** Since my day-to-day work has specific outcomes, it is more important to me than behavior that has distant outcomes.

Source: Strathman, Gleicher, Boninger, & Edwards, 1994.

To score yourself, first reverse the numbers you gave in response to statements 3, 4, 5, 9, 10, 11, and 12 (1 = 5, 2 = 4, 3 = 3, 4 = 2, 5 = 1). Then add up the numbers in front of all 12 items. Total scores can range from 12 to 60 with higher scores reflecting greater consideration of future consequences. Students in an introductory psychology course at the University of Missouri obtained a mean score of 42.5.

Do scores on the Consideration of Future Consequences Scale make a difference? The researchers found that high scorers were more conscientious, hopeful, and optimistic. They demonstrated greater concern for their health, including less cigarette smoking and lower alcohol consumption. Those with higher scores were also more likely to be environmentally conscious, as shown by recycling, driving a fuel-efficient car, and using a water-saving showerhead.

Self-Control: Master Virtue?

Learning to delay gratification is both a mark of maturity and a key to a productive and socially responsible life.

Health psychologists tell us that we would all live longer if we did just three things: exercise regularly, stop smoking, and eat the right foods (Twenge & Baumeister, 2002). But it's not easy. The pleasures of the moment might lead us to spend the night on the couch watching TV, smoking cigarettes, and consuming a box of chocolates.

Studies of the marshmallow kids and research with the Consideration of Future Consequences Scale both highlight the importance of self-control to academic achievement and job success. June Tangney and Roy Baumeister (2000) found that high scores on their trait measure of self-control were linked to success across many activities, including higher college grades. Underachievement in school and work can often be traced to failure to see a task through to the end. The ever-present lure of procrastination—a temptation as enticing as chocolate—can also undo us (Twenge & Baumeister, 2002). Self-control even pays for college and professional football players. Coaches rated players with greater self-restraint as having better football ability, as being more highly motivated, and as showing stronger leadership (Goleman, 1998).

Self-regulation is also important to happy and stable interpersonal relationships. The capacity to delay gratification has been linked to stronger family cohesion, more secure attachments to others, and better anger management (Tangney & Baumeister, 2000). In contrast, people who fail at self-control bring unhappiness not only to themselves but also to those people who are close to them. Neglecting the future consequences of one's actions underlies most antisocial conduct. Indeed, deficient self-control may be the major contributing factor to criminality (Gottfredson & Hirschi, 1990).

Self-control, suggest Roy Baumeister and Julie Exline (1999), is the master virtue. In fact, Baumeister and his colleagues (1994) argue that instilling strong self-control should be the single most important objective of socializing children. They recommend "that parents regard the inculcation of self-control as the premier goal in child-rearing" (p. 259). This is more important, they suggest, than cultivating self-esteem, creativity, obedience, sociability, or even love for parents.

IN REVIEW

Self-control often requires that we ignore immediate rewards in favor of larger, delayed rewards. Compared to the children who failed the marshmallow test, the children who passed it demonstrated greater personal and social competence in adulthood. Consideration of the future consequences of one's behavior seems to be associated with better health, greater job success, and stronger interpersonal relations. Self-control may be the master virtue.

Controlling Our Internal States

How did some of the kids in the marshmallow test manage to reap the double treat? Some covered their eyes so that they wouldn't have to look. Others talked or sang to themselves. A few even tried to go to sleep. By using distraction, they maximized their reward (Mischel, 1974).

Hot "Go" Versus Cool "Slow"

Self-control may be best understood in terms of the operation of "hot" versus "cool" systems (Metcalfe & Mischel, 1999). A hot, emotional system signals "go." It is simple, reflexive, fast, and fully developed at birth. It seeks immediate rewards—the quick gratification of our needs and impulses. In contrast, a cool, thinking system signals "slow." It is complex, reflective, flexible, and develops with age. It applies the brakes to our automatic reactions. It considers the future consequences of action and thereby enables self-control.

The hot/cool system analysis helps us to understand why the use of distraction strategies was the best predictor of successful delay in the marshmallow test. Those who attended to the rewards, thus activating the hot emotional system, were unable to wait. Those who focused their attention elsewhere, thereby activating the cool system, passed the test.

In one clever variation on the original study (Mischel, 1974), investigators found that merely instructing the children to think differently about marshmallows affected their capacity to delay. They told some of the kids to think of the marshmallows they were waiting for as puffy, round clouds—in other words, to focus on the cool, abstract qualities of the rewards. Other children were told to think about how sweet and chewy the marshmallows would be in their mouth, that is, to focus on the hot, pleasurable aspects of the rewards. The results? The children who thought about the rewards in hot terms were able to wait only 5 minutes on average. Those who thought about them in cool terms were able to wait an average of 13 minutes.

In everyday life, the operation of the hot versus cool systems is most vivid in anger management. In a 1997 heavyweight boxing match, Evander Holyfield's head-butting enraged former champion Mike Tyson. It brought back memories of Holy-field's doing the same thing 8 months earlier in a match Tyson lost. Tyson had complained bitterly. This time, his hot system activated, he reacted instantaneously. Shocking all boxing fans, Tyson bit off a chunk of Holyfield's ear. It cost him $3 million and a year's suspension from boxing.

Compare Tyson's hot reaction to the cool response of 6-year-old Ruby Bridges, one of the first African-American children to enter an all-white New Orleans school. In 1960, an angry white crowd jeered the little girl as she started first grade. One of the U.S. marshals later reflected, "For a little girl going into a strange school with four strange deputy marshals, a place she had never been before, she showed a lot of courage. She never cried. She didn't whimper. She just marched along like a little soldier." Clearly Ruby had a right to be angry—and afraid. But as Michele Borba (2001) notes, she showed enormous self-control. Hostile mobs remained for weeks. But every day she walked calmly to class. Isolated in her own room in the school, she learned to write and read with only the company of her teacher.

One morning Ruby stopped in the middle of the screaming crowd and actually seemed to talk to them. The mob only became more furious. Ruby finished and walked calmly into class. The teacher wondered what she had said. Ruby explained that she had said nothing. She had prayed. Indeed, she went on, it was something she did before and after school each day to help her maintain control.

Clearly, self-control includes managing our thoughts and feelings as well as our behavior. Rather than shaping our external environment to meet our needs, sometimes we must shape our internal world to fit our environment.

To what degree do you believe you have control over your own internal states? The following scale assesses the extent to which people believe they can absorb the impact of aversive events on their emotions, thoughts, and physical well-being. Try it for yourself.

SELF-ASSESSMENT ■

Perceived Control of Internal States Scale

Use the following scale to indicate your level of agreement with each statement:

1 = strongly disagree   2 = disagree   3 = neutral   4 = agree   5 = strongly agree

_____ **1.** I don't have much control over my emotional reactions to stressful situations.

_____ **2.** When I'm in a bad mood, I find it hard to snap myself out of it.

_____ **3.** My feelings are usually fairly stable.

_____ **4.** I can usually talk myself out of feeling bad.

_____ **5.** No matter what happens in my life, I am confident of my ability to cope emotionally.

_____ **6.** I have a number of good techniques that will help me cope with any stressful situation.

_____ **7.** I find it hard to stop myself from thinking about my problems.

_____ **8.** If I start to worry about something, I can usually distract myself and think about something nicer.

_____ **9.** If I realize I am thinking silly thoughts, I can usually stop myself.

_____ **10.** I am usually able to keep my thoughts under control.

_____ **11.** I imagine there will be many situations in the future where silly thoughts will get the better of me.

_____ **12.** I have a number of techniques that I am confident will help me to think clearly and rationally in any situation I might find myself.

_____ **13.** Even when under pressure I can usually keep calm and relaxed.

_____ **14.** I have a number of techniques or tricks that I use to stay relaxed in stressful situations.

_____ **15.** When I'm anxious or uptight, there does not seem to be much that I can do to help myself relax.

_____ **16.** There is not much I can do to relax when I get uptight.

_____ **17.** I have a number of ways of relaxing that I am confident will help me cope.

_____ **18.** If my stress levels get too high, I know there are things I can do to help myself.

Source: Palant, 2000.

To score your scale, first reverse the numbers you gave in response to statements 1, 2, 7, 11, 15, and 16 (1 = 5, 2 = 4, 3 = 3, 4 = 2, 5 = 1). Then add up the numbers in front of all 18 statements. Scores can range from 18 to 90, with higher scores reflecting greater perceived control of one's internal states. A sample of 250 adults representing all ages and educational levels obtained a mean score of 64.08 (Palant, 2000).

Although we may not be able to control the occurrence of negative events in our lives, we can learn to control our thoughts, feelings, and reactions during stressful encounters, which helps us deal with stress more effectively. People who perceive that they have the skills and ability to control their internal states appear less likely to succumb to the negative effects of major life stressors.

Research with the Perceived Control of Internal States Scale has found that people with higher scores experience less depression and anxiety as well as fewer physical symptoms; possess higher self-esteem; feel they are more effective in dealing with their external environment; hold more optimistic expectations; and in general show greater satisfaction with life. People with a high sense of control are less likely to view stressful situations as threatening (Palant, 2000). In situations requiring action, they are less likely to be hampered by a hot "go" system clouding their decision-making process. Their confidence provides a significant advantage in choosing the most appropriate coping strategy and executing it effectively. In contrast, low-control people are more likely to see aversive events as threatening and are less likely to cope adaptively.

Misregulation

Of course, perceived control does not guarantee *effective* emotional regulation. Misregulation occurs in various ways. For example, socializing with friends is sometimes an effective way to improve a bad mood. In other cases, the strategy backfires. Sad people who talk with others to lift their depression may find they feel no better; they have only made others feel worse. Similarly, talking about one's anger and life's unfairness may merely elicit anger in the listener (Tice & Bratslavsky, 2000).

The marshmallow study suggests that use of distraction to take one's mind off a distressing problem can sometimes be a useful means of controlling thoughts and emotions—but not always. In one variation, the researchers told some children to think fun thoughts: "If you want to, while you're waiting, you can think about Mommy pushing you on a swing." When the children were led to think pleasant, distracting thoughts, they were able to wait a long time. However, other kids who were instructed to think sad thoughts ("Think about the last time you fell off the swing") were actually less able to resist temptation. Distraction didn't work. Children thinking sad thoughts could not wait as long.

If the distractions are themselves troubling, then we are merely exchanging one source of distress for another. Depressed people tend to think negative thoughts in their efforts to distract themselves from their depression, which only compounds their depression. In general, negative thoughts increase stress and frustration, thus lowering resistance to temptation.

Sometimes we misregulate by giving emotional regulation priority over other forms of self-control. Seeing a movie or going out with friends is hardly an effective strategy for dealing with the anxiety associated with procrastination. Indeed, many people admit to a variety of maladaptive coping responses, including eating, drinking, smoking, shopping, and gambling to "feel better" (Tice & Bratslavsky, 2000).

Underregulation

Some people feel that they *could* control their emotions but don't think they *should*. In fact, the conventional wisdom in many Western cultures seems to support the idea that healthy people must freely express their emotions.

On entering my social psychology class, many of my students agree: "To be mentally healthy, people need an opportunity to act out and thus to vent their aggression." They are unaware that venting is typically ineffective in lifting a negative mood. In fact, findings suggest that venting prolongs and sometimes even increases negative affect.

Expressing angry aggression amplifies it. One possible reason is that venting one's anger prevents people from effectively distracting themselves. Rather, venting focuses attention on precisely the wrong thing, namely, on one's distress and what is producing it. In addition, the physical feedback involved in emotional expression that comes from facial muscles, posture, and the rest of the body plays a role in prolonging the negative mood (Baumeister et al., 1994).

Irresistible Impulses?

Are we sometimes helpless victims of our internal states? Are some impulses irresistible? Or do we acquiesce and permit our self-control to lapse?

Self-regulation failures often involve our active participation. Although we may feel overwhelmed and that our strength is depleted, we still take an active role in indulging ourselves.

When completely stressed out, some people go on an eating binge. But doing so demands that they actively seek food, put it in their mouth, chew it, and swallow it. They may have felt overwhelmed and weak, but while they eat they are anything but helpless. Similarly, given the many restrictions on when and where smokers can light up, they often need to be genuinely creative to indulge in uncontrolled smoking. Loss of self-control is more a matter of giving in than of being overwhelmed. "Self-regulation failure," suggests Baumeister and his colleagues (1994), "seems to involve a relinquishing of control because the exertion of controlling oneself is too unpleasant, and not because the impulse is too powerful" (p. 249).

American soldiers who were heroin addicts in Vietnam often recovered immediately and without treatment for addiction when they returned home (Peele, 1989). Some even used heroin in the United States without resuming their addiction. Similarly, drinking binges among alcoholics may be due more to beliefs and expectations of being unable to resist than of actual physiological dependency. American Jews often drink but rarely become alcoholic. Why? This may be due to a cultural emphasis on personal responsibility that does not exempt drinkers (Peele, 1989).

In the Malay peninsula of southeast Asia, people who become wildly destructive, attacking anyone and anything in their path, are described as *running amok*. Within the culture, stress, sleep deprivation, and extreme heat were thought to be important causes of this "irresistible" behavior. Close examination, however, indicated that the targets of aggression were hardly arbitrary. And when the government instituted severe penalties for running amok, the Malay suddenly found that they could control it after all, and the problem declined dramatically (Tice & Bratslavsky, 2000).

Interestingly, research participants whose self-control had been "depleted" on a first experimental task do manage to show self-control on a second task if they were offered substantial amounts of money for doing well (Muraven, 1998). In fact, when offered 25 cents an ounce for drinking Kool-Aid laced with vinegar, one participant drank 40 ounces for a cool reward of $10. When they were offered only 1 cent per ounce, the control-depleted participants decided not to exert their self-control and drank fewer ounces of vinegar Kool-Aid compared to a control group.

Procrastination: A Special Case of Misregulation

Bruce Tuckman (1991) defines procrastination as "the tendency to put off or completely avoid an activity under one's control" (p. 474). Procrastination illustrates the important role that emotional distress plays in self-control. Whether it's working on a difficult project (a course paper) that elicits worry and anxiety or a too-simple task (mowing the lawn) that leads to boredom, putting the work off provides ready escape, however temporary, from a bad mood. The marshmallow test illustrates how self-control sometimes demands that we wait for a long-term goal. Procrastination shows how, at other times, self-control requires that we get moving.

SELF-ASSESSMENT ■

Procrastination Scale

Respond to each statement using the following scale:

4 = That's me for sure.   3 = That's my tendency.   2 = That's not my tendency.
1 = That's not me for sure.

_____ **1.** I needlessly delay finishing jobs, even when they're important.

_____ **2.** I postpone starting in on things I don't like to do.

_____ **3.** When I have a deadline, I wait until the last minute.

_____ **4.** I delay making tough decisions.

_____ **5.** I keep putting off improving my work habits.

_____ **6.** I manage to find an excuse for not doing something.

_____ **7.** I put the necessary time into even boring tasks, like studying.

_____ **8.** I am an incurable time waster.

_____ **9.** I'm a time waster now, but I can't seem to do anything about it.

_____**10.** When something's too tough to tackle, I believe in postponing it.

_____ **11.** I promise myself I'll do something and then I drag my feet.

_____**12.** Whenever I make a plan of action, I follow it.

_____**13.** Even though I hate myself if I don't get started, it doesn't get me going.

_____**14.** I always finish important jobs with time to spare.

_____**15.** I get stuck in neutral even though I know how important it is to get started.

_____**16.** Putting something off until tomorrow is not the way I do it.

Source: Tuckman, 1991.

To obtain your total score, first reverse the responses (4 = 1, 3 = 2, 2 = 3, 1 = 4) for items 7, 12, 14, and 16. Then add up the numbers for all 16 items. Scores can range from 16 to 64, with higher scores reflecting a greater tendency to procrastinate. The average score for college undergraduates appears to be about 40, right at the midpoint of the scale.

The majority of us admit to procrastinating at least some of the time (Tice & Baumeister, 1997). A substantial minority acknowledge that it's self-defeating. Not everyone, however, thinks it's a problem. In fact, some claim, "I do my best work under pressure." Others more modestly ask, "If one puts in the same amount of work, what difference does early or late make?"

In examining procrastination among college students, Diane Tice and Roy Baumeister (1997) found that while procrastinators seemed to benefit from their carefree, casual attitude in the early phases of a project, their advantage did not last. Overall, total stress and even illness proved greater for procrastinators than for those who started on time. And what about quality of work? Procrastinators ended up doing inferior work. Postponing seems to lead to compromises and sacrifices in quality. Tice and Baumeister (1997) concluded that "procrastination is not a neutral or innocuous form of time management, let alone a helpful or beneficial one (as some people claim)" (p. 457).

Procrastination provides a fascinating puzzle in self-control. We know what we want to do, in some sense can do, at times even try to do; yet we don't do it (Sabini & Silver, 1982). Why? Psychologists' efforts to answer this question provide three important insights into the challenges of self-control more generally. And identifying the causes of this self-control failure also points us to a possible cure.

First, Baumeister and Tice's findings with college students suggest that, like many other forms of self-defeating behavior, procrastination is marked by short-term benefits and long-term costs. Investing ourselves in a task, like writing a course paper, can elicit anxiety over eventual performance evaluation, depression over not meeting ideals, or just plain boredom (Baumeister et al., 1994). Better to postpone. Putting it off provides a quick fix for a bad mood. Tasks that we find painful or difficult to understand are especially likely to elicit distress and thus are also likely candidates for delay. Baumeister argues for *transcendence*—stepping back to see beyond the immediate here and now to long-range goals. Transcendence is an important key to overriding current distress.

Second, procrastination can occur when we don't know what to do. We have failed to identify a long-range goal. But even more often, it happens when we fail to set short-term goals. Think about it. A course paper is a monumental task! However, breaking it down into subtasks makes it manageable. A literature search, then an outline, next an introduction, finally a rough draft. Amazing! A course paper!

Third, procrastination occurs when we set unrealistically high goals. Ironically, perfectionists are particularly susceptible to delay. Creating a masterpiece, locating the perfect job, finding just the right birthday present, meeting the ideal partner—all lead to delays in writing, job hunting, gift buying, and marriage. If we delay long enough, we can congratulate ourselves for our high standards and never despair over having made a wrong choice.

Implementation plans, suggests Peter Gollwitzer (1999), help people get started. Such plans tell when, where, and how to begin. We link a specific situation to a specific response: "When situation x arises, I will perform response y." A long-delayed exercise program may finally take off with a simple implementation plan: "I will ride the exercise bike tonight while watching the evening news."

Gollwitzer and Veronika Brandstätter (1997) asked university students to name two projects—one easy, the other difficult—that they intended to complete during a holiday break. When the students were asked whether they had formed intentions on when and where to get started, some said they had. After the break, the researchers checked on who had completed their projects. For difficult projects, two-thirds of the participants who had formed plans had actually carried them out. Those without plans mostly failed to complete their projects. For the easy projects, formulating plans had little effect on whether a project was completed. In short, plans seem most important when starting is difficult.

Gollwitzer and Brandstätter next gave participants a task that was difficult to implement. Prior to the holiday break, they were asked to write a report on how they spent December 24. The report had to be written and mailed to the researchers no later than 48 hours after that day. Presumably they were studying how people spend the holidays in modern times. Half the participants were instructed to form implementation plans, indicating when and where they intended to write the report during the critical 48 hours. The other half were not. Who completed the task? Three-quarters of those who did and only one-third of those who did not have implementation plans actually wrote the reports.

For those who normally let things slide, plans trigger action. With a plan in place, the critical time and situation "initiate" the action immediately, even without our conscious intent.

IN REVIEW

Self-control involves the regulation of our thoughts and feelings as well as the regulation of our behavior. Perceived control of internal states is linked with successful coping and less depression and anxiety. Misregulation of emotion is a frequent cause of self-control failure. Procrastination provides one example. Like other forms of self-defeating behavior, it is marked by short-term benefits and long-term costs. Procrastination often occurs when we fail to set clear objectives or when we have unrealistically high goals. Implementation plans help people get started.

Fostering Self-Control

How do we develop the capacity for self-control that is essential to our well-being? In answering this important question, we will first examine a helpful theory and its applications. Then we will consider a specific plan for addressing problems in self-regulation.

Self-Regulation Theory

Self-regulation theory assumes that behavior is directed from within the person. More specifically, self-regulation consists of three components: standards, monitoring, and strength (Carver & Scheier, 1981).

Standards are the targets of self-regulation. To control your emotions effectively, you first need to identify clearly what feelings or expressions are appropriate. Having no standards or having unrealistic or conflicting standards creates self-management problems. Having both short-term and long-term goals for reaching your standards is also important. People who lack either type of goal typically experience failure in self-control. Being explicit about setting rewards and punishments in meeting established standards seems to be an effective strategy for fostering self-control. So, if engaging in regular exercise is your goal, you might contract with yourself: "If I run my scheduled two miles before evening, I get to watch my favorite television program tonight. If I don't meet my objective, I watch no television until at least tomorrow."

Effective self-regulation also requires *monitoring* yourself—comparing your behavior to the standards. People seem to vary in their self-consciousness. How many of the following are true of you?

T F **1.** I generally pay attention to my inner feelings.

T F **2.** I'm constantly thinking about my reasons for doing things.

T F **3.** I sometimes step back in my own mind in order to examine myself from a distance.

T F **4.** I'm quick to notice changes in my mood.

T F **5.** I know the way my mind works when I work through a problem.

Source: Selected items from Martin & Debus, 1999.

To monitor ourselves effectively, we need to either hone our self-consciousness or develop some alternative way of acquiring knowledge of our responses. For people who have difficulty monitoring themselves—those who would have very few "true" responses to the questions above—some form of external monitoring, such as recording progress on the calendar, may help. Involving family or friends provides another helpful means of external, unbiased monitoring.

Sometimes even a mirror will help. Stacey Sentyrz and Brad Bushman (1998) found that people eat less unhealthy food when they see their own reflections. The researchers asked college students to test full-fat and no-fat cream cheese spreads on bagelettes. Students in a mirrored room ate less of the full-fat spread than did students in a room with no mirror. Sentyrz and Bushman then asked grocery shoppers to try full-fat, reduced-fat, and fat-free margarine. Those snacking over a mirrored tabletop ate less of the fatty type. A looking glass prompts self-focused attention. We don't like to catch ourselves violating our own standards.

Strength represents the third important component of self-regulation. We need to have the capacity to make desired changes—to alter our behavior to conform to our standards. For example, we need the strength to override the inappropriate emotions that foster procrastination.

Recent research suggests that self-control may be more like lifting weights than playing chess—more like exercising a muscle than mastering a strategy (Muraven & Baumeister, 2000). For example, exerting self-control temporarily reduces the capacity for subsequent self-control efforts. Thus, people who exercise self-control, say, by eating carrots rather than cream puffs subsequently quit sooner when given unsolvable puzzles. Those who first exercise thought control (researchers tell the participants "not to think about a white bear") have greater difficulty in controlling their emotional responses to a video clip.

Sometimes events stretch us too far. Consider an example of a loss of control from J. K. Rowling's *Harry Potter and the Order of the Phoenix* (2003). Throughout an afternoon of athletic competition, Harry and teammate George had been taunted by archrival Draco Malfoy and his comrades about the poor playing of Ron, Harry's best friend and George's brother. After losing the match, Malfoy sadistically berates George and Ron's parents. When he starts in on Harry's mother, the provocation becomes too much for Harry, who had been restraining both George and himself:

> Harry was not aware of releasing George, all he knew was that a second later both of them were sprinting at Malfoy. He had completely forgotten the fact that all the teachers were watching: All he wanted to do was cause Malfoy as much pain as possible. (p. 413)

For losing control, Harry and George paid dearly. The boys could have avoided the school administrator's harsh punishment if they had immediately distanced themselves from Malfoy's insults, which were so effective in depleting their capacity to exercise self-control.

Self-control seems to be a limited resource. Coping with stress and attempting to control negative emotions depletes limited willpower reserves. In everyday life, impulsive crimes, addictive relapses, and eating binges are more likely to occur when people are tired or under heavy work pressures.

From all this we can learn that it's best not to try to control many things at once. If we make multiple New Year's resolutions, we are likely to fail. Moreover, we should keep in mind that demands such as adapting to a new environment (a new school) or unusual work pressures (a new job or an unexpected work assignment) may severely tax self-control efforts in other spheres. Conversely, relaxation, rest, sleep, meditation, and positive emotions seem to replenish one's strength.

Like a muscle, self-control is also strengthened by exercise. Setting up small but frequent challenges for self-improvement seems to foster greater capacity for self-discipline. Students given various self-control drills over a period of two weeks (improving posture, regulating moods, monitoring eating) subsequently showed greater stamina in self-regulatory capacity (Muraven, Baumeister, & Tice, 1999). More significantly, success in overcoming alcohol addiction is followed by greater success in quitting smoking (Breslau, Peterson, Schultz, Andruski, & Chilcoat, 1996).

Cultivating better control over our attention or focus is a special challenge that meditation can help us address (Baumeister et al., 1994). Although it is not easy to take time to meditate once or twice a day, the investment may pay important dividends. At first, the effect may seem to be contrary. In early attempts to meditate, we may seem to have little control over our mind and attention. But practice makes our efforts more fruitful.

Remember that careful pursuit of *accurate* self-knowledge is an important part of self-management (Baumeister et al., 1994). Most of us think we already do this. Research indicates, however, that we don't. Rather, we seem to prefer hearing positive things about ourselves, regardless of whether they are accurate or not! It can be daunting to make a realistic list of our strengths and virtues, as well as our weaknesses and vices. Nonetheless, this exercise promotes effective self-control.

A Well-Defined Plan

To change a problem behavior—procrastination, smoking, a sedentary lifestyle, overeating, nail biting, poor dental hygiene, or some other troubling habit— psychologists argue that you need a well-structured plan and strong motivation (Insel & Roth, 2002).

Implement the following steps:

1. Identify *one* behavior you want to change, for example, overeating, excessive drinking, not exercising, poor study habits, not saving money, or poor use of leisure time. Remember that self-control is a limited resource and that trying to change too many behaviors at once is likely to fail.

2. Set a target behavior that is realistic and measurable. Setting a goal of losing 10 pounds per week, of boosting daily study time by 2 hours, or of biking 30 minutes daily may not be realistic. However, losing 16 pounds in 8 weeks, boosting daily study time by an hour over the course of a month, or working up to biking for 30 minutes daily in 6 weeks are reasonable targets. You can break the larger targets down into incremental targets so that by the end of each week you are studying 15 minutes more per day, or you have lost 2 pounds, or you are biking 5 minutes longer each day.

3. Identify the potential benefits of reaching your target, such as being healthier, happier, or more self-confident, feeling less stress, or having more time to spend with family and friends. Also identify the costs of not reaching your target!

4. Take the following target behavior test designed by the National Wellness Institute.

1. Changing this behavior is important to me.	☐ Yes	☐ No
2. I have a positive attitude about my ability to successfully change my behavior.	☐ Yes	☐ No
3. I am likely to be healthier or live in a healthier environment if I change this behavior.	☐ Yes	☐ No
4. If necessary, I am able and willing to spend the money necessary to help change this behavior.	☐ Yes	☐ No
5. I am willing to devote the time necessary to change this behavior.	☐ Yes	☐ No
6. I have chosen a target behavior that I will be able to measure or count.	☐ Yes	☐ No

7. I have selected an achievable goal (e.g. "I will lose 1 pound per week by   ☐ Yes   ☐ No
increasing my level of exercise." is probably a realistic goal. "I will lose
20 pounds this month" is probably an unrealistic goal and may be unsafe.)

8. I can identify others who will provide support for my behavior change.   ☐ Yes   ☐ No

Source: National Wellness Institute, 1992.

If you answer with even one "no," consider choosing another behavior or setting a more realistic goal that will enable you to answer "yes" to all the statements.

5. Select a start date and set up a daily schedule that utilizes your favorite activities as rewards. What is rewarding for you? Purchasing a favorite newspaper, taking a hot shower, hiking in the woods, making a long-distance phone call to a friend? Pick one that could be the day's or week's reward for meeting your goal.

6. Enlist social support from family and friends. Use the following contract for behavior change.

I, _____, pledge to meet the following goal:

_____

My friend who signed this contract below, agrees to provide me with the following supportive actions:

1. _____

2. _____

3. _____

We will meet on _____ (date) to discuss my behavior change progress and to confirm support for my behavior change efforts.

_____   _____
Your Signature   Date   Signature of Supporting Friend   Date

Source: National Wellness Institute, 1992.

7. Identify the specific obstacles you are likely to encounter in reaching your target and construct strategies for overcoming them. For example, for the obstacle: "Every day I pass the bakery on my way from school—the doughnuts are irresistible," construct a solution: "I will put a piece of fruit in my pocket for a snack," or "I will take an alternate route home."

Remember that your greatest challenge will be to minimize the influence of immediate rewards and to maximize the impact of later rewards. To remind yourself of the future consequences of your behavior, post the specific benefits of change in an obvious place. To avoid overspending, tape the amount you owe on the face of your credit card. Post a magazine article on long-term health benefits of eating fruits and vegetables on your refrigerator. Paul Insel and

Walton Roth (2002) write: "If you want to manage time more effectively, picture yourself as a confident, organized person who systematically tackles important tasks and sets aside time each day for relaxation, exercise, and friends" (p. 23).

8. Use the following tracking system:

| Date | What I planned to do | What I did | Why it happened the way it did | | How I can overcome this obstacle in the future |
			What helped me	What got in my way	
(Example) 1/20/03	Have a daily "to do" list	Prepared the "to do" list the night before	Having the list first thing in the morning helped	— — —	— — —
(Example) 2/21/03	Prioritize my "to do" list	I did not prioritize my list	— — —	Although I worked on my list, I did not get done what I needed to do.	I will set priorities when I prepare my list.

Source: National Wellness Institute, 1992.

9. If you slip, keep trying. Remember that behavioral change takes time. Four out of five people will experience some backsliding when they try to change behavior (Insel & Roth, 2002). Only one in four succeed the first time around. They note that if you retain your commitment to change even when you lapse, you are further along than before you made the commitment. Try again. And again, if necessary. If the behavior is something you know you'd be better off changing, it is worth the effort.

IN REVIEW

Self-regulation requires setting clear standards, carefully monitoring behavior, and building the strength to make desired changes. Changing a problem behavior requires a well-structured plan in which we clearly specify a target behavior and identify the advantages of change. A start date, a daily schedule, and the enlistment of social support facilitate enactment of the plan. Anticipating obstacles and careful tracking of progress increase the likelihood of success.

wisdom 4

Intelligence enabled people to build a nuclear bomb. Wisdom keeps them from using it and even makes them consider the folly of building it in the first place.
—ROBERT J. STERNBERG, 1997

People can be intelligent but not wise. Smart people often do foolish things. In fact, they can make a total mess of their own lives and the lives of family and friends. Living wisely requires more than the academic aptitude assessed by traditional IQ tests. Such tests overlook important human traits, including emotional and practical intelligence. Because other strengths contribute to wisdom, its development represents a lifelong challenge.

■ Emotional Intelligence

When researchers examined the factors that distinguish successful from unsuccessful managers in the workplace, they found that the most important differences related to the managers' interpersonal relations (Lombardo et al., 1988). Those who had been terminated were judged to be insensitive and arrogant. The employees who worked under these supervisors perceived them as overly ambitious and emotional, as demanding but unsupportive. Unlike their successful counterparts, the managers who messed up seemed to lack what some psychologists call *emotional intelligence*.

The following scale attempts to assess this strength. Try it for yourself.

Measuring Emotional Intelligence

Indicate the extent to which each item applies to you using the following scale:

1 = strongly disagree   2 = disagree   3 = neither agree nor disagree   4 = agree
5 = strongly agree

_____ **1.** I know when to speak about my personal problems to others.

_____ **2.** When I am faced with obstacles, I remember times I faced similar obstacles and overcame them.

_____ **3.** I expect that I will do well on most things I try.

_____ **4.** Other people find it easy to confide in me.

_____ **5.** I find it hard to understand the nonverbal messages of other people.

_____ **6.** Some of the major events of my life have led me to reevaluate what is important and not important.

_____ **7.** When my mood changes, I see new possibilities.

_____ **8.** Emotions are some of the things that make my life worth living.

_____ **9.** I am aware of my emotions as I experience them.

_____ **10.** I expect good things to happen.

_____ **11.** I like to share my emotions with others.

_____ **12.** When I experience a positive emotion, I know how to make it last.

_____ **13.** I arrange events others enjoy.

_____ **14.** I seek out activities that make me happy.

_____ **15.** I am aware of the nonverbal messages I send to others.

_____ **16.** I present myself in a way that makes a good impression on others.

_____ **17.** When I am in a positive mood, solving problems is easy for me.

_____ **18.** By looking at their facial expressions, I recognize the emotions people are experiencing.

_____ **19.** I know why my emotions change.

_____ **20.** When I am in a positive mood, I am able to come up with new ideas.

_____ **21.** I have control over my emotions.

_____ **22.** I easily recognize my emotions as I experience them.

_____ **23.** I motivate myself by imagining a good outcome to tasks I take on.

_____ **24.** I compliment others when they have done something well.

_____ **25.** I am aware of the nonverbal messages other people send.

_____ **26.** When another person tells me about an important event in his or her life, I almost feel as though I have experienced this event myself.

_____ **27.** When I feel a change in emotions, I tend to come up with new ideas.

_____ **28.** When I am faced with a challenge, I give up because I believe I will fail.

_____ **29.** I know what other people are feeling just by looking at them.

_____ **30.** I help other people feel better when they are down.

_____ **31.** I use good moods to help myself keep trying in the face of obstacles.

_____ **32.** I can tell how people are feeling by listening to the tone of their voice.

_____ **33.** It is difficult for me to understand why people feel the way they do.

Source: Schutte et al., 1998.

To obtain a total score, first reverse the numbers that you have placed in response to items 5, 28, and 33 (1 = 5, 2 = 4, 3 = 3, 4 = 2, 5 = 1), and then add the numbers in front of all 33 items. Total scores range from 33 to 165, with higher scores suggesting greater emotional intelligence. The authors reported means of 131 and 125 for females and males, respectively.

The researchers recommend caution in interpreting results from this scale. They emphasize that the scale provides only a rough measure of one's emotional intelligence. Thus, it should not be used in making important life decisions such as selecting people for employment. Rather, like many of the self-report scales in this book, it provides a helpful introduction to a new and important concept. Hopefully, it also helps you reflect on your strengths and weaknesses as you set and pursue life goals.

Research with the scale in the U.S. suggests that higher scores are associated with measures of psychological well-being such as greater optimism and less depression and impulsiveness. Scores also predict first-year higher education achievement, but curiously, are unrelated to the SAT or ACT scores that measure academic aptitude in U.S. secondary school students. This suggests that emotional intelligence and academic intelligence may be different concepts.

A Model of Emotional Intelligence

Peter Salovey and John Mayer's important model of emotional intelligence (Salovey, Mayer, & Caruso, 2002) highlights four important components:

1. *Emotional perception and expression:* This component involves the ability to identify your own emotions and to recognize them in others. If you see the fleeting look of fear in another's face, you will understand much more about that person than if you miss the signal. This component also includes the capacity to express both positive and negative emotions accurately. If we always turn our attention away from our unpleasant emotions, we will learn little about emotional life.

2. *Emotional facilitation of thought:* Although emotions can disrupt thinking, they can also be harnessed for more effective problem solving and decision making. They energize us and help us attend to what is important. Sometimes mood changes enable us to appreciate multiple points of view. For example, when our perspective shifts from skeptical to accepting, we think about a problem more deeply and creatively.

3. *Emotional understanding:* This component involves the ability to label emotions with words, to understand the causes and consequences of the various emotions, and to recognize the relationships between them. Understanding complex and sometimes contradictory feelings and how they change over time is an important dimension of emotional intelligence.

4. *Emotional management:* People use a broad range of techniques to regulate their moods. Sometimes this means reducing troublesome feelings in ourselves or others. More often, effective emotional regulation calls for harnessing emotions, as when persuasive speakers "move" their listeners. Emotional self-regulation includes the ability to reflect on our feelings and disclose them appropriately to others.

Using their recently constructed Multifactor Emotional Intelligence Scale, Salovey, Mayer, and David Caruso (2002) report several significant results. For example, emotional intelligence seems to be linked with:

- higher levels of prosocial behavior and lower levels of aggression in adolescents and college students;
- lower levels of substance abuse by adolescents including cigarette smoking and alcohol consumption;
- higher ratings of leadership effectiveness in the workplace;
- higher ratings of employees' performance in the handling of consumer complaints. (Interestingly, emotional intelligence was negatively associated with the speed of addressing complaints. Dealing effectively with customers' feelings, speculate the researchers, probably requires time.)

For more than a decade, Daniel Goleman (2002) has argued that emotional intelligence may be the distinguishing feature of good leaders. They are not brighter or tougher. Rather, they are good at perceiving, understanding, and managing emotions. In the aftermath of September 11, 2001, New York City Mayor Rudy Giuliani connected with the country's unspoken feelings in response to a reporter's question of how many died in the collapse of the World Trade Center. "We don't know the exact number," Giuliani said, "but whatever the number, it will be more than we can bear."

Whether they head a country, a city, a company, or a classroom, great leaders inspire people, suggests Goleman, by touching their emotions. They bring out the best in others. They listen empathically, they build relationships, they resolve disputes. They get others to laugh so that they enjoy what they do. Their successful management of emotion may be simple yet subtle.

Goleman tells how a group of businessmen headed to the Super Bowl were delayed on a Sunday flight. Already late for the start of this big football game, they were further frustrated when the plane stopped several hundred yards from the gate. With all the passengers standing in the aisle, the pilot could not inch to the final destination. Normally the flight attendant issues a stern, formal command, "You must sit down before we can taxi to the gate." But not this time. Sensing her passengers' anger, she used an affectionate singsong voice (as though talking to a mischievous child) to merely observe, "You're staaaanding. . . ." And with that, the passengers laughed and sat down. "That's real leadership," concludes Goleman.

IN REVIEW

Wisdom involves more than academic intelligence. Some psychologists suggest that emotional intelligence is distinct from academic aptitude and is an important key to a productive life. The major components of emotional intelligence include the capacity to perceive, express, understand, and manage emotions. Research findings suggest that this capacity is an important human strength that allows for more effective functioning in many realms.

Successful Intelligence

Robert Sternberg (1996) believes that the aptitude that IQ tests assess contributes to productive living, but that aptitude is not enough. To be successfully intelligent, he suggests, one must think well in three different ways: *analytically, creatively,* and *practically.*

On September 11, 2001, window-washer Jan Demczur demonstrated successful intelligence (Goleman, 2002). Trapped in a stalled elevator in New York's besieged World Trade Center with five other men (mostly executives), Jan, carrying his bucket and squeegee on a pole, engineered an escape. In analyzing the nearly hopeless situation, he figured that the men could use his pole to get out. Working together, they pried open the elevator door, only to find a thick wall with a giant number "50" facing them. But again Jan met the challenge. Under his direction, the men used the sharp edge of the squeegee handle to scrape away the wall. Taking turns at the tedious task, the six men used analytical, creative, and practical intelligence and finally bored through three layers of drywall to freedom.

Tacit Knowledge

The core element in practical intelligence is tacit knowledge (Sternberg, 1996; Sternberg & Horvath, 1999). It is a matter of "knowing how" more than "knowing what." This knowledge is procedural—intimately related to action—and it is instrumental to the attainment of everyday goals. Tacit knowledge is typically acquired without direct instruction from others, although observing models certainly helps.

CRITICAL THINKING ■

"Knowing How" at School and Work

You can get a sense for tacit knowledge by trying the following exercise. Identify one or two things it takes to succeed at your school or at your work that you would never read in textbooks or in your job description:

_____

_____

_____

_____

_____

Tacit knowledge can be expressed in terms of "if–then" conditionals. For example, *if* you need to deliver bad news to your boss, and *if* the boss's golf game was rained out the day before, and *if* the staff seems to be walking on eggshells, *then* it is better to wait until later to deliver the bad news to avoid spoiling the boss's week (Sternberg, 1996).

Adaptation, Shaping, Selection

Sometimes practical intelligence requires that we change or *adapt* ourselves to an existing environment. Other times it demands that we *shape* an environment to make it more compatible with ourselves or others. Still other times it calls for us to *select* a new environment.

Consider the following situations to understand and appreciate the differences between adapting, shaping, and selecting.

Real-World Problems

In each of the following cases, one option represents adaptation—an attempt to adjust to the environment. A second option represents shaping—trying to accommodate the environment to yourself. A third option represents selection—deciding to leave the environment and find a new one. Consider the limited information that is given and choose the solution that you think is best. In each case, Sternberg (1986) suggests you pose the following questions:

1. Given who you are, could you alter yourself in order to make your responses more adaptive?

2. If that is not possible, can you see ways of changing the situation so that it is more suitable for you?

3. If neither alternative is possible, might it be better to find a new environment altogether? If so, what alternative environments might be available to you?

Again, there are no right or wrong answers. The right answer depends on the individual, the situation, and the interaction between them. Your goal should be to identify the choice that is right for you. Thinking about the options, and about how your personality and abilities interact with the situation, may foster more practically intelligent decisions in situations such as those presented here. For each item, choose a, b, or c.

1. The nation of Dragonia is characterized by its authoritarian structure, elitist culture, brutal repression of dissent, and general intolerance. Life in this undeveloped third-world nation is predictable, monotonous, and gray. The small class of elites holds the bureaucratic and military positions while an army of second-class citizens wrests a living working in urban factories and on collectivized farms. You are a young person of high birth who has just completed your education at a prestigious institution of higher learning in Europe. Upon returning to Dragonia, do you:

   a. accept the calling of your birth, resolving to perform your duties to the best of your ability?

   b. renounce the culture of elitism and seek to build a more just order?

   c. decide you cannot live amid such hypocrisy and moral depravity and move to a large cultural metropolis elsewhere, where you can live in relative freedom and obscurity?

2. Aunt Gertrude gives you a shirt for Christmas that is not quite your style. Poor Aunt Gertrude is always giving the most hideous gifts, and this one is no

exception: an ugly, red, plaid, 100-percent polyester nightmare. In this delicate situation, do you:

 a. exchange the shirt for a nice oxford cloth button-down?

 b. take Aunt Gertrude aside to discuss in private the nature of the gifts that in the future you would like to receive?

 c. hang the shirt in the back of the closet and resolve to wear it at the next Halloween party you attend?

3. Your best friend, Jill, always cheats when the two of you play tennis. She reflexively calls any ball out that falls even remotely near a line. In the face of this inexplicable ridiculousness, do you:

 a. refuse to play tennis with her (after all, you have plenty of other tennis partners who do not cheat)?

 b. decide that tennis is only a game to be enjoyed, and knowing in your heart that you are a better player, elect to tolerate her foolishness?

 c. take Jill aside, tell her with all the tact you can muster that this type of behavior is abominable, and make her promise to play squarely?

4. The cafeteria at your place of work serves virtually inedible food. Everyone in the company agrees that the food is horrible, but nobody can agree on a solution. Do you:

 a. buy their fruit and yogurt, which are rather difficult to ruin?

 b. petition for a new, improved food service?

 c. eat at the diner down the street?

5. Imagine you are a high school math teacher. One morning, you discover that the eraser for the blackboard is missing. In light of this calamity, do you:

 a. send one of the students to look for another one?

 b. wipe the board clean with your hand?

 c. decide to use the opaque projector instead?

The alternative approaches to each problem reflect adaptation, shaping, and selection. Compare your answers with the following key to assess whether your specific choices reflect adaptation, shaping, or selection.

1. *a. adaptation*	3. *a. selection*	5. *a. shaping*
b. shaping	*b. adaptation*	*b. adaptation*
c. selection	*c. shaping*	*c. selection*
2. *a. selection*	4. *a. adaptation*	
b. shaping	*b. shaping*	
c. adaptation	*c. selection*	

Source: Sternberg, 1986, pp. 316, 318–319.

In these cases, did you primarily adapt, shape, or select? Do you believe your choices are "wise" ones? If we only adapt, our own personal needs remain unmet and constructive social change never occurs. If we only shape, we ignore others' needs and generate unnecessary social conflict. If we only select, we undermine long-term commitments that ensure social stability. Wisdom, argues Robert Sternberg, demands that we balance adaptation, selection, and shaping. Most of all, wisdom involves balancing diverse interests.

IN REVIEW

Successful intelligence, suggests Robert Sternberg, requires that we think analytically, creatively, and practically. Tacit knowledge is an important component of successful intelligence. It involves "knowing how" more than "knowing what" and is crucial to achieving important life goals. Successful intelligence sometimes requires that we adapt to our environment, at other times that we shape our environment, and at still other times, that we select a new environment.

■

Understanding Wisdom

Academic aptitude, emotional intelligence, and tacit knowledge contribute to wisdom. But are they enough?

A cunning terrorist may be analytically intelligent in assessing the advantages and disadvantages of various targets and even practically intelligent in delivering his attacks (Sternberg, 2002a). An unscrupulous businesswoman may possess sufficient emotional intelligence to sell a worthless product and thus betray a trusting public. An evil tyrant may use his tacit knowledge to control land and resources that are not his own. Terrorists, traitors, and tyrants may be successful but, we would all agree, are not wise. One way to understand wisdom is to consider its exemplars.

CRITICAL THINKING ■

Wisdom's Exemplars and Characteristics

When you think of wise people, not friends or family members, but people who are well known—living or not—who comes to mind? Name three.

1. _____

2. _____

3. _____

Now pause for a moment and reflect: Why did you select those particular people? Take a few minutes to identify a few characteristics of an especially wise person.

1. _____

2. _____

3. _____

4. _____

5. _____

6. _____

When undergraduate students were asked to provide exemplars of wisdom, the top nominees included the following: Ghandi, Confucius, Jesus Christ, Martin Luther King, Jr., Socrates, Mother Teresa, Solomon, Buddha, a pope, Oprah Winfrey, Winston Churchill, the Dalai Lama, Ann Landers, Nelson Mandela, and Queen Elizabeth (Paulus et al., 2002). When asked to provide exemplars for intelligence and creativity, the students generated very different lists. Curiously, only one name occurred as an example of both wisdom and intelligence: Oprah Winfrey. There was no overlap between the exemplars of wisdom and those of creativity.

After Robert Sternberg (1985) asked respondents to identify the characteristic behaviors of wise people and then had others sort the 40 top behaviors into as many or as few piles as they wished on the basis of which behaviors are "likely to hang together" in a person, he identified the six patterns below. How does your list compare?

1. *Reasoning ability:* Has the capacity to look at a problem and solve it, has a logical mind, has a huge store of information, is able to apply knowledge to particular problems.

2. *Human understanding:* Understands human nature through dealing with a variety of people, displays concern for others, is a good listener, and considers advice.

3. *Learns from experience:* Attaches importance to ideas, learns from others' mistakes.

4. *Superior judgment:* Thinks before speaking or acting, is sensible, acts within his or her own physical and intellectual limitations.

5. *Efficient use of information:* Is experienced, mature; seeks out information, especially details.

6. *Accurate perspective:* Is intuitive, is able to see through things and read between the lines, offers solutions that are on the side of right and truth.

Both lists of wise people and wise characteristics recognize the importance of analytical ability (having the capacity to look at a problem and solve it), emotional intelligence (understanding human nature, being a good listener), and tacit knowledge (applying knowledge to particular problems); but there is more.

All the exemplars of wisdom are people who have looked beyond their immediate self-interest. No terrorists, tyrants, or traitors taint our list. Why? Because such people pursue outcomes that are good for themselves but bad for others. Characteristics of wisdom include "concern for others" and choosing "solutions that are on the side of right and truth."

The Balance Theory of Wisdom

The essential goal of wisdom, suggests Sternberg, is to serve a common good. Wise individuals balance (a) intrapersonal, (b) interpersonal, and (c) extrapersonal interests. In Sternberg's (2001) words, wisdom is "not simply about mazimizing one's own or someone else's self-interest, but about balancing various self-interests (intrapersonal) with the interests of others (interpersonal) and of other aspects of the context in which one lives (extrapersonal), such as one's city or country or environment or even God" (p. 231). Carefully considering the common good, the wise person uses tacit and explicit knowledge to adapt to existing environments, sometimes to shape them, and at still other times to select new environments.

How is wisdom expressed in everyday life? Sternberg poses the example of a teacher who has been instructed by her principal to spend almost all of her time teaching in a way that will maximize students' scores on a statewide assessment test. The teacher believes that the principal is essentially forcing her to abandon the true education of her students. What are the critical factors affecting her choice of a wise course of action?

1. *Balancing goals and interests:* People vary not only in the extent to which they seek a common good but also in what they view to be the common good. The teacher may believe that it is not in the children's best interests to engage only in rote memory tasks for a state-mandated test. The principal may see the children's interests differently. Moreover, both teacher and principal see their own integrity and reputation at stake. Finally, what students learn has implications for their parents and their community. The teacher is left with the responsibility of deciding what is in the best interest of all parties concerned.

2. *Balancing short- and long-term interests:* The teacher may believe that, in the long run, good education involves more than rote memorization. However, she may also recognize that performance on the state assessment test impacts the students' immediate well-being as well as that of the principal and school.

3. *Balancing responses to the environmental context:* The teacher may adapt to the environment by doing what the principal has instructed. She may shape the

environment by doing precisely what she believes she should do, or by trying to find some balance that meets both the principal's and her own goals. Finally, she may decide she cannot live with the principal's teaching philosophy: she may select another teaching position elsewhere.

4. *Acquiring and using tacit knowledge:* As we saw earlier, people vary in the extent to which they have acquired tacit knowledge and in how fully they use it. The teacher may have fairly sophisticated tacit knowledge of how to teach, which means she could decide to teach in a way that represents a compromise between her own views and those of the principal. Or she may have little tacit knowledge of teaching and thus have no choice but to do what the principal says. Clearly the teacher's knowledge of how to balance the various interests of the involved parties will shape her course of action.

Apply what you've learned about Sternberg's balance theory to the following challenge.

A Challenging Case

Identify the critical issues in another of Sternberg's (2002a) challenging examples:

Charles and Margaret are both engineers and have been married for five years. Three years ago Charles was offered a job in Europe. Margaret agreed to quit her job in the U.S. and move to Europe with Charles. The job was an excellent career move for Charles. Soon after the move, they had a baby. After the birth, Margaret decided to start working again and, with effort, found a very exciting job that paid well and promised real security. Meanwhile Charles was offered a transfer back to the United States. Margaret feels she needs another year or two in her new job to meaningfully advance her career. She is also tired of moving. She has already given up a lot of time following Charles around. Charles knows that his wife's job is as important as his own, but he thinks returning to the U.S. would help both their careers in the end. What should Charles do?

Source: Sternberg, 2002a.

In responding to this challenge, try to apply Sternberg's balance theory of wisdom. Include responses to the following questions:

1. Whose interests should Charles take into account?

2. How might the short- and long-term interests of each party be different?

3. How might Charles' actions reflect adaptation or shaping of the environment? What would it mean for him to select a new environment?

4. How might tacit knowledge or emotional intelligence be relevant to understanding and resolving this difficult situation?

_____

_____

_____

_____

_____

_____

_____

_____

_____

_____

_____

_____

_____

_____

_____

In contrast to the problems posed on the typical intelligence test, these real-life dilemmas have multiple solutions, each associated with liabilities and assets. Most importantly, values are integral to the balance theory of wisdom (Sternberg, 2001). Values penetrate the consideration of interests, the identification of the appropriate response to the environment (i.e., to adapt, shape, or select), and even one's understanding of the common good. Obviously there will be great differences of opinion. Still, argues Sternberg, we can surely reach agreement on certain universal values such as respect for human life, social justice, and enabling people to reach their full potential.

Is it possible for people to agree on what constitutes a "wise" judgment? This is a question that Paul Baltes and his colleagues at the Max Planck Institute for Education and Human Development have attempted to answer.

Studying Wisdom

Baltes and his colleagues define wisdom simply as good judgment and advice about important but uncertain matters of life (see Baltes & Smith, 1990). It is a definition not far from that in Webster's Dictionary (Goldman & Sparks, 1996, p. 1025): "good judgment that comes from knowledge and experience in life."

Baltes' research team has attempted to move the study of wisdom from the theoretical to the empirical. In the laboratory, they ask their German participants to "think aloud" about difficult life dilemmas. They are simply asked to discuss the problem and offer advice. Here is an example. How would you respond?

Another Challenging Case

A 15-year-old wants to get married right away. What should she consider and do?

_____

_____

_____

_____

_____

_____

_____

_____

_____

_____

Source: Baltes & Staudinger, 2000.

Baltes and his colleagues have hypothesized five components to wise judgment:

1. *Factual knowledge about matters of life:* This includes knowledge about human nature, interpersonal relations, and social norms.

2. *Procedural knowledge:* This involves strategies for dealing with life's problems and weighing goals, methods of handling conflict, and ways of offering advice.

3. *Lifespan contextualism:* Knowledge about the different roles and contexts of life (e.g., family, friends, work, recreation) and how these may change over the life span.

4. *Recognition and management of uncertainty:* The awareness that human knowledge is limited, the future cannot be fully known in advance, and life is unpredictable. The recognition that there may be no perfect solution.

5. *Relativism regarding solutions:* The acknowledgement of individual and cultural differences in values and life priorities.

In their studies, Baltes and his colleagues asked some research participants to read the responses others had given to the life dilemmas and to provide a global judgment of their wisdom. Other participants were trained to rate the responses on one of the five wisdom criteria. Results indicated that the global wisdom judgments were highly correlated with other participants' ratings on each of the five criteria. Such findings support the notion that wisdom can be reliably identified and assessed.

This is one of Baltes' examples of a low wisdom response:

> A 15-year-old wants to get married? No, no way, marrying at age 15 would be utterly wrong. One has to tell the girl that marriage is not possible. (After further probing) It would be irresponsible to support such an idea. No, this is just a crazy idea.

This is one of Baltes' examples of a high wisdom response:

> Well, on the surface this seems like an easy problem. On average, marriage for 15-year-old girls is not a good thing. But there are situations where the average case does not fit. Perhaps in this instance, special life circumstances are involved, such as the girl having a terminal illness. Or, the girl may have just lost her parents. And also, this girl may live in another culture or historical period. Perhaps she was raised with a value system different from ours. In addition, one has to think about adequate ways of talking with the girl and consider her emotional state.

Among the important findings of the Max Planck studies of wisdom are the following (Baltes, Gluck, & Kunzmann, 2002; Kramer, 2000):

1. Only about five percent of subjects tested achieved high scores in wisdom. Mean performance for all those tested was about three out of a possible seven on any given criterion.

2. Wisdom seems to increase sharply during adolescence and young adulthood. Although it remains relatively stable during middle adulthood and young old age, peak performances are more likely when people are in their fifties and sixties.

3. Age combined with professional experience seems to give some people an advantage in wisdom. Wise people tend to come from the human service professions, from leadership positions, or to have had some exceptional intrapersonal or interpersonal experiences, such as preparing their autobiography or being resisters during the Third Reich. Even specific professional specialization made a difference in reasoning on a wisdom task; for example, clinical psychologists performed better than nonclinical psychologists.

4. Wisdom is positively related to certain thinking styles. For example, those who like to evaluate and compare, or who show higher tolerance for ambiguity and willingness to go beyond existing rules, do better on the wisdom tasks.

5. Openness to experience—being imaginative, independent, and preferring variety over routine—is one of the strongest personality predictors of wisdom.

6. The opportunity to talk with another (even an imaginary inner dialogue with a person of choice) about difficult life dilemmas improved performance on wisdom tasks. Older adults profited more from actual interaction than did younger adults.

7. Instructions to take an imaginary journey around the world on a cloud thinking about life in different cultures improved performance on two of the five wisdom criteria.

IN REVIEW

A study of wisdom's exemplars and defining characteristics suggests that this human strength includes analytical ability, emotional intelligence, and tacit knowledge. In addition, wise people look beyond their immediate self-interest and are committed to the values of truth and justice. Balance theory argues that wisdom includes a careful balancing of one's own short- and long-term interests with those of others and with one's own values and other situational factors. Wise judgments seem to require strong factual and procedural knowledge as well as an understanding of life's uncertainty, of its diverse social roles, and of important value differences.

Learning Wisdom

What does the research on wisdom teach us about its development? Are certain attitudes and actions conducive to its acquisition? Here are a few tips:

1. *Expect to work at acquiring wisdom.* The capacity for sound judgment and judicious action is an acquired strength. The idea that intellectual potential can be developed is an important belief that fosters the growth of genius over time (Dweck, 2002). Wisdom is not a fixed trait. What is true of intelligence is even more true of wisdom: Making wise judgments is not just a product of genetic good fortune, it's also a result of effort and experience. Expect to follow a long process of self-development and self-discovery in working toward wisdom.

2. *Be open to experience.* This may be the most influential factor in the development of wisdom (Kramer, 2000). Be adventurous and inquisitive about many different things. Reflect on life's dilemmas and challenges and play with ideas. Develop interest, perhaps even sophistication, in art, music, and literature.

3. *Stay keenly aware of the limits of human knowledge and intuition.* Tolerate ambiguity and learn to accept the unpredictability of life. There are often different ways of looking at a problem, and life's complexity and uncertainty sometimes means there may be no perfect solution.

   In positions of power, we are especially vulnerable to three errors in intuition: thinking that we know more than we do, believing we are all-powerful, and feeling that we will always be protected (Sternberg, 2002b). Be aware of the human capacity for such self-deceptions, and give up illusions of omniscience, omnipotence, and invulnerability.

4. *Seek to understand significant problems from many different points of view.* Discussing life's important challenges with others enables you to uncover and critique your own values as well as those of others. Interaction with others we respect enables us to identify and correct errors in social judgment and consider alternative courses of action. By going public with our decision-making processes, we better understand how knowledge may be used for good or ill, and that the end to which knowledge is put, matters.

5. *Master wisdom by studying its exemplars.* Study the classic works of literature and philosophy and reflect on the collective wisdom of the ages and its application to the present. Seek out contemporary role models as well. This will help you understand the tacit knowledge that allows us to adapt to our specific environments.

6. *Learn to strike an appropriate balance between knowing when to adapt and when to select a new environment.* Suppose, hypothesizes Sternberg (1996), you go to work for a computer company because you are eager to write software for educators, but you find that your new job involves stealing ideas from competitors. Wise people don't adapt; they leave. Wise people also recognize a third option—to shape the environment. You don't leave your job because of a single aggravating coworker, you don't abandon your family because the kids behaved badly, and you don't divorce after your first big fight. Instead you hang in there and find ways to shape the environment in the best interests of all. You need to effectively balance the need for stability and continuity with the need for change.

7. *Work at mastering the steps of effective problem solving.* Sternberg (1996) has identified five key skills in successfully intelligent people. Work on these areas as you strive for wisdom:

   a. Recognize the existence of a problem before it gets out of hand.

   b. Define problems correctly and decide which ones are worth solving.

c. Carefully formulate long-range strategies for solving problems.

d. Think carefully about allocating resources for the immediate and long-term future, and choose allocations that will maximize return.

e. Monitor and evaluate your decisions so that you can correct errors as you discover them.

8. *Balance your own interests with those of others.* Demonstrate warmth and compassion (Kramer, 2000), and develop your emotional intelligence so that you can understand and manage human feelings. Effective living and self-fulfillment mean more than being conventionally successful. It is important to learn to manage ourselves. Learning to delay gratification protects us from impulsiveness. Discovering and pursuing the common good puts us more at ease with ourselves and with others.

IN REVIEW

Developing wisdom is clearly not an easy task! Yet it is not an elusive goal, either. By following specific guidelines, we make progress on the long path to living wisely. For example, we cultivate wisdom by being open to experience as well as by accepting the inherent ambiguity and unpredictability of life. We can seek to understand significant problems from multiple points of view, check our judgments against those of others, and reflect on the collective wisdom of the ages. Mastering tacit knowledge and learning the steps of effective problem solving are also important ingredients in making wise judgments. Wise people effectively balance the need for stability and continuity with the need for change, and they are keenly aware of the human capacity for self-deception.

5 commitment

I haven't failed. I've found 10,000 ways that don't work.
—THOMAS EDISON, 1902

When people ask, "Why are you doing that?" we typically answer in terms of our underlying motives. Some psychologists refer to our motives as "strivings" (Emmons, 1999). In this chapter, you will first be asked to give some thought to your own personal strivings and factors that influence your level of perseverance. Then we will examine the central role of *commitment* in goal attainment, including some ways to foster commitment.

Strivings

Here are some examples of common strivings:

- Gaining others' acceptance
- Earning a college degree
- Achieving independence
- Seeking novel and stimulating experiences
- Avoiding feeling lonely
- Avoiding feeling inferior to others

Note that these strivings are phrased in terms of what we are "trying" to do, regardless of whether we are actually successful. For example, a person might be "trying to get others to like me" without succeeding.

Strivings can be fairly broad, such as "trying to make others happy," or more specific—"trying to make my partner happy." Also, strivings can be either positive or negative. That is, they may be about something we try to obtain or keep or about something we try to avoid or prevent. For example, we might be trying to gain attention from others, or we might be trying to avoid calling attention to ourselves.

Note that this way of describing yourself is different from the usual style of employing trait adjectives (friendly, intelligent, honest). In the following Self-Assessment, do not use trait adjectives. You may have never thought of yourself in this way, so think carefully before writing anything down.

What Are Your Strivings?

Provide a list of at least ten of your strivings. Keep your attention focused on yourself. Do not mentally compare the things that you typically seek with what other people pursue. Think of yourself and your motives alone. Be as honest and as objective as possible.

Take your time with this task; spend some time thinking about your motives before you begin.

I typically try to _____

I typically try to _____

I typically try to _____

I typically try to _____

I typically try to _____

I typically try to _____

I typically try to _____

I typically try to _____

I typically try to _____

I typically try to _____

I typically try to _____

I typically try to _____

Source: Adapted from Emmons, 1999, pp. 181–182.

Approach Versus Avoidant Goals

To what degree does your list include positive (approach) rather than negative (avoidant) goals? That is, to what extent do your strivings reflect movement *toward* desirable outcomes, and to what degree do they reflect movement *away from* undesirable outcomes? For example, trying to "earn a job promotion" reflects an approach goal; trying to "avoid failure" is an avoidant goal. Attempting to "cope with stress" represents a positive striving; trying to "avoid letting anything upset me" is a negative one. For a person trying to lose weight, "to jog three times a week" involves a desirable outcome, whereas "to stay away from sweets" means avoiding an undesirable one. Although the goals seem similar, framing makes a difference.

Compared to people with predominantly positive goals, people with mostly avoidant goals are more distressed and anxious (Emmons & Kaiser, 1996). They experience a lower sense of subjective well-being (Elliot, Sheldon, & Church, 1997) and suffer more physical distress (Elliot & Sheldon, 1998). People with avoidance strivings are also less likely to achieve their goals (Coats, Janoff-Bulman, & Alpert, 1996). Failure may focus our attention on avoiding negative outcomes in the future. However, it may also create a cycle of negativity in which we expect, and therefore achieve, less success.

To reach a positive goal, we need identify only one route (Schwarz, 1990). To avoid an undesired outcome, we must identify and block numerous possibilities. "Getting closer to someone" requires us to identify only a single path to the goal (Emmons, 1999). "Avoiding offending others" requires continuous monitoring of everyone's reactions. The most effective weight control methods rely more on approach goals, such as exercising, than on avoidance goals, such as dieting (Coats et al., 1996).

Positive and negative strivings even affect the quality of our interpersonal relations. People are less satisfied with their marriage when their spouse is more concerned with avoiding negative outcomes than with achieving positive ones (King & Emmons, 1991).

Reasons for Striving

Some gardeners strive to grow roses for the sheer pleasure of it. Others do so to earn a living. Most golfers pay to play. Some professionals play only for the pay. My son finds his daily five-mile run exhilarating. My painful two miles keep me in shape. What one person finds to be an end in itself another sees merely as a means to an end.

In psychology an important distinction is made between *intrinsic* and *extrinsic motivation* (Ryan & Deci, 2000). Intrinsically motivated behaviors are inherently enjoyable and satisfying. Extrinsically motivated actions are a means to an end; that is, our behavior enables us to obtain some reward or avoid a punishment.

This distinction has practical importance. Educators, employers, and coaches all recognize it. Children who find challenge and satisfaction in study persevere. They learn more and are fun to teach. Employees who enjoy their work not only produce a better product, they require less supervision. And athletes who relish the game practice on their own. Consider your own reasons for striving in the following exercise.

Four Kinds of Strivings

In reality, intrinsic and extrinsic motivations are ends of a continuum. People may be motivated to pursue a goal for at least four different reasons (Ryan & Deci, 2000). You will best understand these reasons by examining your own strivings. For each of the ten strivings you identified earlier, indicate the major reason for your striving (write the identifying word next to it).

Extrinsic: *You strive for this goal because somebody else wants you to or thinks you ought to, or because you'll get something from somebody if you do. Stated differently, you probably wouldn't strive for this goal if you didn't get some kind of reward, praise, or approval for it.*

Introjected: *You strive for this goal mostly because you would feel ashamed, guilty, or anxious if you didn't. Rather than striving because someone else thinks you ought to, you feel that you ought to strive for that something.*

Identified: *You hold this striving because you really believe that it's an important goal to have. Although this goal may once have been taught to you by others, now you endorse it freely and value it wholeheartedly.*

Intrinsic: *You strive purely because of the fun and enjoyment that striving provides. While there may be other good reasons for the striving, the primary reason is simply your interest in the experience itself.*

Source: Adapted from Emmons, 1999, p. 187.

If you are like most people, your strivings probably reflect a mix of these four reasons.

Like extrinsic motivation, "introjected" motivation is more constrained. We feel less ownership of our goals, even somewhat coerced. In extrinsic activity, we experience external pressure. With introjected activity, we sense internal pressure.

Like intrinsic motivation, "identified" motivation is undertaken willingly and with a clear sense of choice. Although identified activity may not be pleasurable (e.g., changing a child's diapers), it's consistent with a person's deeper beliefs. Freely chosen goals flow from developing interests or from core values.

Levels of extrinsic or intrinsic motivation also reflect personal investment. When intrinsically motivated, we pursue goals naturally and persistently. Your ratings of four kinds of strivings give you an idea of how your intrinsic motivation and extrinsic motivation levels balance. The following scale focuses only on your levels of intrinsic motivation, identifying key ingredients.

Intrinsic Motivation: Feelings I Have

Please read each of the following items carefully, thinking about how it relates to your life, and then indicate how true it is for you. Use the following scale to respond:

1	2	3	4	5	6	7
Not at all true			Somewhat true			Very true

____ **1.** I feel I am free to decide for myself how to live my life.

____ **2.** I really like the people I interact with.

____ **3.** Often, I do not feel very competent.

____ **4.** I feel pressured in my life.

____ **5.** People I know tell me I am good at what I do.

____ **6.** I get along with people I come into contact with.

____ **7.** I pretty much keep to myself and don't have a lot of social contacts.

____ **8.** I generally feel free to express my ideas and opinions.

____ **9.** I consider the people I regularly interact with to be my friends.

____ **10.** I have been able to learn interesting new skills recently.

____ **11.** In my daily life, I frequently have to do what I am told.

____ **12.** People in my life care about me.

____ **13.** Most days I feel a sense of accomplishment from what I do.

____ **14.** People I interact with on a daily basis tend to take my feelings into consideration.

____ **15.** In my life I do not get much of a chance to show how capable I am.

____ **16.** There are not many people that I am close to.

____ **17.** I feel I can pretty much be myself in my daily situations.

____ **18.** The people I interact with regularly do not seem to like me much.

____ **19.** I often do not feel very capable.

____ **20.** There is not much opportunity for me to decide for myself how to do things in my daily life.

____ **21.** People are generally pretty friendly toward me.

The scale measures the degree to which you experience fulfillment of three fundamental needs. Autonomy *is feeling that you are in charge of your own actions. Items 1, 4, 8,*

11, 14, 17, and 20 assess your feeling that you have a voice in determining your own behavior. Reverse the numbers you wrote in response to items 4, 11, and 20 (1 = 7, 2 = 6, 3 = 5, 4 = 4, 5 = 3, 6 = 2, 7 = 1), and then add up the numbers in front of the seven items composing the subscale. The total can range from 7 to 49, with higher numbers representing a greater sense of autonomy in your everyday life. Scores above the midpoint of 28 suggest that you generally have feelings of being in charge of your actions; scores below the midpoint indicate that you do not.

Competence is your sense of effectiveness in dealing with your environment. Items 3, 5, 10, 13, 15, and 19 assess your experience of competence. Reverse the numbers you gave in response to items 3, 15, and 19 before adding up the numbers in front of all six items. This time, scores can range from 6 to 42, with higher scores reflecting a greater sense of effectiveness in dealing with your world. This time the midpoint is 24. Higher scores suggest feelings of competence. Lower scores indicate that you struggle with a sense of effectiveness.

Relatedness reflects your experience of satisfying interpersonal relationships, including the feeling that others genuinely care about you. Items 2, 6, 7, 9, 12, 16, 18, and 21 assess your feelings of relatedness. Reverse the numbers you gave in response to items 7, 16, and 18 before adding them to items 2, 6, 9, 12, and 21 to obtain a score. Scores can range from 8 to 56, with higher scores reflecting a greater experience of relatedness. Scores above the midpoint of 32 indicate that you experience considerable satisfaction in your interpersonal relationships. Lower scores indicate that you are somewhat dissatisfied with your relationships.

Adding up the scores on the three subscales gives a measure of overall intrinsic motivation in your life, that is, the degree to which needs for autonomy, competence, and relatedness are being met. Total scores can range from 21 to 147 (with 84 the midpoint), with higher scores reflecting greater intrinsic motivation.

Source: The Basic Need Satisfaction in General Scale at http://psych.rochester.edu/SDT/measures/needs_scl.html is currently being developed and researched by Dr. Richard M. Ryan, Department of Clinical and Social Sciences in Psychology, University of Rochester, Rochester, NY.

IN REVIEW

Our strivings include both approach and avoidant goals. Compared to approach goals, avoidant goals are linked with greater distress and prove harder to achieve. Intrinsically motivated behaviors are inherently enjoyable and satisfying. In contrast, extrinsically motivated activities are only a means to an end. Intrinsic motivation meets fundamental needs for competence, relatedness, and autonomy.

Commitment in Our Strivings

Now that you have given some thought to your strivings, consider how *committed* you are to your goals. Try the following exercise.

What Is Commitment?

If you were asked to list the characteristics of the concept extraversion, *you might list liveliness, vivaciousness, sociability, and so on. When you think of the concept* commitment, *what three characteristics come to mind?*

1. _____

2. _____

3. _____

   When Beverly Fehr (1988) asked her research participants to identify commitment's essential features, the terms they identified most frequently were "perseverance," "responsibility," and "living up to your word." Words such as "liking" and "contentment" were near the bottom of the list, even falling behind "feeling trapped." The most common theme that pervaded the set of features was one of making a decision and following through on it. Commitment means consciously and deliberately getting beyond the urge to do only what is immediately satisfying.

Route to Competence, Relatedness, and Autonomy

Consider the following examples:

> Here we stand arm-in-arm in our oldest child's backyard on a beautiful summer evening, surrounded by friends and family. Candles are twinkling, tables are piled high with food, and big band music is playing out of speakers on the patio. It is our fortieth wedding anniversary party, and as our daughter toasts our love and our commitment to each other and everyone raises their glasses above their heads, I catch the sight of a tear glimmering in the corner of my wife's eye. We didn't make it this far because it was easy. We made it through forty years of marriage because we vowed that we would. That meant never backing out, even when it was hard or uncomfortable or painful. We learned to compromise, and we discovered that difficult situations can make you stronger and more patient. Staying committed to your goals and dreams doesn't guarantee you'll have an easy road, but you'll be working toward something important with

every step you take in that direction. Tonight, the smile on my wife's face is all I need to tell me it has been worth it.

Source: www.forbetterlife.org/values/value_commitment.php.

It was a couple of months after I decided to be a full-time freelance writer and the first time I submitted an unsolicited manuscript. I studied the magazine's guidelines carefully, and I was certain they were going to accept my article for their "Personal Experiences" department. Two months passed before they sent me a short explanation of why they couldn't use my article. I was devastated. I wanted to stop writing, thinking myself crazy for having decided to pursue a writing career in the first place. Then my son reminded me of something I had totally forgotten. He said, "Mom, you only lose when you quit trying." As I buried the rejection letter, I felt the spark of determination burn in my blood. I won't be a loser. I won't quit writing. I became determined to be more competent in writing my articles, in marketing my skills, and in interacting with the publishing world. I believe that a man is not measured by how tall he stands, but by how many times he stood up when life made him buckle to the ground. We can stay crumpled in the middle of the road, grieving. Or we can use the pause to calibrate our compass and build strength to avoid stumbling again. It's our choice. Adversities are inevitable. We can quit and lose—or we can keep trying and win. And, by the way, the article that was rejected? I pitched it to another magazine and it's getting published next month.

Source: Ruby Bayan. Used by permission from Suite101.com.

One inch at a time. That is how I climb and that is how I live. Sure, the summit is my goal, but without each carefully calculated move, I could never make it to the top. Each small step and giant reach presents a unique challenge. As I move up the cliff, I recognize characteristics of the rock and adapt learned techniques to advance further toward the goal. My father taught me perseverance by his example. I remember him going back to college when I was a little boy. He worked all day, attended classes in the evening, and then came home to study. I don't know how he did it, but somehow the yard work got done and he kept the car maintained. I never have asked him how he did it, but he did. When I was just 10 years old, my father got his degree. It took him many years, but he reached his goal and then moved on to other challenges. As I reach the summit, I look back down and enjoy the moment. Then I gather my gear and start planning my next climb. One inch at a time.

Source: www.forbetterlife.org/values/value_perseverance.php.

As these everyday examples illustrate, our strivings in relationships, in work, and even in leisure activity are not always joyful or exciting. Clearly, they are not always intrinsically motivating. If they were, there would be no need for commitment. We face conflict, encounter obstacles, and even experience failure. Alternative strivings often look attractive.

The most absorbing of activities at times contain stressful elements. Surgeons, mountain climbers, and scientists make heavy sacrifices for their skills and run risks—both material and psychological—in the exercise of their skills (Brickman, 1987).

Patients die, climbers fall, experiments fail. Even the development of skill in activities that are intrinsically motivating demands hard work and effort that is not always enjoyable. In challenging times, commitment keeps us on course. It runs interference against all those things that might distract us from our striving and thereby increases the probability of success. Commitment is essential to us in meeting our need for competence.

Commitment also enables community. The freedom of early childhood to do only what's inherently satisfying is quickly replaced by pressures to assume a variety of social responsibilities. By the time we reach adulthood, much of what we do we have to do. Every day we find ourselves engaged in activities that are necessary but not exciting. From washing dishes to changing diapers, from helping a neighbor paint her house to nursing a sick child back to health, we fulfill social obligation.

Imagine a society in which people never pledged loyalty. Imagine, suggests Lewis Smedes (1987), that the best we could get from anyone was "I'll try to be there if I can, but don't count on it" (p. 12). Every functioning social unit depends on commitment—from two roommates sharing an apartment to international organizations keeping peace. Commitment makes social life possible. Commitment serves our need for relatedness, our need to belong.

Does commitment also serve our need for autonomy? At first glance, commitments seem constricting. A year before his death, Irish actor Richard Harris reflected on his promise to play Professor Albus Dumbledore, the wise old wizard, in all the Harry Potter movies. "I hate that kind of commitment," he complained. "I hate the idea that my life in any way is sort of restricted." Twice divorced, he quickly added, "That's why my marriages broke up. I hate commitment, and I'm totally unreliable anyway" ("Star of 'Camelot,'" 2002, p. D9).

However, it is important to remember that commitment is always chosen, never coerced. Thus, it does meet our need for autonomy. Commitment frees us from the whims of our own fluctuating moods—of being buffeted by the everyday ups and downs of life. Making a decision and following through on it also frees us from manipulation by others. We are least vulnerable to social pressure when we make our commitments public. Indeed, by choosing our commitments carefully and consciously, we take charge of our future. And by exercising our freedom to choose our loyalties, we develop a much clearer sense of self.

In Robert Bolt's (1960) brilliant play *A Man for All Seasons*, Thomas More, the second most powerful man in England, privately challenges King Henry VIII's decision to divorce his wife, Catherine of Aragon. As a result, More loses his position and finally his life. Why? His strong personal commitment shaped his self-identity. While he is in prison, his daughter, Margaret, visits. She pleads with her father to voice allegiance to the king in spite of what he thought. But More objects: "When a man makes a promise, Meg, he takes himself into his own hands, like water. And if he opens his fingers then, he need not hope to find himself again" (p. 140).

Linking the Negative with the Positive

Commitments have both positive and negative elements (Brickman, 1987). Sometimes the positive element of enthusiasm (something valuable, even enjoyable) is evident; at other times the negative element of persistence (an obligation) dominates.

The following scale measures people's tendency to make or avoid commitments. Items reflecting persistence and items reflecting enthusiasm contribute equally to a total commitment score. Try it for yourself.

Commitment Scale

Check each statement that is true for you.

_____ **1.** I will do anything to keep a promise.

_____ **2.** I am easily distracted.

_____ **3.** I know what the top priority in my life is.

_____ **4.** I will suffer for what I love.

_____ **5.** I feel I have made much progress toward fulfilling my life's goals.

_____ **6.** I do not stop until the job is done.

_____ **7.** The things that I am involved with often make me a different person than I was before.

_____ **8.** I do not mind making sacrifices for something I believe in.

_____ **9.** My life is exciting to me.

_____ **10.** It is hard for me to make up my mind.

_____ **11.** I am committed to a few special things in my life.

_____ **12.** I do things as a matter of principle.

_____ **13.** Even when I am unhappy, I hardly ever quit until things are finished.

_____ **14.** I see my life as having a definite purpose and meaning.

_____ **15.** I sacrifice for what I believe in.

_____ **16.** There are many things that would tempt me to abandon my current life.

_____ **17.** I do my best even if the situation seems hopeless.

_____ **18.** I am willing to make commitments in my life.

_____ **19.** When I get going on something, I cannot quit until it is done.

_____ **20.** I find things lose their excitement over time.

_____ **21.** I never get into anything halfway.

_____ **22.** I will give up other things I want to do in order to do something that really matters to me.

_____ **23.** I value the things I love more than I value my freedom.

_____ **24.** I often have doubts about what I am doing.

_____ **25.** I give everything I have to whatever I do.

_____ **26.** I start more things than I finish.

_____ **27.** I feel I have a mission in life.

_____ **28.** I am committed to my work.

_____ **29.** I believe in meeting deadlines.

_____ **30.** I usually find a point in activities that seem pointless.

Source: Brickman, 1987, p. 11.

In scoring the scale, give yourself one point each if you did not *check items 2, 10, 16, 20, 24, and 26. Give yourself a point for each of the other items you* did *check. Total scores range from 0 to 30. The midpoint of the scale is 15, with lower scores reflecting a tendency to avoid commitments and higher scores reflecting greater willingness to make them.*

Commitments seem to last when we come to want to do what we feel we must do (Brickman, 1987). In terms of our earlier discussion of intrinsic/extrinsic motivation, what is introjected (we feel internal pressure) becomes internalized (we embrace it). Obligation merges with enthusiasm when we find that the object of our commitment has lasting value or meaning. Let's see how this might apply to our life's work.

Commitment to Work

For most adults, work involves more than half of waking life (Wrzesniewski, Rozin, & Bennett, 2003). For the overwhelming majority of us, it is an obligation—we must work to earn a living. However, our actual work experience may range from daily drudgery to genuine joy. We may count the minutes to our next paycheck or secretly wonder why we are being paid for doing what we most enjoy. Closely linked to the enjoyment of our work is the sense that it brings *fulfillment*—the firm belief that, because of our work, we are better people and the world is a better place (Wrzesniewski et al., 2003).

Job, Career, or Vocation?

Read each of the following paragraphs and consider how much you are like Mr. A, Mr. B., and Mr. C. If you are a full-time student, imagine how you will experience your most likely full-time employment after completing school.

Mr. A works primarily to earn enough money to support his life outside his job. If he were financially secure, he would not continue with his current line of work but would do something else instead. Mr. A's job is basically a necessity of life, a lot like breathing or sleeping. He often wishes the time would pass more quickly at work. He greatly anticipates weekends and vacations. If Mr. A lived his life over again, he probably would not go into the same line of work. He would not encourage his friends and children to enter his line of work. Mr. A is very eager to retire.

Mr. B basically enjoys his work but does not expect to be in his current job five years from now. Instead, he plans to move on to a better, higher-level job. He has several goals for his future pertaining to the positions he would eventually like to hold. Sometimes his work seems like a waste of time, but he knows that he must do sufficiently well in his current position to move on. Mr. B can't wait to get a promotion. For him, a promotion means recognition of his good work and a sign of his success in competition with his coworkers.

Mr. C's work is one of the most important parts of his life. He is very pleased that he is in this line of work. Because what he does for a living is a vital part of who he is, it is one of the first things he tells people about himself. He tends to take his work home with him and on vacations, too. The majority of his friends are from his place of employment, and he belongs to several organizations and clubs relating to his work. Mr. C feels good about his work because he loves it and because he thinks it makes the world a better place. He would encourage his friends and children to enter his line of work. Mr. C would be pretty upset if he were forced to stop working, and he is not particularly looking forward to retirement.

How much are you like Mr. A, Mr. B, and Mr. C?

3 = very much   2 = somewhat   1 = a little   0 = not at all

_____ Mr. A?

_____ Mr. B?

_____ Mr. C?

Source: Wrzesniewski, McCauley, Rozin, & Schwartz, 1997, p. 24.

Amy Wrzesniewski and her colleagues (1997) found that most adults tend to experience their work as a *job* (Mr. A), a *career* (Mr. B), or a *vocation* (Mr. C). In fact, they report that people found it relatively easy to make a choice, with roughly a third falling into each category. Do you see your own employment (present or future) as a job, a career, or a vocation?

Work as a Vocation

Wrzesniewski and her research team (1997) found that how you view your work makes a difference. When work becomes a vocation, obligation merges with enthusiasm. Those who regard their work as a vocation report both higher work satisfaction and greater life satisfaction than those who see their work as a job or as a career. Not surprisingly, people who feel a vocation or "calling" devote more time to their work, compensated or not. Interestingly, they also report that work brings greater satisfaction than does leisure. In contrast, those with "jobs" and "careers" rate the satisfaction they receive from leisure higher than the satisfaction they get from work. For people with a vocation, work becomes life's passion; for people with a job or career, the deepest satisfactions come from hobbies and relationships outside the workplace (Wrzesniewski et al., 2003).

So is it the worker or the workplace that makes work a vocation? Is it personality traits or job characteristics that make our primary occupation fulfilling? The person and the situation are both important.

Worker engagement is linked to a variety of situational variables (Harter et al., 2003). For example, people are more likely to be committed when managers communicate clear expectations, provide the materials and equipment for them to do their work, praise good performance, encourage development, and care about them as persons. Furthermore, when employees feel their opinions count, believe that they have the opportunity to do their best every day, and know that their associates are also committed to doing quality work, they experience greater satisfaction in their work and, as one might predict, are more productive.

At the same time, it is clear that the person shapes the work experience. We play an active role by shaping the meaning of our own work. Wrzesniewski and her colleagues (2003) report all three work orientations—job, career, and vocation—among administrative assistants, and evidence of both job and vocation orientations among hospital cleaners. They speculate that traits such as optimism and conscientiousness may be linked to a sense of vocation. Indeed, a person's attitudes toward work are highly stable over time and across different kinds of occupations (Staw, Bell, & Clausen, 1986). Perhaps, conclude Wrzesniewski and her colleagues, "a calling orientation is a portable benefit of those who tend to have a more positive outlook on life in general."

Perhaps what's most important to commitment is the match of the person to the situation. When people identify with the purpose of their role and the mission of their organization, they become deeply committed to their work. "Employees who know their own guiding values or purposes," suggests Daniel Goleman (1998), "will have a clear, even vivid sense about whether there is a 'fit' with an organization. When they feel a match, their commitment is spontaneous and strong" (p. 120). Clearly, self-awareness is one building block of commitment. The other is for companies and organizations to have a well-formulated mission—one that clearly defines how its efforts make the world a better place. People are likely to show little allegiance to organizations whose vision statements are merely public relations ploys.

Discovering the match, of course, is not automatic. Sometimes it takes time to find one's calling. The feature film *Mr. Holland's Opus* traces the remarkable transformation in a high school teacher's motivation over three decades of his professional life. Glenn Holland comes to JFK High School in the 1960s to teach music. His goal? To accumulate a nest egg quickly so that he can return to his true passion—composing. Teaching is a job. When his wife Iris becomes pregnant, Mr. Holland continues working at JFK High School. He makes teaching his career. Professional success and recognition become important goals. As the years pass, however, the commitment of obligation becomes one of enthusiasm. What he has to do becomes something he wants to do. He discovers that teaching students to appreciate music brings its own rewards. By the end of the story, teaching is Mr. Holland's calling, his vocation.

IN REVIEW

Often our strivings are neither joyful nor exciting. Commitment enables us to persevere in meeting our needs for competence, relatedness, and autonomy. Obligations merge with enthusiasm when our goals have lasting meaning or value. We may view our work as a job, a career, or a vocation. When our work is a vocation, we experience the highest levels of commitment and the greatest satisfaction in work and life.

■

Fostering Commitment

How do we nurture lasting commitment in ourselves and in our children? Psychological research suggests specific directions, including the following nine:

1. **Look for meaning.** People become vitally engaged in activities that they find have long-term importance. Mere enjoyment is not enough. Even teenagers who find the arts absorbing are likely to withdraw if they do not find that their involvement serves some larger purpose (Csikszentmihalyi et al., 1993). Similarly, people persist even in a boring laboratory task if they are provided a meaningful rationale. Edward Deci and his colleagues (1994) asked introductory

psychology students in their laboratory to press a bar whenever a light appeared on a screen. If told that this was a task air controllers used to enhance their signal detection ability, the students continued the task in a free activity period following the laboratory assignment. When asked, they reported that they found the task both meaningful and enjoyable.

Parents strengthen their children's commitment to an otherwise onerous task by providing a meaningful rationale. Children are more likely to clean their room if they have a credible reason—"so your toys won't get lost or stepped on." We fulfill an obligation if we grasp its meaning and find that it is consistent with other goals and values.

2. **Transform a "should" to a "want."** Some people perceive value in social obligations more easily than others. For example, some teenagers see a visit to relatives as an unpleasant but necessary obligation, while others see the potential for good conversation and positive feelings. Some students regard going to class as merely a requirement, while others see it as a unique opportunity to learn. And some parents find that driving their children to activities is a monotonous task that simply erodes precious time, whereas other experience it as an opportunity to enjoy their children's company.

When challenged to find value in social obligation, most research participants in one study could (Berg, Janoff-Bullman, & Carter, 2001). People listed obligatory tasks such as studying for a test, visiting a sick friend, going to work, and cleaning a room. After being asked to identify reasons why these tasks might be regarded as "wants" rather than "shoulds," almost two-thirds of the participants produced at least one reason. Research findings further indicated that transforming a "should" to a "should + a want" increased not only the likelihood of attaining the goal but also one's level of life satisfaction.

3. **Choose commitments.** Centuries ago, Samuel Butler observed, "He who agrees against his will, is of the same opinion still." We prize a sense of freedom. People lose interest in even intrinsically satisfying activities if they feel pressured to engage in them. Parents and teachers can learn an important lesson from Jonathan Freedman's (1965) experiment with elementary school children. He found that either a severe threat or a mild threat could keep kids from playing with an attractive toy—a battery-controlled robot—but only temporarily. Some weeks later, when the children were given another opportunity to play with the toy, the children who had been severely threatened succumbed to temptation and played freely with the robot. The children given the mild deterrent did not. Feeling that they had freely chosen not to play with the toy, they internalized their decision.

In the laboratory task in which students were instructed to press a bar whenever a light came on, Deci's research team (1994) found that conveying choice as well as a meaningful rationale fostered commitment. A simple change in instruction from "You should start the activity by pressing the space bar" to "If you are willing to continue, all you need to do is start pressing the space bar" promoted internalization. Acknowledging the conflicting feelings that subjects might experience also strengthened commitment. Stating, "I know that doing this is not much fun; in fact many subjects have told me that it's pretty boring. So I can perfectly understand and accept that you may not find it very interesting" conveyed respect for the person's inclinations and right to choose.

Wise parents strengthen their children's commitment to moral values, such as honesty, by providing them with just enough reason to do the right thing. As Robert Cialdini (2001) observes, a powerful threat like "It's bad to lie, honey, so if I catch you at it, I'll cut your tongue out" will be effective as long as you are present. A subtler approach that provides only enough reason for the child to tell the truth—"Things go more smoothly when people are honest" —is more likely to strengthen conscience. In addition, teachers and parents who communicate empathy by saying "I know that it's not fun for you to spend time picking up your room" convey that the children's feelings are legitimate and not necessarily inconsistent with doing the activity.

4. **Enact commitments.** Sometimes we need to "just do it." We strengthen our commitments not only by changing our thoughts but also by altering our actions (Myers, 2002). Psychologists have long recognized that not only does belief shape behavior, but behavior shapes belief. Sometimes actions even precede commitments. In *Mr. Holland's Opus*, it was only in the act of teaching that Glenn Holland discovered its value.

Consider the following:

- Doing a favor for another person, including tutoring a student, increases liking of that person (Blanchard & Cook, 1976).

- When asked, voters almost always indicate they will vote. Compared to voters who are not asked, voters expressing their intentions are significantly more likely to vote (Greenwald, Carnot, Beach, & Young, 1987).

- Older children who teach a moral norm to younger children subsequently follow the moral code better themselves (Parke, 1974).

- People who agreed (everyone asked did) to wear a lapel pin publicizing a Cancer Society drive were later twice as likely to donate (Pliner, Hart, Kohl, & Saari, 1974).

As Sir Thomas More suggested in *A Man For All Seasons*, we come to know ourselves through our own actions. "I write," claimed popular author Flannery O'Connor, "because I don't know what I think until I read what I say" (cited by Cytowic, 1993, p. 213).

5. Go public. If we make our commitments public, we are more likely to keep them. We want to appear consistent not only to ourselves but to others. Society rightly values integrity. When Charles DeGaulle was asked why his announcement to quit his heavy smoking obliged him to quit forever, he proudly proclaimed, "DeGaulle cannot go back on his word." It is no wonder that many weight reduction clinics require their clients to write down their weight loss goal and show it to as many friends, relatives, and neighbors as possible. This simple strategy sometimes works when all else has failed (Cialdini, 2001).

6. Set priorities. Our specific strivings and commitments sometimes conflict with each other. If so, we need to set priorities. If we are committed to too many things, we end up being committed to none. Lewis Smedes (1987) notes that some people "are committed to commitment, or to their run at praise for being highly committed people."

When Mark Starr (2003) asked premier figure skater Michelle Kwan about her commitment to her sport, she wisely responded: "Skating can take control of your life. I've learned that you have to take control—to try to balance having a boyfriend, going to school, friends, and family. Skating is a huge part of my life, but the rest is just as important. Skating is not going to keep you company. It's not going to make you laugh. The ice doesn't talk to you."

7. Review commitments. Commitments serve us well by giving our lives direction. We are more efficient when we don't have to revisit the merits of every action. But periodically we do need to review our prior decisions and actions. At the end of his life, Nazi Albert Speer, architect of the Third Reich asked, "How could I have given my life to this monstrous evil?" He provided his own answer: "I committed myself early on and never allowed myself to examine or criticize my commitment" (Smedes, 1987, p. 51). Sometimes commitments should be broken.

Robert Cialdini (2001) shows how compliance professionals sometimes manipulate us by securing a commitment from us that serves their own ends, not our own. A good example is the low-ball technique. Car dealers may get a customer to commit to buying a new car because of its great price. In completing the sales forms, the salesperson removes the price advantage by charging for options the buyer thought were included, or by checking with the sales manager who disallows the deal: "We would be losing money." Because of their intial commitment, customers accept a higher price than they would have agreed to at the outset. Cialdini recommends that we always ask ourselves, "Knowing what I now know about the real price, if I go back in time, would I make the same choice again?"

8. Maintain hope. We are most likely to persevere when a striving is meaningful and we believe that the objective is attainable. Hope enables us to endure temporary setbacks. Our interpretation of negative events plays a crucial role in continued commitment to our strivings. Hope reflects *willpower*—the motivation to keep moving toward our goals—and *waypower*—the perceived ability to generate routes to achieve them. Hope nourishes commitment, and commitment fosters hope.

Many thought Michelle Kwan's second failure to win an Olympic gold medal in 2002 would end one of America's greatest skating careers. Younger and talented rivals were positioned to replace her as grande dame of the ice. But Kwan remained hopeful. When asked, "Do the two Olympic losses weigh heavily?" she responded, "I don't think so. I've had so many great years of skating, it doesn't all ride on two Olympic competitions." She went on to whip her younger rivals for her seventh national championship and her fifth world title in 2003.

9. Use structured, voluntary activities. Reed Larson (2000) suggests that we need to provide adolescents with more opportunities to learn *initiative*. The devotion of cumulative effort over time to achieve a goal, Larson argues, is a key component of creativity, leadership, altruism, and civic engagement. Neither traditional schoolwork nor unstructured leisure provide the ideal conditions for learning commitment.

In doing schoolwork, adolescents report low levels of intrinsic motivation. Adults typically control the structure of academic work. Although adolescents may report high intrinsic motivation during unstructured leisure, often it is not associated with high concentration or challenge. For example, watching TV and interacting with friends consume a huge proportion of the average adolescent's waking hours. So the context best suited for the development of commitment, suggests Larson (2000), is structured voluntary activities such as sports and the arts. These activities occur within a structure of constraints, rules, and specific goals. Students are likely to learn and practice commitment where they value the activity and where they must invest time and effort in achieving some skill. Participation in school extracurricular activities is associated with higher self-esteem, feelings of control over one's life, lower rates of delinquency, and higher educational aspirations.

IN REVIEW

Finding meaning in our strivings and transforming our "shoulds" to "wants" strengthens commitment. Lasting commitments are chosen, enacted, and made public. Periodically, we need to review our commitments and set priorities. Hope strengthens commitment, and adolescents may best learn initiative through structured voluntary activities.

happiness

6

Assessing Happiness
Satisfying Life Experiences
Pursuing Happiness

Happiness is the meaning and the purpose of life, the whole aim and end of human existence.
—ARISTOTLE (384–322 B.C.)

Everything we do, suggested Aristotle, is motivated by our drive to experience happiness. In fact, he argued, it is the supreme good. We pursue health, fame, and wealth because we think they will make us happy. We seek happiness as an end in itself.

Test the idea with this mental challenge: Imagine someone could grant you fame and fortune *or* happiness. You could have the world's respect and own everything you could dream of but without happiness. Or you could live each day joyfully, having only your basic needs met. Which would you pick (Fordyce, 1977)?

For virtually everyone, it's no contest: Happiness wins hands down. No wonder that college students report thinking of happiness often, rating it 6.58 on a scale of 1 to 7, where 1 is "of no importance" and 7 is "extraordinarily important and valuable" (Diener, 2000). In almost every culture that researchers have examined, happiness ranks as one of life's most cherished goals (Lyubomirsky, 2001).

Assessing Happiness

The following scale was designed to gather data on people's general satisfaction with life (Diener et al., 1985a). Try it yourself.

SELF-ASSESSMENT ■

Satisfaction with Life Scale

There are five statements on the next page with which you may agree or disagree. Using the scale provided, indicate your agreement with each item by placing the appropriate number on the line preceding that item. Please be open and honest in your responses.

7 = strongly agree   6 = agree   5 = slightly agree   4 = neither agree nor disagree
3 = slightly disagree   2 = disagree   1 = strongly disagree

_____ **1.** In most ways my life is close to my ideal.

_____ **2.** The conditions of my life are excellent.

_____ **3.** I am satisfied with my life.

_____ **4.** So far I have gotten the important things I want in life.

_____ **5.** If I could live my life over, I would change almost nothing.

Source: Diener et al., 1985a.

Add up your answers to the five items to obtain your total score. Scores can range from 5 to 35. Scores above the midpoint of 20 suggest satisfaction with life. As we will see in the next section, most folks are pretty satisfied!

Are Most People Happy?

Is life a tragedy? Sophocles thought so. "Not to be born surpasses thought and speech," he observed. "The second best is to have seen the light and then to go back quickly whence we came." Centuries later, Rousseau agreed: "Our pains exceed our pleasures so that, all things considered, human life is not at all a valuable gift."

So, how happy are people? Below are some faces expressing various feelings (Andrews & Withey, 1976). Which face comes closest to expressing how you feel about your life as a whole?

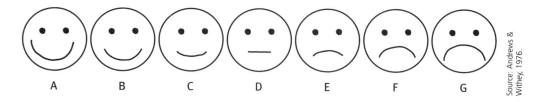

Source: Andrews & Withey, 1976.

Which face do most respondents select? Contrary to the idea that most people are unhappy, a whopping 92 percent of respondents in the United States picked a happy face (Myers, 2000). Nearly two-thirds picked A or B.

And how do people score on the Satisfaction with Life Scale? Most Americans score in the 21 to 25 range. In other words, you would need a score above 25 to be more satisfied than most Americans. A recent Harris poll (Reilly & Simmons, 2003) reported that 57 percent of Americans indicated that they were "very satisfied" with life, and 34 percent said they were "fairly satisfied." A relatively small 6 percent were "not very satisfied," and a miniscule 2 percent were "not at all satisfied."

Americans are not uniquely happy. Research from around the world suggests that most people are happy. Although cultural differences exist—the Swiss are happier than Bulgarians, and Danes seem happier than South Koreans—people of most nations average above the midpoint on happiness scales (Diener, 2000).

Still the idea that *others* are probably not happy persists. For example, more than two-thirds of respondents in Minnesota rated their capacity for happiness to be in the upper 35 percent of people their own age and sex (Lykken, 1999). And when Americans were asked "Who of the following people do you think is the happiest?" they responded Oprah Winfrey (23 percent), Bill Gates (7 percent), the Pope (12 percent), Chelsea Clinton (3 percent), and yourself (49 percent). The remaining 6 percent did not know (Black & McCafferty, 1998). Most people see themselves as even happier than the popular, powerful, and wise!

Why Be Happy?

The benefits of happiness extend beyond the enjoyment of good feelings. In fact, research indicates that joy pays major physical and psychological dividends.

Compared to their dour counterparts, happy people (Seligman, 2002):

- are healthier and live longer.
- are more productive at work and have higher incomes.
- are more tolerant and creative and make decisions more easily.
- select more challenging goals, persist longer, and perform better in a variety of laboratory tasks.
- demonstrate greater empathy, have more close friends, and enjoy better marriages.

Barbara Frederickson's (2001) theory of positive emotions states that a certain level of joy helps individuals build a variety of personal resources including physical (skills, health, longevity), social (friendships, social support networks), intellectual (expert knowledge, intellectual complexity), and psychological (resilience, optimism, creativity) resources. Her theory emphasizes that positive emotions strengthen resources that are drawn on throughout life to improve coping and our odds of survival.

Perhaps, then, Robert Louis Stevenson was right when he said, "There is no duty we so underrate as the duty of being happy. By being happy we sow anonymous benefits upon the world." The "feel-good do-good effect" is in fact now a well-established psychological principle. People who are in a good mood not only display more empathy, they are also more helpful. Happy people are less self-focused, like others more, and seek to spread their good cheer.

Who Is Happy?

Helen Keller claimed, "External conditions are the accidents of life, its outer trappings. Success and happiness lie within you." Was she right? What do you think? Are there are also important demographic predictors of well-being?

Happiness

Complete the following true-or-false quiz.

T   F   **1.** Men have a greater sense of well-being than do women.

T   F   **2.** The teen and elderly years are the least happy times of life.

T   F   **3.** More years of formal education are linked with a more joyful life.

T   F   **4.** White people are happier than members of minority race groups.

T   F   **5.** By and large, the single life is happier than the married life.

T   F   **6.** Compared to religiously active people, the nonreligious tend to enjoy a greater sense of well-being.

T   F   **7.** In North America and Europe, those with higher annual incomes, and especially the very rich, live happier lives.

Researchers have addressed all of these issues, and all of the above statements are false!

Gender provides little clue to happiness levels. Although women may be more susceptible to depression and anxiety, and men more often experience antisocial disorders or become alcoholic, numerous studies indicate that the genders are equally likely to report being "very happy" and "satisfied" with their lives.

Like gender, age tells little about a person's level of happiness. Contrary to the conventional wisdom that adolescent stress or physical decline in old age makes a person miserable, repeated surveys show that people of all ages report similar feelings of well-being. Unhappiness does not surge in women during menopause or when children leave home. (The "empty nest" for most parents is actually a happy place.) Nor do most people experience a mid-life crisis. One study of nearly 10,000 men and women found "not the slightest evidence" that distress peaks in the early forties (McCrae & Costa, 1990).

Years of formal education, IQ, and skin color are not significant predictors of happiness either. "People who go to work in their overalls and on the bus," concludes David Lykken (1999, p. 17), "are just as happy, on the average, as those in suits who drive to work in their own Mercedes." Studies in both North America and Europe show that education and race account for very little of the person-to-person variation in happiness. For example, in spite of decades of disadvantage, African-Americans report about the same sense of well-being as do white Americans.

Surveys of both Americans and Europeans report that married people experience greater happiness and life satisfaction than those who are single or widowed, especially compared to those who are divorced or separated. For example, among the thousands of Americans surveyed by the National Opinion Research Center over the past 30 years, 40 percent of married adults declared themselves very happy, almost double the 24 percent of never-married adults who said the same (Seligman, 2002). Data from national surveys in 19 countries confirm this marriage–happiness link. The idea that the marriage–happiness link is gender specific—strongly predictive of men's but not women's happiness—is also a myth. Throughout the western world, both sexes report greater life satisfaction than those never married, divorced, or separated.

Active religious practices are also linked with happier and healthier lives. In reviewing the research on faith and well-being, David Myers (2000) notes how active religiosity is associated with several mental health criteria. Actively religious North Americans are much less likely than the nonreligious to become delinquent, to abuse drugs and alcohol, to divorce, or to commit suicide. The religiously devout also seem to cope with stress more effectively. Compared with religiously inactive widows, recently widowed women who attend worship services regularly report greater life satisfaction. People of faith also tend to retain or regain greater happiness after suffering divorce, unemployment, or serious illness. For the elderly, the two best predictors of life satisfaction seem to be health and religiousness.

Basic needs must be met for us to be happy. However, once we have life's necessities, income makes little difference. For example, in those nations whose gross national product is more than eight thousand dollars per person, there is little relationship between wealth and well-being. Moreover, within wealthier countries such as the United States and Canada, the correlation between income and personal happiness, reports Ronald Inglehart (1990, p. 242), "is surprisingly weak (indeed virtually negligible)." A survey of the Forbes 1000 list of the wealthiest Americans found the very rich to be only slightly happier than the average American (Diener et al., 1985b). In fact, 37 percent were less happy.

Given that age, gender, race, educational level, and income play little role in happiness, might we gain better clues from knowing people's personality traits?

CRITICAL THINKING ■

Personality and Happiness

Think of a person you know well who seems especially happy. Identify at least three of that person's distinguishing traits:

_____

_____

_____

_____

_____

_____

When asked to name one condition for happiness, psychologist Ed Diener (Elias, 2002) responded, "The happiest people all seem to have good friends." When Diener and Martin Seligman (2002) studied very happy people—those who scored about 30 on the Satisfaction with Life Scale at the start of this chapter—they found that they were highly social. In contrast to those who were only moderately happy or very unhappy, the happiest people spent the least amount of time alone and the most time socializing. Outside observers rated the happiest people highest in interpersonal relationships.

Indeed, happy people are *extraverts*. They are sociable, outgoing people. Extraverts are more successful in meeting the fundamental need to belong. Happy people have both the desire and the ability to foster strong social relationships. This motivation and competence seems linked to their basic *trust* in others. They assume the best, seeing others as fundamentally honest and trustworthy. In contrast, those who are skeptical, cynical, and assume that others may be dishonest or dangerous tend to be unhappy. Extraverts' greater sensitivity to positive information also seems to foster their sense of well-being. Told that they have done well on a test or to imagine they have won a lottery, they are happier than introverts given the same news. Interestingly, extraverts' and introverts' reactions to negative news (hearing about a poor test performance or imagining being expelled from school) are the same (Larsen & Ketelaar, 1991).

Happy people are also *conscientious*. One study of the happy personality found that the trait of conscientiousness was the strongest positive correlate of life satisfaction (DeNeve & Cooper, 1998). The researchers suggest that engaging in goal-directed activity—exerting control over ourselves and our environment—enhances quality of life. Conscientious people set higher goals for themselves and tend to achieve more in work settings. When they are highly challenged and have the skills to meet the challenge, they are especially likely to report *flow*, an optimal experience we will focus on later in this chapter.

Linked closely to conscientiousness is a sense of *personal control*. In reviewing the University of Michigan's nationwide surveys, Angus Campbell (1981, p. 218) concluded that "having a strong sense of controlling one's life is a more dependable predictor of positive feelings of well-being than any of the objective conditions of life we have considered." Those with a strong desire for control are assertive, decisive, and are more likely to attain their personal goals. They take credit for their successes but also accept responsibility for their failures.

Happy people also enjoy high *self-esteem* (Schimmack & Diener, 2002). They like themselves. People who feel good about themselves are less susceptible to insomnia and ulcers, are more persistent after failure, and are less likely to conform. The University of Michigan surveys (Campbell, 1981) have shown that satisfaction with self is a more powerful predictor of well-being in America than is satisfaction with family life, friendships, or income. Self-esteem is, however, a stronger predictor of well-being in countries that value personal autonomy, such as the United States and Europe, than in collectivist cultures such as China, Korea, and India, where people think more about how their families are doing.

Have you noticed the common thread that runs through these personality characteristics? Happy people tend to make optimistic interpretations in everyday life. They see the best in others, in their work, and in themselves. Optimists don't deny their setbacks but rather seem to interpret them differently. Because they are convinced that effort and self-discipline make a difference, they believe the future is bright. They are *hardy* individuals who utilize more effective coping strategies in managing stress. Ironically, those who deny threatening life events and the existence of negative emotions are among the unhappiest (DeNeve, 1999).

IN REVIEW

Happiness is one of life's most important goals. Happy people live longer, are more productive, and enjoy better interpersonal relations. Most people report relatively high levels of life satisfaction. Gender, age, race, formal education, and income level seem to make little difference in people's level of happiness. On the other hand, those who are married, actively religious, extraverted, conscientious, and self-confident express greater life satisfaction.

■

Satisfying Life Experiences

Some psychologists have attempted to understand happiness by studying specific life experiences.

SELF-ASSESSMENT ■

Satisfying Life Event

Consider the past month of your life. Think back to the important occurrences of this period of time. Bring to mind the single most personally satisfying event *that you experienced. Use your own definition of "satisfying." That is, think of "satisfying" in whatever way makes sense to you. Take a couple of minutes to come up with a very impactful experience and then describe it (Sheldon et al., 2001).*

_____

_____

_____

_____

_____

What do people find most satisfying? Ken Sheldon and his colleagues (2001) report that American students most commonly recount experiences in which they felt a strong sense of self-respect, successfully completed a difficult task, experienced intimacy with other people, or had been free to do things their own way. They were less likely to report their most satisfying experiences as having involved buying the things they wanted, physical pleasure, or exercising strong influence over others' beliefs and behaviors. When people reflect on their most satisfying experiences, they think primarily of times when they felt worthy, competent, related to others, or free of external pressure. Our experiences of position, pleasure, or power are less important.

This pattern seems to hold across time and place. Sheldon found that this same order emerged when he asked people to reflect on a shorter period of time ("think of the most satisfying experience in the past week") as well as a much longer period ("think of the most satisfying experience in the entire semester"). South Koreans offered similar reflections. Compared to their American counterparts, however, South Koreans were somewhat more likely to report that feelings of relatedness were a crucial aspect of their most satisfying life events and somewhat less likely to identify self-esteem as being important.

Tim Kasser and Richard Ryan (1993, 1996) wondered if prominent elements of the American dream—striving to become rich, famous, and attractive—really foster happiness. In a series of studies, they examined how different aspirations were related to well-being. Adults, including college students, rated the relative importance and likelihood of attaining seven different goals. They also ranked the goals in terms of how much each one was a "guiding principle" in their lives. Results indicated that strivings for financial success, social recognition, and an appealing appearance were associated with lower vitality, less self-actualization (fulfillment of one's potential), and greater physical distress. In contrast, the pursuit of self-acceptance, affiliation, community feeling (helpfulness), and physical fitness were linked with greater psychological and physical well-being. Kasser and Ryan concluded: There may well be a "dark side to the American dream." Ed Diener agrees: "Materialism is toxic for happiness" (Elias, 2002).

We know this and yet we don't. Most of us agree—you can't buy happiness. Still we are not so sure. In a University of Michigan survey, people were asked what would improve the quality of their life. The first and most frequent answer was "more money" (Campbell, 1981). To fulfill their dreams, Americans claim they need an annual income of $102,000 (Myers, 2000). Moreover, nearly three-quarters of college freshman consider being "very well-off financially" to be a "very important" or "essential" goal. Among 19 possible objectives, they ranked it highest, well ahead of "developing a meaningful philosophy of life," "raising a family," or "becoming an authority in my field."

In relating the story of an American investment banker's visit to a small Mexican fishing village, Mike Albrecht (2001) comically captures our confused feelings about money and happiness.

> After complimenting one fisherman on his quick catch of several large yellowfin tuna, the banker asked what he did with the rest of his time. "I sleep late," explained the fisherman, "fish a little, play with my children, take siestas with my wife, Maria, stroll into the village where I sip wine, and play guitar with friends. I live a full and busy life."
>
> The American scoffed, "As a Harvard MBA, I could help you. You should spend more time fishing and with the profits buy a bigger boat. Eventually you could acquire a fleet and move to New York where you could run an expanding enterprise. Eventually you would have millions." "Then what?" asked the fisherman. "You could retire," said the banker. "Move to a small fishing village where you could sleep late, fish a little, play with your kids, take siestas with your wife, stroll to the village in the evenings where you could sip wine and play guitar with your friends."

Flow in Work and Leisure

Mihaly Csikszentmihalyi (1990) claims that what makes experiences genuinely satisfying is a state of consciousness called *flow,* in which our concentration is so focused that it amounts to absolute absorption in an activity. "This is happiness," said American novelist Willa Cather, "to be dissolved into something completely great." Consider your own experience with flow in the following activity.

CRITICAL THINKING ■

Flow

Do you ever get involved in something so deeply that nothing else seems to matter and you lose track of time?

Often ﹘﹘﹘﹘   Sometimes ﹘﹘﹘﹘   Rarely ﹘﹘﹘﹘   Never or don't know ﹘﹘﹘﹘

If you have had such an experience, briefly describe it.

﹘﹘﹘﹘﹘﹘﹘﹘﹘﹘﹘﹘﹘﹘﹘﹘﹘﹘﹘﹘﹘﹘﹘﹘﹘﹘﹘﹘﹘﹘﹘﹘

﹘﹘﹘﹘﹘﹘﹘﹘﹘﹘﹘﹘﹘﹘﹘﹘﹘﹘﹘﹘﹘﹘﹘﹘﹘﹘﹘﹘﹘﹘﹘﹘

﹘﹘﹘﹘﹘﹘﹘﹘﹘﹘﹘﹘﹘﹘﹘﹘﹘﹘﹘﹘﹘﹘﹘﹘﹘﹘﹘﹘﹘﹘﹘﹘

﹘﹘﹘﹘﹘﹘﹘﹘﹘﹘﹘﹘﹘﹘﹘﹘﹘﹘﹘﹘﹘﹘﹘﹘﹘﹘﹘﹘﹘﹘﹘﹘

﹘﹘﹘﹘﹘﹘﹘﹘﹘﹘﹘﹘﹘﹘﹘﹘﹘﹘﹘﹘﹘﹘﹘﹘﹘﹘﹘﹘﹘﹘﹘﹘

﹘﹘﹘﹘﹘﹘﹘﹘﹘﹘﹘﹘﹘﹘﹘﹘﹘﹘﹘﹘﹘﹘﹘﹘﹘﹘﹘﹘﹘﹘﹘﹘

Now think about how you felt while engaged in the experience and answer the questions below. Using the following scale, select the number that best describes your experience.

1 = strongly disagree   2 = disagree   3 = neither agree nor disagree   4 = agree
5 = strongly agree

_____ **1.** I was challenged, but I believed my skills would allow me to meet the challenge.

_____ **2.** I made the correct movements without thinking about trying to do so.

_____ **3.** I knew clearly what I wanted to do.

_____ **4.** It was really clear to me that I was doing well.

_____ **5.** My attention was focused entirely on what I was doing.

_____ **6.** I felt in total control of what I was doing.

_____ **7.** I was not concerned with what others may have been thinking about me.

_____ **8.** Time seemed to alter (either slowed down or speeded up).

_____ **9.** I really enjoyed the experience.

Source: Jackson & Marsh, 1996, p. 34.

The more items that you agree with, the closer you came to experiencing flow. Csikzentmihalyi formulated the flow concept after studying artists who worked with enormous concentration. Immersed in a project, they would work as if nothing else mattered and then would promptly forget about it once it was finished. The work was so engrossing and enjoyable that it was worth doing for its own sake, even though it may have had no consequence outside itself.

Do only highly skilled and creative people experience flow? No, ordinary folks fully absorbed and engaged in a favorite activity report the flow experience. When a representative sample of Americans was asked what you were just asked ("Do you ever get involved in something so deeply that nothing else seems to matter, and you lose track of time?"), about one in five said that this happens to them often, as much as several times a day. Only 15 percent said that this never happens (Csikszentmihalyi, 1997). Cross-cultural comparisons suggest these frequencies are quite stable and universal.

Flow comes in playing touch football, repairing a broken appliance, preparing a good meal, conversing with friends, dealing with customers, and even driving a car. One college student even seemed to find it in taking a final exam. He transformed his answer to an essay question into a rap (Frantz, 2003)!

In describing her source of deepest enjoyment, one mother reported the following (Allison & Duncan, 1988):

(It happens when) I am working with my daughter, when she's discovered something new. A new cookie recipe that she has accomplished, that she has made herself, an artistic work that she's done and she is proud of. Her reading is something that she is really into, and we read together. She reads to me and I read to her, and that's a time when I really lose touch with the rest of the world. I am totally absorbed in what I am doing. (cited by Csikszentmihalyi, 1997, p. 112)

Clearly, flow is not achieved by passively accepting whatever comes our way, or in leisure that's merely relaxing or enjoyable. For example, people rarely report flow when watching TV or while "just sitting relaxing." The flow experience comes with mindful challenge rather than mindless passivity.

The nine sample items from the flow scale that you completed earlier capture the key dimensions of the flow experience (Jackson & Marsh, 1996). Which ones describe your experience?

_____ **1.** *Challenge–skill balance* The situational demands match skill level. (Challenges that are too high lead to anxiety. Challenges that are too low lead to boredom.)

_____ **2.** *Action-awareness merging* Engagement in the activity becomes so strong that it becomes spontaneous or automatic.

_____ **3.** *Clear goals* Goals may be set in advance or evolve while engaged in the action.

_____ **4.** *Unambiguous feedback* Immediate and clear feedback provides information about progress.

_____ **5.** *Concentration* There is a total focus on the task at hand.

_____ **6.** *Sense of control* There is a sense of being in control without actively trying to exert control.

_____ **7.** *Loss of self-consciousness* Concern for the self disappears. One is "unselfconsciously" involved.

_____ **8.** *Transformation of time* Time alters perceptibly, either slowing down or speeding up. Alternatively, time may be out of awareness.

_____ **9.** *Autotelic experience* An activity is "autotelic" if it is done for its own sake, with no expectation of reward. In other words, the experience is intrinsically motivating.

For the most part, people are happy not because of what they do, but because of how they do it (Csikszentmihalyi, 1999). Happy people tend to immerse themselves in their daily activities—generally doing things for their own sake rather than to achieve some external reward. Fully absorbed in the current of life, they actively attend to what is happening around them. They notice more and relish the experience.

The first step in achieving flow is to have a clear goal. Without a goal, it is difficult to concentrate and avoid distraction. The second step is practicing the habit of

doing what needs to be done with concentrated focus—with skill rather than iner-
tia. Even routine tasks like washing windows, vacuuming, and driving to work become rewarding when done with focus.

Interpreting Life Events

Abraham Lincoln once observed, "Most people are about as happy as they make up
their minds to be." Was he right? Is it our life experiences or how we interpret them
that make the difference? Our earlier examination of personality traits and happiness suggested that our interpretations can be important.

We all know people who just seem upbeat. They see the world through rose-tinted
glasses, discover the silver lining in the worst of times, and find happiness in everyday occurrences. Others seem chronically unhappy. Nothing is ever right, they always feel the thorns in the roses, and each day seems to bring disaster (Lyubomirsky,
2001). What is the real difference between these two types of people? We'll address
that question by considering how people differ in their levels of maximizing, regret,
savoring, and gratitude.

Maximization and Regret

In considering life's many choices—from selecting toothpaste to choosing a college—are you more likely to ask, "Is this alternative acceptable?" or "Is this the best?"
Are you a *satisficer* or a *maximizer*? The following scale assesses these two contrasting orientations to goals.

SELF-ASSESSMENT ■

Maximization

Use the following scale to respond to each statement:

1 = completely disagree   2 = disagree   3 = disagree somewhat   4 = neither
disagree nor agree   5 = agree somewhat   6 = agree   7 = completely agree

_____ **1.** When I watch TV, I channel surf, often scanning through the available
options even while attempting to watch one program.

_____ **2.** When I am in the car listening to the radio, I often check other stations
to see if something better is playing, even if I'm relatively satisfied with
what I'm listening to.

_____ **3.** I treat relationships like clothing; I expect to try a lot on before I get the
perfect fit.

_____ **4.** No matter how satisfied I am with my job, it's only right for me to be on
the lookout for better opportunities.

_____ **5.** I often fantasize about living in ways that are quite different from my actual life.

_____ **6.** I'm a big fan of lists that attempt to rank things (the best movies, the best singers, the best athletes, the best novels, etc.).

_____ **7.** I often find it difficult to shop for a gift for a friend.

_____ **8.** When shopping, I have a hard time finding clothing that I really love.

_____ **9.** Renting videos is really difficult. I'm always struggling to pick the best one.

_____ **10.** I find that writing is very difficult, even if it's just writing a letter to a friend, because it's so hard to word things just right. I often do several drafts of even simple things.

_____ **11.** No matter what I do, I have the highest standards for myself.

_____ **12.** I never settle for second best.

_____ **13.** Whenever I'm faced with a choice, I try to imagine what all the other possibilities are, even ones that aren't present at the moment.

Source: Schwartz et al., 2002, p. 1182.

To score, add up the numbers you circled. Total scores range from 13 to 91. Higher scores reflect a greater tendency to be a maximizer—someone who tries to get the very best or absolute most out of every situation. Several samples of adults obtained a mean score slightly above 50.

What difference do these contrasting orientations make? In some cases, maximizing is the better strategy for making decisions. For example, in responding to a serious health threat, seeking and settling for only the best treatment increases your chances of survival. Maximizers plan more carefully in solving problems, and their high standards may spur them on to greater achievement, but maximization can come at a significant cost to well-being. The following scale assesses feelings of regret.

SELF-ASSESSMENT ■

Regret

Use the following scale to respond to each statement:

1 = completely disagree   2 = disagree   3 = disagree somewhat   4 = neither disagree nor agree   5 = agree somewhat   6 = agree   7 = completely agree

_____ **1.** Whenever I make a choice, I'm curious about what would have happened if I had chosen differently.

_____ **2.** Whenever I make a choice, I try to get information about how the other alternatives turned out.

_____ **3.** If I make a choice and it turns out well, I still feel like something of a failure if I find out that another choice would have turned out better.

_____ **4.** When I think about how I'm doing in life, I often assess opportunities I have passed up.

_____ **5.** Once I make a decision, I don't look back.

Source: Schwartz et al., 2002, p. 1182.

Reverse the number you gave to item 5 (i.e., 1 = 7, 2 = 6, 3 = 5, 4 = 4, 5 = 3, 6 = 2, 7 = 1), then add up the numbers you gave in response to all five items. Scores range from 5 to 35, with those above the midpoint of 20 reflecting a tendency to experience some regret about your life choices.

Schwartz and his team found that the tendency to want to maximize outcomes is highly correlated with potential regret. In several samples of adults, the researchers also found that maximization was negatively related to happiness, life satisfaction, optimism, and self-esteem. Maximizers seem especially susceptible to two common psychological processes—social comparison and adaptation—that sometimes drain joy from life. And maximizers tend to keep their options open, which can lower life satisfaction.

To some degree we all compare our life's outcomes with those of others. The gap between what we have and what our friends and neighbors possess can foster feelings of relative deprivation. An important reason why money fails to boost life satisfaction is our strong tendency to compare ourselves with those who have more. Especially as we climb the ladder of success, we tend to compare ourselves with those one rung higher rather than those a rung lower and often become dissatisfied.

Maximizers, in their eagerness to decide whether they have attained the "best" life outcomes, need some standard for making that judgment. Often, an objective criterion is not available, so they compare themselves with others. Research confirms that, relative to satisficers, maximizers do engage in more social comparison and experience greater feelings of relative deprivation.

Our remarkable capacity to adapt also short-circuits happiness. Good experiences—a promotion, a new car, gaining entrance to a prestigious school—boost our spirits only briefly. Similarly, bad experiences—a car accident, a rejected job application, a low score on an entrance exam—deflate us, but only temporarily.

Although we may understand the adaptation principle, we underestimate its power. We adapt more quickly than we think. Researchers at the University of Illinois asked people to report on every significant positive or negative experience in the preceding year. If the good or bad events occurred only three months back, their effects on present mood were nearly impossible to distinguish. After six months there was no difference between mood prior to the good or bad event and current mood (Suh, Diener, & Fujita, 1996). In a survey of 128 accident victims who had experienced paralysis of all four limbs a year or so earlier, researchers found that most described their quality of life as good or excellent. Although many admitted having considered suicide shortly after their injury, only 10 percent now considered their quality of life to be poor (Myers, 2001).

Because they have higher standards of acceptability than do satisficers, maximizers find adaptation more distressing. Given the huge investment they have made in weighing alternatives before making a choice, maximizers feel that they deserve a higher rate of return. Expecting more from every situation, maximizers more often experience disappointment.

Finally, maximizers strive to keep their options open. For this they may pay an unanticipated price. Dan Gilbert and Jane Ebert (2002) conducted an intriguing series of studies in which participants made a reversible or irreversible choice. Participants strongly preferred keeping their options open to having their choice made final. Surprisingly, however, the researchers found that participants were less satisfied with the outcomes of reversible decisions than with those that were irreversible. Why? Perhaps when we make a final decision, we work to convince ourselves that we have made the right choice. In keeping our options open, as maximizers tend to do, we remain ambivalent.

Savoring and Gratitude

Now that you've considered how you may be affected by the way you plan when setting goals, and your levels of regret as a result, examine your style of reflecting on past life events. Consider your levels of savoring and gratitude.

SELF-ASSESSMENT ■

Savoring

Assess each question by selecting the number that best describes your response. To what degree do you savor the present moment?

1. When good things have happened in your life, how much do you feel you have typically been able to appreciate or enjoy them?

   1 = not at all   2 = a little bit   3 = some   4 = a lot   5 = a great deal

2. Compared to most other people you know, how much pleasure have you typically gotten from good things that have happened to you?

   1 = none   2 = a little bit   3 = some   4 = a lot   5 = a great deal

3. When something good happens to you, compared to most other people you know, how long does it usually affect the way you feel? Provide a number ranging from 1 (not for very long) to 7 (for a very long time): _____

4. When good things have happened to you, have there ever been times when you felt like everything was really going your way; that is, when you felt on top of the world, or felt a great deal of joy in life, or found it hard to contain your positive feelings? How often would you say you felt like that?

1 = many times   2 = sometimes   3 = once in a while   4 = never

5. How often would you say that you feel like jumping for joy?

1 = never   2 = rarely   3 = sometimes   4 = often

Source: Bryant, 1989, p. 782.

Reverse the number you gave to question 4 (i.e., 1 = 4, 2 = 3, 3 = 2, 4 = 1) and then total your numbers for the five items. Scores can range from 5 to 25, with higher scores reflecting greater savoring of positive outcomes. Undergraduates in an introductory psychology course scored a mean of 18.76.

Martin Seligman (2002) laments how the rush of contemporary life as well as our future-mindedness keeps us from savoring the present moment. Read Joe Veroff's reflections on his grown children's letters to understand the difference savoring makes:

> I find a quiet moment when I can linger a bit with them, and read them in order and let the words roll very slowly over me like a long warm gentle shower. I read each one slowly. Sometimes they are highly sentimental, and I can't hold back the tears. Sometimes they are profoundly insightful about what has been happening to them and the world around them, and I am amazed. I can almost feel the children gathered in the room in which I am reading. (Seligman, 2002, p. 108)

By adding clarity and vividness to experience, savoring contributes directly to well-being and happiness (Brown & Ryan, 2003). Without attention and awareness, fleeting but important moments pass us by. In reflecting from the Columbia shuttle a few days before its scheduled landing, mission specialist Laurel Clark described her delight at the simple, unexpected wonder of a sunset in space: "There's a flash; the whole payload bay turns this rosy pink," she observed. "It only lasts about 15 seconds and then it's gone. It's very ethereal and extremely beautiful."

Can you recall having such a moment—a perfect surprise? Oprah Winfrey recently shared having experienced such a beautiful moment. And what was it? A walk down a Santa Barbara lane, a hummingbird, and the smell of orange blossoms. It was one of those rare times, she related, when she could say she was truly happy. A mere ten seconds, suggests Craig Wilson (2003), can stretch a smile for a lifetime. We all have the opportunity at one time or another but whether we are wise enough to catch the moment may be another matter.

Noticing and appreciating even small benefits relates to another important attribute of happy people assessed by the following questionnaire.

Gratitude

Use the following scale to respond to each question:

1 = strongly disagree   2 = disagree   3 = slightly disagree   4 = neutral
5 = slightly agree   6 = agree   7 = strongly agree

_____ **1.** I have so much in life to be thankful for.

_____ **2.** If I had to list everything that I felt grateful for, it would be a very long list.

_____ **3.** When I look at the world, I don't see much to be grateful for.

_____ **4.** I am grateful to a wide variety of people.

_____ **5.** As I get older I find myself more able to appreciate the people, events, and situations that have been part of my life history.

_____ **6.** Long amounts of time can go by before I feel grateful to something or someone.

Source: McCullough et al., 2002.

Reverse the numbers you gave in response to items 3 and 6 (i.e., 1 = 7, 2 = 6, 3 = 5, 4 = 4, 5 = 3, 6 = 2, and 7 = 1), then add up the numbers for all six statements. Scores range from 6 to 42, with higher scores suggesting a more grateful disposition. A sample of 156 undergraduate psychology students obtained a mean score of about 35.

Gratitude is rooted in the experience of positive outcomes and in seeing oneself as the recipient of another's generosity. Stretching our attributions for success to include the wide range of people who contribute to our well-being leads us to feel affirmed, esteemed, and valued (McCullough et al., 2002). Such an interpretation boosts our self-esteem and our feelings of social support. Highly grateful people may possess a worldview in which everything they have, indeed life itself, is a gift. Such appreciation helps people to avoid taking benefits for granted. They may be less likely to adapt to positive life circumstances and thus may sustain happiness and well-being over time.

Research with the gratitude questionnaire identifies several important correlates of a grateful disposition. In addition to experiencing greater life satisfaction, grateful people are less prone to negative emotions such as depression, anxiety, and envy. Furthermore, they are more empathic, forgiving, and helpful. Grateful people seem less focused on materialistic goals.

Do these correlations reflect a causal relationship? Does a grateful outlook actually contribute to health and happiness? In a recent Gallup (1998) survey, American teens and adults certainly thought so. Over 90 percent of the respondents indicated that expressing gratitude helped them to feel happy.

A series of studies asked different groups of volunteers to remember "things in your life you are grateful for," hassles, life events, or "ways in which you are better off than others" (Emmons & McCullough, 2003). Both undergraduate students without disabilities and persons suffering from neuromuscular disease participated in the research and kept records of their moods, life satisfaction, physical symptoms, and coping behaviors. Relative to other groups, those with a grateful mindset, regardless of their physical disabilities, exhibited heightened well-being, especially on the measures of positive affect.

IN REVIEW

People report their most satisfying experiences to be the times when they felt worthy, competent, related to others, and free of external pressure. Aspirations of fame, fortune, and image are linked with a lowered sense of well-being. A state of consciousness called *flow* occurs when our concentration is so focused that we are completely absorbed in an activity. It is most likely to happen when we have clear goals, when the challenge matches our level of skill, and when we receive immediate feedback.

People's perceptions of their lives are more important to their well-being than objective circumstances. The desire to maximize all of our outcomes is often associated with feelings of regret and decreases our life satisfaction. Savoring life's best moments fosters joy. Those who have a grateful outlook on life and see themselves as the recipients of others' generosity report greater positive feelings.

Pursuing Happiness

Current happiness research points to a number of recommendations. Here's a quick summary:

1. *Don't confuse well-being with being well-off.* Don't equate stuff with success. Remember: A growing income, along with all it can purchase, is not associated with an iota of increased well-being. We quickly adapt to our changing circumstances, including income increases, and only notice momentary variations from it. Rather, acknowledge the joy of non-material experiences. "When you're outside at night with your kids," counsels Jane Hammerslough, "say 'I love it when the stars are out and the snow looks so beautiful.' Put emphasis on things that aren't stuff—on the nonpurchasable" (cited in Hamilton, 2001).

2. *Make wise comparisons.* Research suggests that as we climb the ladder of success we tend to compare ourselves with those a rung or two above. Choose not to. Instead, compare yourself with those who have less. Psychologist Abraham Maslow (1972, p. 108) suggested, "All you have to do is to go to a hospital and hear all the simple blessings that people never before realized *were* blessings—being able to urinate, to sleep on your side, to be able to swallow, to scratch an itch, etc. Could *exercises* in deprivation educate us faster about all our blessings?" Even imagining others' misfortune produces renewed life satisfaction (Dermer, 1979). College women who merely viewed vivid depictions of how grim life was in 1900 or who imagined and then wrote about various personal tragedies such as being burned or disfigured expressed greater life satisfaction.

3. *Keep a gratitude journal.* Savor the present moment and say thank you often. When you say thank you, argues Hammerslough, "you're reminding yourself that something good has come to you" (Hamilton, 2001). In her book *Simple Abundance*, Sarah Ban Breathnach (1995) suggests that each night you write down five things that happened that day for which you are thankful. These need not be major surprises or achievements but simple gifts such as finding a good parking space, enjoying a sunny day, meeting a work deadline, tasting a delicious dessert, or watching a child laugh. Robert Emmons found that those who did this in daily or even weekly journals were not only more joyful; they were healthier, less stressed, more optimistic, and more likely to help others (Morris, 2001).

4. *Discover your flow.* Keep a diary of the high points and low points of each day. Notice patterns. We all experience life differently. An important step in improving the quality of our lives is to pay close attention to what we do every day and to notice how we feel doing different things, in different places, at different times, and with different people (Csikszentmihalyi, 1997). It may be helpful to experiment with one's surroundings, activities, and companions. There may be surprises. It may be that you really like being alone, that you like work more than you thought, that grocery shopping is really not so bad, that reading makes you feel better than watching television, that socializing with friends is actually more satisfying than going to the movies. When it becomes clear which activities produce the high points for you, increase their frequency.

5. *Finish what you start and wholly experience it along the way.* Be conscientious and accomplish something every day. Strive for excellence, not necessarily perfection. Heed Father Laurence's sage advice (Monks of New Skete, 1999, p. 311):

> Being happy means entering wholeheartedly into everything—no matter what kind of challenge it presents, no matter what the possible difficulties involved—entering into it body, soul, mind, and spirit. We have to enter into it in such a way that we're

no longer separate from what we're doing. We forget ourselves at the same time that we give ourselves completely. And when we do enter into life totally and completely, then, if we stop and reflect for just a moment, we'll notice that somehow we're beginning to experience happiness. This is what we're made for.

David Niven (2001) relates how a Chicago Transit Authority motorman has made his work a true expression of himself. Victor loves his job. "Thank you for riding with me this evening on Electric Avenue. Don't lean against the doors, I don't want to lose you," he tells his passengers as the train departs. He points out all the interesting sites and identifies the connecting buses in the street below. "Our equipment may be junky," the veteran motorman admits, "but for a dollar-fifty, I want to give a Lincoln Town Car ride." Victor's commitment has deep roots: "My father is a retired motorman, and one day he took me to work with him and I was so impressed looking out that window. Ever since I was 5 years old, I knew I wanted to run the trains" (p. 98).

6. *Find a hobby.* Turn off the TV. It fosters our hunger for possessions while reducing our personal contentment (Wu, 1988). Most important, television steals time from engagement in more mindful leisure challenges. Researchers of flow found that only 3 percent of those watching TV reported flow, while 39 percent felt apathetic. In contrast, of those engaged in arts and hobbies, 47 percent reported flow and 4 percent experienced apathy. The less expensive and more involving a leisure activity, the happier people tend to be while pursuing it. Most people are happier gardening than power boating, conversing than watching TV (Myers, 1992).

7. *Cultivate family ties.* Remember your roots. "The sun looks down on nothing half as good," observed C.S. Lewis (1949, p. 32), "as a household laughing together over a meal." As we grow older and typically more distant from our origins, this is easy to forget. We do better when bonds are maintained. "Call your mother," is the final word of advice from "Life's Little Instructions," a poster on my office wall.

8. *Know your neighbors.* Join a group. Build friendships. Aristotle labeled us the "social animal." Research concurs: we have a fundamental need to belong. Relative to more communal societies, those in individualist societies who learn independence at an early age often end up experiencing greater loneliness, alienation, and stess-related diseases. Those who enjoy close relationships cope better with life's challenges.

9. *Volunteer.* Do something that turns attention from yourself. As we have seen, researchers of altruism have uncovered a "feel-good, do-good effect," that is, happy people are helpful people. However, the link goes both ways. Kind acts lead one to think more kindly about oneself. Service to others contributes to well-being by decreasing boredom and increasing a sense of meaning in life.

10. *Practice spirituality.* "Don't let your religious beliefs fade," suggests author David Niven (2001). "Take care of the soul," advises psychologist David Myers (1992). A wealth of research has found that religious people are happier. They cope better with life's challenges. For many, faith provides a supportive community, a sense of meaning, the experience of acceptance, and a focus beyond self.

IN REVIEW

To foster life satisfaction, research suggests that we not confuse well-being with being well-off. Comparing ourselves with those who have less rather than more is likely to foster gratitude and happiness. Monitoring the daily activities that bring us the most satisfaction may enable us to increase life's flow. Clearly, the mindful challenge of a hobby is preferable to the mindless passivity of watching television. Strengthening family ties, fostering friendships, and volunteer service are all likely to increase well-being. Practicing spirituality can infuse life with meaning and provide a focus beyond self.

7

self-respect

When you're as good as I am, it's hard to be humble.
—MUHAMMAD ALI, 1963

No man, deep down in the privacy of his heart, has any considerable respect for himself.
—MARK TWAIN, 1897

No topic is more interesting to us than people. Most fascinating of all is ourselves. It is not surprising then that the self is one of the most researched topics in psychology (Baumeister, 1999).

Self-Concept

Start by taking a moment to reflect on your own self-concept.

SELF-ASSESSMENT ■

Who Am I?

Begin by writing 20 different statements in response to the simple question "Who am I?" Begin each statement with "I am. . . ." Respond as if you are giving answers to yourself, not to someone else. Write your answers in the order that they occur to you. Do not worry about importance or logic. Go fairly fast.

I am _____ .

I am _____ .

I am _____ .

I am _____ .

I am _____ .

I am _____ .

I am _____ .

I am _____ .

I am _____ .

I am _____ .

I am _____ .

I am _____ .

I am _____ .

I am _____ .

I am _____ .

I am _____ .

I am _____ .

I am _____ .

I am _____ .

I am _____ .

Taken as a whole, your answers to the question "Who am I?" define your self-concept. We'll return to your answers in a moment, but first consider the idea of a self-concept more generally. Our sense of self organizes our thoughts, feelings, and actions. Our self-concept affects our memories, our present perceptions, and our future goals (Myers, 2002).

Consider the *self-reference effect*. When we think about something in relation to ourselves, we remember it better. For example, if asked whether a specific word, such as "thoughtful," characterizes us, we subsequently remember the word better than if we are asked whether it describes someone else. Memories form around our primary interest, namely, ourselves. I hope the self-assessment exercises throughout this book will help you remember research on the human strengths!

Our self-perceptions also affect what we notice and how we process social information. We seek information that helps us appraise our abilities, opinions, and traits. We especially notice and welcome feedback that is consistent with our self-concept. Moreover, our self-concept affects what we attend to in others. If musical skill is a central component of our self-concept, we are more likely to notice others' musical gifts and limitations.

Finally, our self-concepts include not only our current characteristics but also what we might become—our possible selves. They include visions of what we hope for—the wealthy self, the educated self, the famous self—as well as images of what we fear becoming—the unloved self, the unhealthy self, the unemployed self. Such future aspirations and fears shape our everyday actions and directions.

Impact of Culture

Self-concepts differ across cultures. Consider the following responses college students made to the request "Describe yourself briefly."

> I like to live life with a lot of positive energy. I feel like there is so much to do and see and experience. However, I also know the value of relaxation. I love the obscure. I play ultimate Frisbee, juggle, unicycle, and dabble on the recorder and concertina. I have a taste for the unique. I am very friendly and in most situations very self-confident. I'm almost always happy, and when I am down, it is usually because of stress (Markus & Kitayama, 1998, p. 63).

> I cannot decide quickly what I should do, and I am often swayed by other people's opinions, and I cannot oppose the opinions of people who are supposed to be respected because of age or status. Even if I have displeasure, I compromise myself to the people around me without getting rid of the displeasure. When I cannot make a decision, I often do it according to other people's opinions. Also, I am concerned about how other people think about me and often decide based on that consideration. I try to have a harmless life. I calm down by being the same as others (Markus & Kitayama, 1998, p. 64).

An American student gave the first self-description; a Japanese student provided the second. They reflect very different themes. To an American observer, the first student shows self-reliance, energy, and optimism. The second student is tentative, passive, and even insecure. A Japanese reader would see the accounts quite differently. The first student seems self-serving, inflated, and too confident. The second student shows proper modesty, deference, and solidarity.

Individualist societies such as the United States promote an *independent self* that emphasizes being unique and expressing the self. Its members are likely to complete "I am. . ." statements with personal traits: "I am ambitious," "I am creative," "I am open-minded." Collectivist societies such as those of East Asia encourage an *interdependent self* that emphasizes social connectedness. Its members are more likely to complete "I am. . ." with their social identities: "I am Jee-Seon's friend," and "I am the second son in my family."

Look back at your responses to the "Who am I?" exercise that opened this chapter. Examine each answer and score it with an S if it implies a social response (for example, I am a son = family; I am a Catholic = religious group; I am a member of the XYZ Athletic Club = club). Respondents who have more than four S scores tend to be *collectivists*—social membership is part of their identity. Those with four or fewer S scores lean more toward being *individualists*—they define themselves in terms of their personal attributes rather than their social groups. The most common total S score on this exercise for a group of University of Illinois undergraduates was zero (Triandis, 1994).

People with an independent self are concerned with personal success, achievement, and self-fulfillment. They shun conformity and affirm that "the squeaky wheel gets the grease." In contrast, those having an interdependent self are focused on group goals, attaining solidarity, and fulfilling social responsibilities. They disapprove of egotism. Their motto might be "The nail that stands out gets pounded down."

As you might imagine, there is a difference between individualists and collectivists in their tendencies to attribute positive versus negative traits to themselves. In comparison to Americans, the Japanese make far fewer spontaneous positive statements about themselves (Herzog et al., 1995). The Japanese are also more likely to express their positive traits in the form of negations: "I'm not lazy." Americans are more likely to say: "I'm a hard worker."

Evaluating the Self

In addition to the knowledge component of self, there is an even more thoroughly studied evaluative component. Not only do we ask, "Who am I?" but we also ask, "How do I feel about who I am?" (Campbell & Lavellee, 1993). Do your answers to "Who am I?" suggest anything about your level of self-regard? One study found that American adults gave four times as many positive attributes as negative (Herzog et al., 1995). In this section you will have three opportunities to evaluate your self-concept more closely.

The Rosenberg Self-Esteem Scale is the most frequently used assessment of global self-esteem—a person's overall evaluation of self or sense of self-worth. Try it for yourself.

SELF-ASSESSMENT ■

Rosenberg Self-Esteem Scale

Indicate your agreement or disagreement with each statement using the following scale:

1 = strongly disagree   2 = disagree   3 = agree   4 = strongly agree

_____ **1.** I feel that I am a person of worth, at least on an equal basis with others.

_____ **2.** I feel that I have a number of good qualities.

_____ **3.** All in all, I am inclined to feel that I am a failure.

_____ **4.** I am able to do things as well as most other people.

_____ **5.** I feel I do not have much to be proud of.

_____ **6.** I take a positive attitude toward myself.

_____ **7.** On the whole, I am satisfied with myself.

_____ **8.** I wish I could have more respect for myself.

_____ **9.** I certainly feel useless at times.

_____ **10.** At times I think I am no good at all.

Source: Rosenberg, 1989, pp. 325–327.

This scale was designed to assess the degree to which people are generally satisfied with their lives and consider themselves worthy people. In scoring it, you should first reverse the numbers you placed in front of items 3, 5, 8, 9, and 10 (4 = 1, 3 = 2, 2 = 3, 1 = 4). Leave the numbers in front of the remaining five items the same. Then add the numbers in front of all ten items to obtain a total score. Scores can range from 10 to 40, with scores above the midpoint of 25 reflecting a greater sense of self-worth.

Now, how do you see yourself in comparison to others? Try the following exercise.

SELF-ASSESSMENT ■

Social Comparisons

When you think of yourself relative to others of the same age, education, and sex as yourself, how do you think you compare? Specifically, how would you rate yourself on the following characteristics? Use the scale in making your response.

1 = well below average   2 = below average   3 = average   4 = above average
5 = well above average

_____ **1.** leadership ability

_____ **2.** ability to get along with others

_____ **3.** energy level

_____ **4.** helpfulness

_____ **5.** responsibility

_____ **6.** patience

_____ **7.** trustworthiness

_____ **8.** sincerity

_____ **9.** thoughtfulness

_____ **10.** cooperativeness

Add up the numbers you placed in front of the ten traits and divide by 10 to find your mean. A mean below 3 suggests that, in comparison to your peers, you see yourself as below average. Scores over 3 indicate that you see yourself as better than average.

Finally, consider your strengths and weaknesses and your attitudes toward your strengths and weaknesses by completing the following scale.

Strengths Versus Weaknesses

Try to respond to the following questions as honestly as you can. Answer each question using the following scale:

1	2	3	4	5	6	7
Not at all						Very much

_____ **1.** How athletic are you?

_____ **2.** How much do you care about whether or not you are athletic?

_____ **3.** How musically talented are you?

_____ **4.** How much do you care about whether or not you have musical talent?

_____ **5.** How physically attractive are you?

_____ **6.** How much do you care about whether or not you are physically attractive?

_____ **7.** How creative are you?

_____ **8.** How much do you care about whether or not you are creative?

_____ **9.** How mechanically skilled are you?

_____ **10.** How much do you care about whether or not you are mechanically skilled?

We tend to value our strengths but see our weaknesses as much less important. Research (for example, Hill, Smith, & Lewicki, 1989) suggests that people care much more about their strengths than about their weaknesses. Do your scores match this pattern?

How highly do most people regard themselves? Do they more commonly have inflated or deflated self-images? Was psychologist Carl Rogers right when he argued, "The central core of difficulty in people . . . is that in the great majority of cases they despise themselves, regard themselves as worthless and unlovable"? Or was Henry Ward Beecher closer to the truth in claiming, "Conceit is the most incurable disease known to the human soul"?

One review (Baumeister, Tice, & Hutton, 1989) of Rosenberg Esteem Scale responses found very few respondents scoring at the low end. Not many people view themselves negatively. Total scores typically run from the midpoint of 25 to the high end of the scale, with a mean of 31. Males score somewhat higher than females.

When people are asked to compare themselves with others on a list of socially desirable traits, as in the Social Comparisons scale, the overwhelming majority see themselves as "better than average." For example, the U.S. College Board invited the million students who take their achievement test yearly to indicate "how you feel you compare with other people your own age in certain areas of ability" (cited by Myers, 2002, p. 62). In "leadership ability," 70 percent rated themselves above average, 2 percent as below average. Sixty percent of the respondents thought themselves better than average in "athletic ability," only 6 percent as below average. And in their "ability to get along with others," 0 percent of the students rated themselves below average while 25 percent saw themselves in the top 1 percent! "Every community seems like Garrison Keillor's fictional Lake Wobegon," concludes David Myers (2002, p. 61), "where 'all the women are strong, all the men are good-looking, and all the children are above average.'"

Is such bias universal? Respondents from cultures that value modesty and self-restraint, such as those of China and Japan, do tend to express less self-serving bias. Nonetheless, most people from around the world seem privately self-enhancing. For example, researchers have observed the self-serving bias among Dutch college students, Belgian basketball players, Australian workers, Hong Kong sports writers, Singaporean schoolchildren, and French people of all ages (Myers, 2002).

The Strengths Versus Weaknesses exercise reveals that in case we actually do have any perceived weaknesses, most respondents conveniently protect their self-esteem by caring less about their weaknesses than about their strengths!

Clearly, research findings challenge the popular notion that most people suffer from a negative self-image. A very positive view of self seems more common than an inferiority complex.

IN REVIEW

Our responses to the question "Who am I?" define our self-concept. Our self-understandings organize our thoughts and actions and affect our memories, perceptions, and future goals. Some cultures encourage the development of an independent self in which people define themselves in terms of their personal traits. Other cultures promote an interdependent self in which people see their identity in terms of their social connections. Globally, most people tend to have a very positive self-image.

■
Self-Esteem

Perhaps the fact that most people enjoy high self-esteem is good news. Research seems to suggest that people who feel good about themselves are less susceptible to insomnia, are not as conforming, and are less shy, lonely, and depressed. People with high self-esteem are also happier. Low self-esteem, on the other hand, seems to be linked to failure in school, substance abuse, eating disorders, teenage pregnancy, and marital discord (Crocker & Wolfe, 2001).

In a poignant account of his early adolescence, Lewis Smedes (2003), author of best-selling books on love, forgiveness, and hope, relates the burden of a negative self-concept. Left fatherless at an early age, he found his mother's sense of unworthiness infectious. "Obsessed with her own lack of virtue worth praising," observes Smedes, "my mother did not have it in her to persuade us children that there was any virtue in us worth noting" (p. 28). When an older sibling dubbed Lewis "rotten" for a minor infraction of the family's strict moral code, his mother only concurred. "Small wonder," Smedes continues, "that as a boy I was thoroughly convinced that God held his nose as he passed me by." Friends and school offered little support. A 6-foot-tall 15-year-old, he weighed in at a mere 95 pounds. "To anyone who saw me undressed," continues Smedes, "I was a sure case of rickets. . . . To be frank about it, I was a lonely loser, something to be pitied." After a tenth-grade English teacher provided a ray of hope—"Lewis, you write well"—he announced to his family over supper that he might become a journalist. "Oh, Lewis," they chimed, "be practical for a change, don't have such big-shot ideas" (Smedes, 2003, pp. 35–36). And with that, the dream died.

Many public officials, teachers, and helping professionals have hoped that fostering self-esteem would solve a variety of personal and social problems. For example, the California Task Force to Promote Self-Esteem and Personal and Social Responsibility (1990) asserted that self-esteem "is the likeliest candidate for a social vaccine" to inoculate individuals and society "against the lures of crime, violence, substance abuse, teen pregnancy, child abuse, chronic welfare dependency, and educational failure." The task force's final report asserted that "the lack of self-esteem is central to most personal and social ills plaguing our state and nation" (p. 4).

Benefits and Dangers of High Self-Esteem

Self-esteem studies have been mostly correlational and thus raise questions about cause and effect. Does low self-esteem destine us to screw-ups and misery? Or does life's misery and our failure cause low self-esteem? Maybe liking oneself follows rather than produces success. Perhaps high self-esteem is the fruit rather than the root of surmounting difficulty.

Such was the case for Lewis Smedes. Early college success accompanied by a small circle of supportive friends encouraged him to revise his self-concept. Stunned to discover that he had received perfect scores in his first term, he writes, "It occurred to me that I may have been wrong about my intellectual deficiency" (Smedes, 2003, p. 57). Together with a few college classmates, he went on to write his first book.

The presumed links between self-esteem and a variety of positive human characteristics are often based on self-report that may not be entirely accurate. People who make favorable statements about themselves on self-esteem scales tend also to provide positive self-reports of other characteristics, including interpersonal skills, attractiveness, and performance at school and work. When researchers use more objective measures of these characteristics, they find that people aren't as wonderful as they think they are (Baumeister et al., 2003)!

Consider physical appearance, for example. Research finds a strong positive relationship between self-esteem and self-reported attractiveness. Those with high self-esteem love what they see in the mirror. But are they gorgeous to others? Hardly. In fact, when observers' assessments of looks are used as the measure of attractiveness, the correlation between self-esteem and appearance doesn't merely shrink. It evaporates. There's no relationship.

In his review of the literature, Roy Baumeister (1996) concludes: "The enthusiastic claims of the self-esteem movement mostly range from fantasy to hogwash. The effects of self-esteem are small, limited, and not all good." Although he acknowledges that high self-esteem has a small number of practical benefits, including making people happier and strengthening their persistence in the face of failure, most social and personal problems are not caused by a lack of self-esteem. Thus, raising self-esteem is unlikely to solve them (Baumeister et al., 2003).

Moreover, continues Baumeister and his colleagues (Baumeister, Smart, & Boden, 1996), high self-esteem has a dark side. People who think very highly of themselves are more likely to be obnoxious, to interrupt, and to talk at other people rather than with them. Even worse, some people with high self-esteem—for example, those who agree with narcissistic statements such as "If I ruled the world it would be a much better place"—are prone to interpersonal violence. Aggression typically occurs in people who have an inflated self-concept (Baumeister, 1998). They lash out at others who criticize or disrespect them as a strategy for avoiding the need to revise downward their sense of self-worth. "People who believe themselves to be among the top 10 percent on any dimension may be insulted and threatened whenever anyone asserts that they are in the 80th or 50th or 25th percentile," observes Baumeister (cited by Slater, 2003). "In contrast, someone with lower self-esteem who regards himself or herself as being merely in the top 60 percent would only be threatened by the feedback that puts him or her at the 25th percentile. . . . In short, the more favorable one's view of oneself, the greater the range of external feedback that will be perceived as unacceptably low." Overall, Baumeister (1996) concludes, "Self-control is worth 10 times as much as self-esteem."

Sources of Self-Worth

We can better understand the paradoxical links between self-esteem and behavior, suggest Jennifer Crocker and Connie Wolfe (2001), by examining possible sources of self-esteem. "Contingencies" of self-worth are the areas of life in which people believe that success means they are worthwhile and failure means they are worthless. Crocker and Wolfe's research has identified seven possible domains in which people may invest their self-esteem.

Contingencies of Self-Worth Scale

The following sample items assess domains that may or may not be relevant to your sense of self-worth. Please respond to each of the following statements by using the scale.

1 = strongly disagree   2 = disagree   3 = disagree somewhat   4 = neutral
5 = agree somewhat   6 = agree   7 = strongly agree

_____ **1.** When my family members are proud of me, my sense of self-worth increases.

_____ **2.** My self-worth is affected by how well I do when I am competing with others.

_____ **3.** When I think I look attractive, I feel good about myself.

_____ **4.** My self-worth is based on God's love.

_____ **5.** Doing well in school gives me a sense of self-respect.

_____ **6.** Whenever I follow my moral principles, my sense of self-respect gets a boost.

_____ **7.** My self-esteem depends on the opinions others hold of me.

Source: Crocker, Luhtanen, Cooper, & Bouvrette, 2003.

The full Contingencies of Self-Worth Scale uses five items, not one, to assess the importance of each domain to one's sense of self-worth. Still, you can make some initial comparisons with Crocker, Luhtanen, & Bouvrette's (2001) sample of 1300 college students. Compare your number for each statement with the following mean scores (also on a scale from 1 to 7) that their sample obtained.

Family support = 5.3
Competition = 5.0
Appearance = 4.9
God's love = 4.2
Academic competence = 5.3
Virtue = 5.5
Others' approval = 4.6

Crocker and Wolfe (2001) do not claim that this is an exhaustive list of the areas in which people find their self-worth or that one contingency is necessarily preferable to another. The list merely reflects some of the more common domains that respondents identify as important to their self-esteem. Can you think of other domains that might be important?

Contingencies of Self-Worth and Behavior

The source of our self-esteem provides a powerful guide for our behavior. If our self-worth is rooted in being virtuous, we will act quite differently than someone whose self-esteem is based on appearance.

In a study of 600 college freshmen (Crocker, Luhtanen, & Bouvrette, 2001), self-esteem based on appearance was linked to spending more hours per week grooming, shopping, and partying. Self-esteem rooted in God's love was linked to spending more hours in religious activities, such as praying and going to church or synagogue, and to fewer hours partying. Self-esteem based on academic competence was associated with greater success in gaining admission to graduate school.

Crocker and Wolfe (2001) argue that major problems such as depression, drug abuse, and aggression may be linked not so much to our general level of self-esteem as to the source of our self-esteem. For example, research indicates that basing one's self-esteem on physical appearance increases one's susceptibility to eating disorders. Similarly, people who have high but fragile self-esteem that is based on social approval seem especially prone to anger and hostility when others challenge them.

People who are unable to secure self-respect on one basis may shift to another source. Frustrated in their pursuit of self-esteem, they may even reject goals that are important to a successful life. For example the high dropout rate among African-American college students may be the result of disconnecting self-worth from academic performance after numerous frustrating attempts to succeed in an environment that assumes they are academically inferior (Steele, 1997). Others who don't have the means to garner a positive image on the basis of good grades in school or strong relations with peers may organize their self-esteem around strength, power, or physical superiority (Staub, 1999). Several factors foster this unfortunate tendency. Experiencing abuse, readily available models of aggression, and a culture that prizes male physical power and superiority can all increase the likelihood of aggression and antisocial behavior.

Shifting sources of self-worth also explains why overall level of self-esteem does not decline as we grow older. As people age, suggest Crocker and Wolfe, contingencies of self-worth typically change from competition and appearance to a more internal and intrinsic basis such as virtue or family.

Contingencies of Self-Worth: Assets or Liabilities?

Are contingencies of self-worth beneficial or limiting?

Some psychologists have argued that high-functioning people have a self-concept that is sensitive to what others in their environment think of them. Others recommend that children be encouraged to base their self-esteem on their objective accomplishments, skills, and abilities. Roy Baumeister and his colleagues (2003) suggest that we try to boost self-esteem as a reward for worthy achievements and ethical behavior. To avoid social comparisons that lead people to boost themselves at the expense of others, they recommend emphasizing *improvement* so that people learn to compare themselves with themselves rather than with their peers.

Some research hints that having multiple contingencies of self-worth is best. People with several independent sources of self-worth may react less extremely to negative life events. Bumps and bruises in one area of life shift one's attention to other important areas where things are going well.

Can self-esteem be "noncontingent"? "I like you for just being you," television's Fred Rogers fondly told the young visitors to his friendly neighborhood. Because contingent self-esteem is so often associated with anxiety, hostility, defensiveness, and the risk of depression, perhaps what people need most is the awareness that they have inherent value. Edward Deci and Richard Ryan (1995) distinguished between contingent and "true" self-esteem, which is more stable and securely based in a solid sense of self. True self-esteem develops, argue Deci and Ryan, when one acts autonomously, experiences a sense of competence, and is loved for who one is rather than for matching some external standard. It follows that environments that satisfy the three fundamental needs for autonomy, competence, and relatedness foster true self-esteem. People with such "noncontingent" self-esteem are pleased when they succeed and disappointed when they fail, but their sense of self-worth is not at risk in the process.

Carl Rogers (1951) emphasized the importance of parents providing their children with unconditional positive regard. Such children mature into adults who never feel that their self-worth is on the line. However, we've since learned that simply telling people with low self-esteem "you can do it" does not truly strengthen their self-confidence. Better to help them understand: "It's all right if you can't do it; it doesn't mean you are a bad person" (Brown, 1998).

Those whose self-worth is not continually put to the test spend less time analyzing themselves. They may even be self-forgetful, which, as we will see next, is one very important ingredient of humility.

IN REVIEW

Psychologists debate the benefits of high self-esteem. Although a positive self-concept seems to promote happiness and perseverance, most personal and social problems are not caused by low self-esteem. In fact, those with an inflated self-concept may be more prone to interpersonal violence. Examining specific sources of self-esteem helps us to understand the links between self-concept and behavior. Those who have several independent sources of self-esteem may have a more stable sense of self-worth. Those with noncontingent self-esteem have an awareness of their inherent value and do not question their self-worth.

Humility

Given the general public's preoccupation with the merits of positive self-views, how do people view humility? Is it a strength or weakness? Consider your own perceptions of humility by answering the following questions.

CRITICAL THINKING ■

Reflections on Humility

1. When you think of the word *humility*, what words, images, or associations come to your mind?

_____

_____

_____

_____

_____

_____

2. Is humility a strength or a weakness? Do your immediate associations with the word tend to be negative or positive (select a number)?

-5 -4 -3 -2 -1 0 1 2 3 4 5
Negative   Positive

3. Think of a person whom you see as being very humble (either someone famous or someone you know). Who is the person? _____

Please give a brief description of the person. What makes you see this person as humble?

_____

_____

_____

_____

4. To what extent do you see humility as being similar to low self-esteem?

0 1 2 3 4 5 6 7 8 9 10
Not at all   Extremely

5. Recall a real-life situation in which you felt humble. Give a brief description of the situation. Why did you feel humble in this situation?

_____

_____

_____

_____

6. What did you learn from this experience, if anything? What emotions did you experience when you recalled this situation?

_____

_____

_____

_____

7. To what extent is this memory pleasant or unpleasant to recall?

	Not at all									Extremely	
Pleasant to recall	0	1	2	3	4	5	6	7	8	9	10
Unpleasant to recall	0	1	2	3	4	5	6	7	8	9	10

8. If you wanted to put yourself in a humble frame of mind right now, what kinds of things would you think about?

_____

_____

_____

9. To what extent do you:

	Not at all									Extremely	
view yourself as a humble person?	0	1	2	3	4	5	6	7	8	9	10
believe that people who know you well view you as a humble person?	0	1	2	3	4	5	6	7	8	9	10
think that it would be good if you were less humble?	0	1	2	3	4	5	6	7	8	9	10
think that it would be good if you were more humble?	0	1	2	3	4	5	6	7	8	9	10

Source: Exline & Geyer, in press.

Results with undergraduates (Exline & Geyer, 2002) on the humility self-evaluation indicated that students' overall views of humility were positive. For example, on the

10-point scale (from −5 to +5), they gave "humility" an average rating of 2.4. Moreover, humility was not seen as reflecting low self-esteem (mean = 2.3 on a scale from 0 to 10). Open-ended definitions of humility suggested substantial overlap with modesty, including "not bragging" and "not taking full credit for success." Humility was associated with a variety of positive attributes including unselfishness and generosity. Rather than viewing humility as a preoccupation with shortcomings, respondents saw humility as reflecting an unassuming attitude toward one's positive qualities.

When asked to recall a real-life situation in which they felt humble, undergraduates reported much higher levels of pleasant than unpleasant feelings. Interestingly, the majority of participants recalled experiences that involved success or accomplishment, that is, doing something good, receiving praise, winning, or getting more credit than they deserved. A minority of students reported situations that involved humiliation, for example, a loss, a failure, or feeling threatened by someone who was more successful.

Asked to identify a humble person, participants picked friends, classmates, roommates, relatives, celebrities, saints, and religious leaders. When asked to indicate why the person was seen as humble, the research participants identified positive characteristics such as kindness or caring toward others, self-sacrifice, competence, and intelligence. Only a small minority suggested that a humble person was timid, quiet, or unassertive. Thus, research participants generally perceived humility as a human strength. They indicated that they themselves wanted to become more humble.

How do your results compare?

These surprising findings contrast sharply with dictionary definitions of humility that link the trait to self-abasement or low self-esteem. At the same time, they are consistent with ancient wisdom that presents humility as a virtue. "It was pride that changed angels into devils," observed St. Augustine; "it is humility that makes men into angels." Confucius agreed. "Humility," he noted, "is the solid foundation of all the virtues."

Humility is a trait we obviously respect. Apparently people especially like to see the attribute in attorneys. A survey in the *National Law Journal* ("Jurors prefer lawyers," 1993) found that humility was the characteristic jurors most admired in lawyers! Similarly, few traits are more grating to us than arrogance—humility's opposite. We relish puncturing the pride of those who know it all and who seem in love with themselves. Most of us take special delight in Javad Hashtroudian's (2003) retelling of the Mullah Nasrudin story, simply entitled "The Boatman."

> The Mullah earned his living by running a ferry across a lake, and one afternoon he took a pompous scholar to the other side. When the learned academic asked if he had read Plato's *Republic*, the Mullah replied, "Sir, I am a simple boatman. What would I do with Plato?" The scholar scoffed, "In that case, half of your life's been wasted." Some time passed before the Mullah inquired, "Sir, do you know how to swim?" "Of course

not," replied the professor, "I am a scholar. What would I do with swimming?" The Mullah replied, "In that case, all of your life's been wasted. We're sinking."

More than an admired personal quality, humility is an important human strength. Consider the following research findings:

- In attempting to understand what transforms a good company into a great one, researchers studied companies that increased their value eight times faster than the stock market (Collins, 2001). They concluded that all great companies share one common factor: they have leaders who blend personal humility with professional willpower. Compellingly modest and never boastful, these "level 5 leaders" shun public adulation. They take personal responsibility for failure and attribute the company's success to others. Most important, they are not self-seeking but show an unwavering, single-minded commitment to the long-term interests of everyone.

- In attempting to answer why some people devote themselves to good deeds, Kathleen Brehony (1999) interviewed dozens of men and women of all ages, ethnicities, and lifestyles who have quietly committed themselves to helping others. In her book *Ordinary Grace,* she highlights how grace is all around us—in both profoundly moving experiences and in small, hardly noticed acts. People who demonstrate social concern, she suggests, share a number of common qualities. Most important, their strong social connections are marked by an abiding faith in others, personal humility, and the belief that helping others is not service but a privilege and blessing.

- In an effort to understand Abraham Maslow's concept of self-actualization more fully, researchers undertook an exhaustive case study of Eleanor Roosevelt (Piechowski & Tyska, 1982). They analyzed biographical accounts of Roosevelt's "years on her own" for the presence of traits that contributed to self-actualization. Among their important conclusions was that Maslow may have overlooked two crucial traits of the self-actualizing person. One was equitableness—the capacity to advocate what is in the best interests of all concerned. The other was humility.

Characteristics of Humility

What are the essential features of humility? June Tangney (2000) identified the following:

- Accurate, realistic estimate of abilities and achievements
- Ability to acknowledge one's mistakes, imperfections, gaps in knowledge, and limitations

- Openness to new ideas, contradictory information, and advice
- Keeping one's abilities and accomplishments in perspective
- Relatively low self-focus or an ability to "forget the self"
- Appreciation of the value of all people and their unique contributions

If asked to complete the Rosenberg Self-Esteem Scale, "humble" people, suggests Tangney, would endorse statements such as "I feel that I am a person of worth, at least on an equal plane with others," and "I feel I have a number of good qualities."

It seems that, in the final analysis, humility reflects a sense of security in which feelings of personal worth are based on stable, reliable sources (such as feeling unconditionally loved or a belief in the value of all life) rather than on more transient, external sources (such as achievement, appearance, or social approval) (Exline et al., in press).

Practicing Self-Forgetfulness

Given what is often a pervasive drive toward self-enhancement in our cultures, how do we begin to cultivate humility? In cultures that emphasize the relative worth of people based on their achievements, appearance, and athleticism, is it possible to practice self-forgetfulness?

Of all the human strengths, humility may be the most elusive. Benjamin Franklin certainly thought so. After he publicly displayed a list of virtues he intended to pursue, a friend suggested that he had overlooked one. Franklin, he bravely noted, was often guilty of pride. So the patriot dutifully added "humility" to his list. Later, Franklin observed that he had never come close: "There is perhaps no one of our natural passions so hard to subdue as pride; disguise it, struggle with it, beat it down, stifle it, mortify it as much as one pleases, it is still alive and will every now and then peep out and show itself" (cited by Isaacson, 2003, p. 47).

Tongue in cheek, Ted Turner agrees. "If only I had a little humility," he laments, "I would be perfect." It's not easy to become one of the humble. As soon as you think you belong, you have excluded yourself. Franklin captured the irony: "Even if I could conceive that I had completely overcome pride, I would probably be proud of my humility."

Nonetheless, the extensive research on the development of self-esteem as well as early work on humility hints at how this human strength unfolds.

1. **Admit bias.** Our self-perceptions may not reflect reality. For the minority of us who may suffer from an unrealistically poor self-concept, it helps to examine its roots. What negative messages might you have received about yourself

early in life? Was there any evidence to support them? Begin to challenge your present negative self-talk and replace it with the truth.

For most of us, however, overcoming bias is a matter of admitting our pride. "If anyone would like to acquire humility, I can, I think, tell him the first step," observes C. S. Lewis (1960, p. 101). "The first step is to realize that one is proud. And a biggish step, too." Research points to a pervasive self-serving bias—a powerful tendency to see oneself favorably. We saw evidence of it earlier in this chapter in our tendencies to see ourselves as better than average and to value our strengths but downplay our weaknesses. As Lewis suggests, it's tough to admit vulnerability. In fact, when most students learn of the self-serving bias, they congratulate themselves on being better than average at not thinking of themselves as better than average (Friedrich, 1996)! Sometimes our expressed modesty barely conceals underlying pride in our better-than-average humility. When students were invited to write about an important success experience, those who anticipated reading their story to others readily acknowledged the help and emotional support they had received from others (Baumeister & Ilko, 1995). Those who wrote anonymously portrayed themselves as having achieved success on their own.

2. **Seek accurate feedback.** Some forms of the self-serving bias are controllable through clear and accurate feedback. Deliberately seeking honest feedback from others—friends, relatives, roommates—gives us one important strategy for assessing both our strengths and weaknesses. It is encouraging to know that when people receive feedback about themselves from others (dating partners and roommates) they prefer accurate feedback even when this information is relatively negative (Katz & Joiner, 2002).

3. **Learn to laugh at ourselves.** Arrogant people have no sense of humor, especially about themselves. Conscientious people may also take their work and themselves too seriously. Certainly we have important tasks to do and others depend on us. To be productive and happy we must believe our actions make a difference. However, the world won't end if we stumble. And others are not noting our every miscue. Cultivate the capacity to laugh at yourself—to admit your weaknesses and not take yourself too seriously.

4. **Learn from other cultures.** Humble people recognize that they are part of a large whole. As we have seen, people in collectivist cultures are keenly aware of their interdependence. They also value modesty. There is little evidence for self-enhancement among the Japanese, for example (Heine et al., 1999). Instead, a self-critical posture is the norm. This effort at self-improvement, suggest the researchers, expresses a strong sense of belonging.

Secure social connections enable us to admit our uncertainty and frailty. One researcher conducted two experiments in which he temporarily led Yale University students to feel accepted or rejected by their peers (Dittes, 1959).

He then gave them a fabricated parable and asked them to interpret it. Although the parable was incoherent, students who experienced rejection proudly declared its meaning. Those who felt accepted and supported were more likely to humbly admit they did not know.

5. **Cultivate the other strengths.** Humility is a natural by-product of pursuing the other human strengths. For example, the practice of gratitude increases life satisfaction and fosters a mindset of humility. The word *gratitude* is the derivative of the Latin word for "grace"—getting something for nothing. In keeping a gratitude journal, people acknowledge the undeserved benevolence of another.

   Similarly, in developing empathy, we recognize our "oneness" or equality with others. A belief in the value of all life enables compassion for others, and also "self-compassion" (Neff, 2003). Perceiving our common humanity enables us to be kind and understanding toward others and ourselves, particularly in times of failure. Like everyone else, we are limited and imperfect human beings. However, cautions Neff, self-compassion does not mean that failings go unnoticed or unchanged. Rather, by showing compassion to ourselves as well as others, we provide the emotional safety needed for self-examination. We are motivated to grow and to change.

6. **Assume a cosmic perspective.** Albert Einstein taught us an important lesson in humility by showing us that we are mere specks in an unfathomably large universe. "A spirit is manifest in the laws of the universe," he once observed, "in the face of which we, with our modest powers, must feel humble." With humility, I can recognize that I am one of several billion people inhabiting this planet, that the historical moment of my life is but a short span in a human history covering millions of years, and that I occupy but a few cubic feet in a vast and continuously expanding universe.

7. **Experience awe.** Awe-inspiring experiences that connect us to the world's beauty and excellence foster a recognition that we are a small part of a much larger whole (Keltner & Haidt, 2003). Most important, the experience of awe fosters self-forgetfulness. A wide range of physical and social stimuli can elicit the experience—a grand cathedral, a marvelous symphony, a beautiful poem, a wondrous landscape, an elegant theory. Famous, exceptionally skilled, or morally admirable people also elicit awe. All these encounters are characterized by "vastness"—the recognition of something larger than ourselves—and by a need for "accommodation" because the experience does not fit into our existing mental structures. Unfortunately, some people go about their daily lives wearing blinders. Others have minds and hearts tuned to what is moving and beautiful around them. It's a sensitivity worth cultivating.

8. **Focus beyond self.** Healthy self-respect makes it easier to forget about ourselves. Proving our worth is no longer a driving concern. At the same time,

trying not to think about ourselves is somewhat like trying not to think about pink elephants. The harder we try, the more memorable they become. Only when we shift our attention from ourselves to something more interesting do we master humility. When we become genuinely invested in others or in a task larger than ourselves we also forget about ourselves.

9. **Promote secure attachment.** Factors that facilitate secure attachment in infants also lay the groundwork for humility (Exline et al., in press). Parents who are responsive to their infants' needs encourage them to approach life with an attitude of trust rather than fear. This basic sense of security enables the older child to tolerate both positive and negative feedback, which is fundamental to accurate self-appraisal.

10. **Practice authoritative parenting.** Several researchers report that children with the highest self-esteem have had warm, concerned, authoritative parents. Such parents set rules and enforce them in an atmosphere of nurturance and genuine respect for the child as a person. They validate the child's intrinsic worth by avoiding perfectionistic performance standards as well as extreme emphasis on appearance, popularity, or competitive comparisons with siblings and peers. Moreover, parental approval of commendable behavior can be communicated in a way that encourages the child to internalize standards of conduct rather than remain dependent on external feedback. Telling him or her, "You must be very pleased with yourself for what you did" will encourage internalization and not just convey personal pleasure that the child did what you wanted (Harter, 2002). Most important, parents who communicate to their children that they have intrinsic merit and thus need not establish their worth enable a healthy sense of self-forgetfulness.

11. **Model humility.** Observational learning is as important to the development of humility as it is to fostering the other strengths. Important models of humility come from adults who are keenly sensitive to the beauty and excellence around them and who clearly communicate that they see themselves as part of a larger whole. Parents who demonstrate healthy self-appraisal are able to admit their weaknesses and accept both positive and negative feedback about themselves without overreacting to either. Teachers who convey the intrinsic worth of all people lay the foundation for students' understanding that they are neither inferior nor superior to their peers.

12. **Demonstrate balance.** Fostering humility, notes Julie Exline and her colleagues (in press), can be risky. Probably more caution needs to be exercised in attempting to induce humility than in the development of the other strengths. Strategies backfire if they cause a person to feel helpless, ashamed, or insignificant. People often defend against ego threat through self-enhancement or even by behaving aggressively. "Successful humility inductions," suggests Exline's

research team, "might require a delicate balance: They may need to prompt a person to reduce self-focus or gain a new perspective on the self without feeling that the self has been obliterated or damaged."

IN REVIEW

Humble people view their strengths and weaknesses realistically. They are able to "forget themselves" because they possess stable, reliable sources of self-worth. We cultivate humility by admitting our pride, by seeking accurate feedback, by learning to laugh at ourselves, and by taking a cosmic perspective. Parents who promote secure attachment, practice authoritative parenting, and model humility help their children to understand their intrinsic worth and to recognize that they are neither inferior nor superior to their peers.

hope 8

Hope is a good thing, maybe the best of things. And no good thing ever dies.
—Andy Dufresne in The Shawshank Redemption (Marvin & Darabont, 1994)

Andy Dufresne has no reason to hope. In fact, he should be depressed. Once a successful banker, he has been wrongly convicted of his wife's murder and sentenced to life in Shawshank prison. It's hardly a place to call home. Taunted by veteran prisoners, beaten by hardened guards, Shawshank's new recruits see no light at the end of the tunnel.

Still, neither maggots in his oatmeal nor gang rape by fellow inmates dims Andy's optimism. After two weeks in solitary, he returns to the prison yard still gushing hope: "We need it so we don't forget . . . that there are places in the world that aren't made out of stone, that there's, there's somethin' inside that they can't get to, that they can't touch. It's yours." Andy's friend, Red, a prisoner more firmly anchored in reality, counters: "Let me tell you something . . . hope is a dangerous thing. Hope can drive a man insane. It's got no use on the inside" (Marvin & Darabont, 1994).

Andy and Red echo the centuries-old debate over the merits of hope. Do you agree with Karl Menninger that hope is a "life instinct," or are you more sympathetic with Benjamin Franklin, who once said, "He who lives upon hope will die fasting"? Was Martin Luther right when he said, "Everything that is done in the world is done by hope"? Or was Friedrich Nietzsche closer to the truth: "Hope is the worst of all evils because it prolongs the torments of man"?

Contemporary psychology provides fascinating new insights into this continuing controversy over the power and peril of positive thinking. First, we will examine optimism—the general belief that a bright future awaits us—and its links to psychological and physical well-being. Next, we will reflect on closely related investigations of hope. We will see how a positive orientation to specific life goals relates to achievement. Finally, we will consider some important strategies for fostering hope in ourselves and in others.

■ Optimism

Do you believe that good things or bad things will generally occur in your life?

To assess your optimism, take the following Life Orientation Test (LOT) by Michael Scheier, Charles Carver, and Michael Bridges (1994).

SELF-ASSESSMENT ■

Life Orientation Test: How Optimistic Are You?

Respond to each statement using the following scale:

0 = strongly disagree   1 = disagree   2 = neutral   3 = agree   4 = strongly agree

_____ **1.** In uncertain times, I usually expect the best.

_____ **2.** If something can go wrong for me, it will.

_____ **3.** I'm always optimistic about my future.

_____ **4.** I hardly ever expect things to go my way.

_____ **5.** I rarely count on good things happening to me.

_____ **6.** Overall, I expect more good things to happen to me than bad.

To score yourself, first reverse the numbers you placed in answer to statements 2, 4, and 5. That is, for each of these items, change 0 to 4, 1 to 3, 3 to 1, and 4 to 0 (a 2 remains a 2). Leave the numbers in front of the rest of the statements unchanged. Then add up the numbers in front of all items to obtain a final score. Scores range from 0 to 24, with higher scores reflecting greater optimism. The average (mean) score is between 14 and 15.

Optimism and Psychological Well-Being

Do optimists fare better than pessimists? Past prophets of positive thinking would be pleased with the findings of recent research. In general, optimism is linked with a positive mood and higher morale. Indeed, numerous studies find that optimism is associated with diverse measures of psychological health. For example, LOT scores are positively related to both a sense of self-mastery and self-esteem and negatively linked to depression and anxiety (Scheier, Carver, & Bridges, 1994).

Even more important, optimism confers resistance to distress. A bright outlook fosters well-being. Optimists cope with stressful events, from dealing with unfamiliar environments to major health concerns, more effectively than pessimists. Consider the following:

- Students who entered college with an optimistic outlook handled the new challenges more successfully (Aspinwall & Taylor, 1992). Those with higher LOT scores at the start of college experienced lower levels of emotional distress at the end of the semester. Optimists seem to experience less stress, depression, and loneliness than pessimists.

- Optimism seems to confer resistance to the development of postpartum depression. Expectant mothers anticipating the birth of their first child completed the LOT and a depression scale during the last weeks of their pregnancy. They took the depression measure a second time three weeks after giving birth. Those who were optimistic before giving birth were less likely than those who were pessimistic to show any increase in depression after the birth (Carver & Gaines, 1987).

- Optimism makes the experience of major surgery less stressful. Optimistic patients having heart bypass surgery experienced less presurgical distress than pessimistic patients. Further, controlling for presurgical life satisfaction, optimism was associated with greater psychological well-being after surgery. Independent of disease severity, a general sense of optimism seemed to funnel into specific confidence regarding the surgery, and from there to greater life satisfaction (Fitzgerald, Tenner, Affleck, & Pransky, 1993). Patients undergoing surgery for breast cancer showed similar effects. LOT scores assessed at the time of diagnosis were used to predict levels of distress. Optimism predicted not only lower initial distress, but resilience to distress during the year following surgery (Carver et al., 1993).

- Optimism positively affects caregivers' well-being (Given et al., 1993). Greater optimism in people caring for cancer patients was linked with lower depression, better physical health, and fewer detrimental effects on caregivers' daily schedules. Optimism in the caregiver spouses of Alzheimer's patients conferred similar benefits.

Optimism and Physical Well-Being

Optimism proves to be good medicine. Numerous case studies hint that hopefulness extends life and hopelessness takes it.

When Bruno Bettelheim (1960) observed Nazi concentration camp inmates, he learned that some measure of hopefulness was necessary for survival:

> Prisoners who came to believe the repeated statements of the guards—that there was no hope for them, that they would never leave the camp except as a corpse—these

prisoners were in a literal sense walking corpses. . . . They were people so totally exhausted, both physically and emotionally, that they had given the environment total power over them. . . . Shortly after the beginning of captivity, these men stopped eating, sat mute and motionless in corners, and finally died (pp. 151–152).

Careful research confirms that people with a positive outlook not only feel better, they also enjoy better physical health than those with a negative outlook. Optimists are bothered by fewer physical illnesses and live longer. When compared to pessimists, optimists make fewer visits to the doctor, receive better ratings of general health from their physicians, have stronger immune system functioning, and show faster rehabilitation from major surgery. Here are some specific examples:

- Optimistic college students reported better physical health at both the start and end of the final month of the semester (Scheier & Carver, 1985). Most important, optimism at the start of the month predicted fewer physical symptoms at the end of the month. The positive link between optimism and good health was not the result of fewer symptoms producing a brighter outlook. Rather, optimism was an independent predictor of good health.

- Optimists were less likely to suffer a heart attack during bypass surgery, and they achieved behavioral milestones more quickly afterward (sitting up in bed, walking around the room, and so on) (Scheier et al., 1989). A six-month follow-up found that optimists were more likely to have resumed vigorous physical exercise and to have returned to work full time. All the "optimism" advantages were independent of the patient's medical status at the outset of the study. That is, optimists didn't do better simply because they were less sick at the time of the surgery.

- Optimism was associated with a lower risk of death in 839 Mayo Clinic patients observed over a 30-year period (Maruta, Colligan, Malinchoe, and Offord, 2000). In fact, optimists enjoyed significantly greater longevity. Moreover, optimistic content in the handwritten early-life autobiographies of Catholic nuns was highly predictive of their longevity (Danner & Snowdon, 2001). More than half of those who wrote with joy and optimism in early adulthood were still alive at 94. In contrast, only 11 percent of those who had expressed little positive emotion in their diaries survived to that age.

- For 660 older adults, attitudes toward aging, measured up to 23 years earlier, were strongly predictive of survival (Levy, Slade, Kunkel, & Kasl, 2002). People with positive perceptions ("I have as much pep as I did last year," "As I get older, things are better than I thought they would be") lived 7.5 years longer than people with less positive perceptions of aging ("As you get older, you are less useful").

Interestingly, pessimists seem particularly more vulnerable than optimists to accidental or violent death (Peterson, Seligman, Yurko, Martin, & Friedman, 1998). The finding recalls the sage advice given the victim lamenting, "I broke my nose in two places." "Well," responded his sympathetic listener, "I'd stay out of those two places if I were you" (Peterson & Bossio, 2001). Male pessimists, especially, seem to have a habit of being in the wrong place at the wrong time.

Realistic Optimism

Clearly, optimism is beneficial, but there is another important angle to take in assessing this strength. Try the Future Life Events scale.

Future Life Events

Compared with other students of your sex at your school, what do you think are the chances that the events listed will happen to you? Use the following scale in making your responses:

1 = 100% less (no chance)   2 = 80% less   3 = 60% less   4 = 40% less
5 = 20% less   6 = 10% less   7 = average (my chances are equal to the average)
8 = 10% more   9 = 20% more   10 = 40% more   11 = 60% more
12 = 80% more   13 = 100% more   14 = 3 times average   15 = 5 times average

Note: *Do NOT respond to events in terms of how likely they are. Instead, be sure to evaluate the likelihood of events for you compared with other students at your school. In other words, for each item think "Compared with other students, I am _____% more (or less) likely to _____."*

_____ **1.** Have a drinking problem

_____ **2.** Like my post-college job

_____ **3.** Own my own home

_____ **4.** Attempt suicide

_____ **5.** Have a heart attack before age 40

_____ **6.** Be fired from a job

_____ **7.** Have a starting salary of more than $24,000 per year

_____ **8.** Travel to Europe

_____ **9.** Graduate in the top third of my college class

_____ **10.** Get lung cancer

_____ **11.** Trip and break a bone

_____ **12.** Live past 80

_____**13.** Control my weight for at least 10 years

_____**14.** Get divorced a few years after my marriage

To score your responses, find your average (mean) response to items 1, 4, 5, 6, 10, 11, and 14: that is, sum the numbers you gave in response to those items and divide by 7. Also find your average (mean) response to items 2, 3, 7, 8, 9, 12, and 13: Total and divide by 7. The first list represents negative life events and the second list contains positive life events. Most respondents to this exercise have a mean below 7.0 for the first list and a mean above 7.0 for the second list. That is, they think that, compared to their peers, they are less likely to experience negative events and more likely to experience positive events.

Many of us, suggests Neil Weinstein (1980, 1982), demonstrate an unrealistic optimism about future life events. The result? In underestimating our risk, we may be less likely to take preventive action. By discounting their personal susceptibility to the risks of smoking, cigarette smokers avoid trying to quit (Gibbons, Eggleston, & Benthin, 1997). Seeing themselves as less vulnerable to unwanted pregnancy than other women of childbearing age, sexually active college women don't consistently use contraceptives (Burger & Burns, 1988). Clearly, optimism has its limits.

So "Don't get your hopes up" is sometimes good advice. At Shawshank prison, Red warns Andy that optimism can disappoint. There's no escape. We are destined to die here and hoping will drive you insane. "Blessed is he who expects nothing," wrote poet Alexander Pope, "for he shall never be disappointed."

In contrast to unrealistic optimism, "flexible" or "realistic" optimism (Seligman, 1990; Schneider, 2001) characterizes hope-filled people who keep their eyes open. In viewing the past they give themselves and others the benefit of the doubt, they see current obstacles as challenges, and they look expectantly to the future. At the same time, they know that wishful thinking by itself does not improve things, nor is everything under personal control. And optimists show acceptance in uncontrollable situations, while pessimists are more likely to engage in active denial (Carver & Scheier, 1999). So, optimism—especially flexible optimism—is beneficial. But why? How exactly does optimism work to provide its advantages?

How Optimism Works

First, realistic optimism motivates. We are more likely to invest effort if we believe that the desirable is attainable. Those who make favorable appraisals of their future are more likely to initiate action. When they encounter obstacles (and everyone does) and progress is temporarily impeded, optimists are also more likely to persist. Why? The key is how we interpret setbacks. Optimists and pessimists, Martin Seligman (1990) explains, provide different explanations for life's disappointments.

Explanatory Styles

Imagine for a moment your bank has just informed you that your checking account is overdrawn. After reflecting a bit on the possible reasons for this notice, write down in a sentence or two what you believe to be the single most important cause.

_____

_____

_____

_____

In thinking about what you have just written, answer the following questions:

1. Is the cause something that is *permanent* or is it *temporary*; that is, will the cause be present in the future?

_____

2. Is the cause something that influences other areas of your life or only your checking account balance?

_____

3. Does the cause you describe reflect more about you or about other people and circumstances?

_____

Seligman reports that pessimists tend to explain troubles in terms that are *stable* ("It's going to last forever"), *global* ("It's going to affect everything I do"), and *internal* ("It's all my fault"). Such explanations leave them feeling helpless. Since life is not controllable, they ask, "Why put forth the effort?" Pessimism paralyzes.

Contrast this style of explaining life's problems with that of the optimistic Andy Dufresne at Shawshank. "Sure, I'm in prison," Andy admits, "but my loss of freedom is temporary. Moreover, imprisonment need not undermine everything I do. My efforts still make a difference. Look," he says to himself, "I write letters, read books, teach students, even continue financial accounting. And what brought me to Shawshank is really not my fault." Clearly, his optimistic outlook energizes.

As Andy illustrates, optimists are more likely to explain negative events in terms that are *temporary* ("This is only momentary"), *specific* ("This is only one small aspect of life"), and *external* ("This is really not my fault"). Such explanations are more likely to invigorate. Clearly, the troubling event can be surmounted.

It's no wonder that this motivating way of explaining things is associated with greater achievement. Seligman and Schulman (1986) evaluated the success of new life insurance salespeople who were more or less optimistic in their outlooks. Those who saw their initial setbacks as flukes or as suggesting the need for a new approach sold more policies and were half as likely to quit.

Still, it is more than sheer persistence that gives optimists their advantage. They also tend to cope well with problems.

Coping Strategies

Take a few minutes to identify the most important problem you faced during the last year. Then, using the scale, indicate how often you used each of the following strategies to deal with it.

0 = not at all   1 = a little   2 = occasionally   3 = fairly often

_____ **1.** Took things one day at a time

_____ **2.** Tried to find out more about the situation

_____ **3.** Tried to reduce tension by drinking more

_____ **4.** Talked with a professional person (doctor, lawyer, cleric)

_____ **5.** Took it out on other people when I felt angry or depressed

_____ **6.** Prayed for guidance and/or strength

_____ **7.** Talked with a friend about the problem

_____ **8.** Tried to reduce tension by taking more tranquilizing drugs

_____ **9.** Told myself things that helped me feel better

_____**10.** Kept my feelings to myself

_____ **11.** Bargained or compromised to get something positive from the situation

_____**12.** Tried to reduce tension by exercising more

_____**13.** Tried to reduce tension by smoking more

_____**14.** Tried to see the positive side of the situation

_____**15.** Considered several alternatives for handling the problem

_____**16.** Made a plan of action and followed it

_____**17.** Went over the situation in my mind to try to understand it

_____**18.** Tried to reduce tension by eating more

_____**19.** Got busy with other things to keep my mind off the problem

_____**20.** Drew on my past experiences

_____**21.** Avoided being with people in general

_____**22.** I knew what had to be done and tried harder to make things work

_____**23.** Tried to step back from the situation and be more objective

_____**24.** Refused to believe that it happened

This questionnaire, abbreviated from one designed by Charles Holahan and Rudolph Moos (1987), assesses three different kinds of strategies for coping with problems. The authors believe that active-cognitive strategies *(assessed by items 1, 6, 9, 14, 15, 17, 20, and 23) represent active efforts to construct thoughts to help cope with the problem.* Active-behavioral strategies *(assessed by items 2, 4, 7, 11, 12, 16, 19, and 22) constitute active efforts to change the situation, and* avoidance strategies *(assessed by items 3, 5, 8, 10, 13, 18, 21, and 24) reflect efforts to keep the problem out of awareness. To determine what strategy you tend to use more, find your mean score for each subscale. That is, add up the numbers you gave in response to the items on each of the three subscales and, for each subscale, divide by 8. Which mean is highest and which is lowest for you?*

Research suggests that optimists cope with stress in more adaptive ways, that is, they tend to use active-cognitive and active-behavioral rather than avoidance strategies. They not only take action but are more focused and more inclined to plan in meeting challenges. Intent on making the best of negative situations, they seek to grow personally from adversity.

Consider optimistic college freshmen, who seem to have an easier time adjusting to college life than pessimistic students. In studying their coping strategies, Aspinwall and Taylor (1992) found that the optimists were more likely to deal with the stress of attending new classes, forming new relationships, and living in a strange environment by trying to do something about these challenges directly. They faced the challenge of an upcoming exam through direct problem solving, such as preparing for the test and talking with other students. Pessimists were more likely to pretend the problems did not exist or to disengage by wishful thinking and social withdrawal.

Pessimism, particularly when it's based in feelings of helplessness, suppresses the immune system and thus leaves people more vulnerable to physical illness (Rodin, 1986). Optimism's positive link to physical well-being also has its basis in attitudes and actions that contribute to good health. Optimists pay more attention to health-relevant information than do pessimists (Aspinwall & Brunhart, 1996) and are less prone to self-destructive habits such as substance abuse (Carvajal, Clair, Nash, & Evans, 1998). They demonstrate greater success in limiting saturated fat in their diet, reducing body fat, and increasing their aerobic capacity (Shepperd, Maroto, & Pbert, 1996). And when diagnosed with a serious illness, such as cancer, optimists are more likely not only to accept its reality but to take active steps to meet the unexpected challenge (Carver et al., 1993).

In short, optimism benefits us by energizing us and fostering more effective problem solving.

IN REVIEW

Philosophers, theologians, and psychologists have long debated the merits of hope. The Life Orientation Test (LOT) of Scheier, Carver, and Bridges (1985) assesses optimism—the extent to which we believe that good as opposed to bad things will generally occur in our lives. Research has linked optimism to both psychological and physical well-being. Optimists seem to cope better with stressful life events and actually live longer than pessimists. Although unrealistic optimism can disappoint and even endanger, flexible optimism energizes and fosters effective problem solving.

■ Exploring Hope

Andy Dufresne: Dynamo with an Agenda

Andy dreams of freedom. Most prisoners at Shawshank do, at least when they first enter. However, an experienced resident like Red knows better. For him and all other veterans, hope is bubble-headed optimism. He warns Andy, "It would take a man 600 years to tunnel through the wall." Most inmates eventually became "institutionalized." "These walls are funny," Red continues, "first, you hate 'em, then you get used to 'em. Enough time passes, it gets so you depend on 'em." Hope withers in a wretched environment.

But not for Andy. His will seeks a way. And some early prison success only fuels his optimism. Six years of weekly request letters to the State Senate secure a $200 check along with boxes of books for a new inmate library. Andy's smart legal advice saves Captain Hadley's inheritance and earns Andy and his coworkers a break with three cold beers each on a hot summer day. Finally, Tommy Williams, a new arrival serving a two-year sentence for breaking and entering, seems to provide the route out. Imprisoned elsewhere, Tommy heard a fellow inmate confess to the murder of Andy's wife.

But hope is short-circuited. Warden Norton, the real criminal in the story, kills Tommy before he can testify and prove Andy's innocence. The road to freedom dead-ends. The lesson? Strong wills do not guarantee fruitful ways.

Nineteen years pass. Then, amazingly, Shawshank's early morning headcount finds Andy's bunk empty. Rushing to the vacant cell, a dumbfounded warden stumbles onto the escape route. Behind a wall-sized poster of Raquel Welch, Andy had meticulously chiseled a passageway to freedom. Patiently over the years, he had toted his wall out to the exercise yard, pocketfuls at a time. His tool of redemption? A small rock hammer carefully concealed in a hollowed-out Bible, the warden's gift to every new Shawshank inmate. Andy's driving hope was realized. Its ingredients? A clearly defined objective, back-breaking determination, and a carefully planned route.

Psychology of Hope

Close your eyes for a moment and think of your future. Write down the first image that comes to mind.

_____

_____

_____

_____

How long does it take to see that something? If you are like most people, suggests C. Rick Snyder (1994), it takes only a few seconds to imagine something you want to happen. We are intrinsically goal directed. Goals are the target of hopeful thinking, from the immediate short term ("I hope to complete today's reading assignment") to the more significant long term ("I hope to earn a college degree"). But goals are only one ingredient of hope, argues Snyder. To appreciate its other elements, complete his Hope Scale (Snyder, 1994, p. 26).

SELF-ASSESSMENT ■

Hope Scale

Read each of the following items carefully. Using the scale, enter the number that best describes you in the blank provided.

1 = definitely false   2 = mostly false   3 = mostly true   4 = definitely true

_____ **1.** I energetically pursue my goals.

_____ **2.** I can think of many ways to get out of a jam.

_____ **3.** My past experiences have prepared me well for my future.

_____ **4.** There are lots of ways around any problem.

_____ **5.** I've been pretty successful in life.

_____ **6.** I can think of many ways to get the things done in life that are most important to me.

_____ **7.** I meet the goals that I set for myself.

_____ **8.** Even when others get discouraged, I know I can find a way to solve the problem.

Hope, suggests Snyder, reflects one's willpower and "waypower" in reaching future goals. Agency is the willpower, or energy needed to keep moving toward your goals. Pathways is the waypower, or perceived ability to generate routes to achieve those goals. Your agency subscale is derived by adding the numbers you place in front of items 1, 3, 5, and 7. The pathways subscale is found by adding items 2, 4, 6, and 8. Add the four agency and four pathways items to obtain a total "hope" score. Mean or average scores on each subscale are 12, making the average total hope score 24. Higher scores reflect more hope, lower scores reflect less hope.

The case of Greg Nash, a real-life version of the ace pitcher in the film *The Natural,* highlights the distinction between hope's willpower and its waypower. Playing Little League baseball in rural Sorrento, Louisiana (pop. 1300), the 12-year-old could hit anything thrown at him. Six years later, "Toe," nicknamed after his size 18 shoes, had become a muscular 6-foot-6-inch, 225-pound slugger with a picture-perfect swing that went along with a near 100-mph fastball. But he played baseball only in a weekly beer and barbecue league. Toe wanted more: "I always *hoped* I could make it to the majors." Although motivated to succeed, he lacked the waypower to get there.

Living in poverty with his father and sister, Toe had dropped out of eighth grade and out of organized baseball. In professional sports, talent and motivation aren't enough. Someone must know you have it. When Nash turned 18, he was not one of the almost 1500 choices in the baseball draft. No one had heard of him. He was destined to join his father as a part-time groundskeeper at the local ballpark.

Only Benny Latino's chance observation of Nash as a Little Leaguer saved the promising ballplayer from obscurity. Promoted to full scout with the Tampa Bay Devil Rays, Benny happened to remember the kid with powerful arms and a blistering fastball. Returning to Sorrento to see what might have happened to him, he located the now mature and superb athlete. A $30,000 signing bonus, a fortune to Nash, rejuvenated his hope (Beaton, 2001). In addition to willpower, now there was waypower.

Goals of Hopeful People

High-hope people seem to set more objectives for themselves than low-hope people (Snyder et al., 1991). They set several goals, not just one, in each of their life's roles, including career, relationships, and recreation. Hopeful people also set more difficult goals for themselves (Snyder et al., 1991). Finally, the objectives of hopeful people tend to be concrete and vivid (Snyder, 1995). They are fully describable to themselves and to others.

Willpower of Hopeful People

High-hope people are routinely optimistic and believe they control their own destiny (Snyder, 1994). Difficult goals are viewed as invigorating challenges rather than as insurmountable obstacles. Hopeful people experience disappointments like everyone else, but they tend to think about them differently. With self-talk like "I'll make it," "I can do it," and "I won't give up," hopeful people endure. Rather than ruminating over setbacks, they focus on what still needs to be done (Snyder, LaPointe, Crowson, & Early, 1998).

Waypower of Hopeful People

In comparison with less hopeful people, those with high hope are more skilled at finding alternative routes to their goals. For example, researchers asked college students what they would do if they were taking a course for which they had set a grade goal of a B but then received a D on their first examination. Hopeful students generated a variety of adaptive strategies, such as going to talk to the instructor, outlining their notes and readings, scheduling specific times each day to study, and hiring a tutor for reaching their goal (Yoshinobu, 1989).

In times of stress, hopeful people seem to have a greater arsenal of coping strategies to draw from. They have a larger support network to use in both good and bad times. In addition, they are more likely to use humor to cope with life's trials and to engage in prayer or meditation to renew their mental energy. Recognizing the importance of health maintenance strategies, they are more likely to exercise.

Hope and Achievement

Those who score high on the Hope Scale do not have higher IQs than low scorers, but they are more successful. They are more likely to persevere and to reach their goals. For example, in one study (Snyder et al., 1991), introductory psychology students took the Hope Scale at the beginning of the semester. A few weeks later they were asked to predict the final grade they would receive for the course. Hope Scale scores were positively correlated with both expected and obtained grades.

Goals are the targets of hopeful thinking. Willpower is the motivation to keep moving toward goals. Waypower is the perceived ability to generate routes to achieve them. These ingredients of hope are interconnected. For example, identifying clear goals energizes a search for appropriate routes.

Hopeful people set more challenging goals for themselves. Moreover, they have objectives that are concrete and vivid. They are routinely optimistic and view obstacles as invigorating challenges rather than as insurmountable obstacles. They are skilled at finding alternative routes to their goals and thus enjoy higher levels of achievement.

Fostering Hope

Hopeful people can tell you what they hope for. Periodically, we all need to take inventory of our hopes and why we hope for the things we do, suggest Diane McDermott and C. R. Snyder (1999).

Identifying Goals

One effective strategy for goal setting is to identify the major areas of your life—perhaps relationships, family, work, health, leisure—and list important goals under each. Doing this even for the first time doesn't take long. Once formulated, put the list away for a week and then take another look. Add or delete goals as you see fit. Try to increase the number of goals in each area. Hopeful people tend to have many objectives across the various arenas of life.

As you identify goals, keep in mind that hopeful people have goals that are vivid and concrete. Vague goals such as "to be successful" are of little use in terms of motivation. Remember also that manageable goals are hope-inducing. It's fine to have inspiring, long-range goals, but try to break them down into step-by-step subgoals. The journey is always more satisfying when you can measure progress along the way.

After you have identified multiple goals in each area, prioritize. Sort the goals from the most to the least important. Give A's to the extremely important things, B's to the quite important, C's to the somewhat important, and D's to the slightly important. Until you do this, you will probably be pulled in too many directions. Following Snyder's guidelines, I didn't find it difficult to generate my own inventory.

Rank	Relationships	Family	Work	Health	Leisure
A	Express more appreciation	Help daughter select high school classes	Finish faculty guide for video series	Purchase new glasses	Purchase season tickets to film series
A	Take computer class together	Visit elderly mother weekly	Write letters of recommendation	Exercise 30 minutes daily	Schedule weekly golf game
B	Finish home repair projects	Help daughter learn to drive	Prepare chapter on empathy	Lose 8 pounds	Read book on aquarium care
B	Remember anniversary	Plan family reunion	Prepare course syllabi for new semester	Eat more balanced diet	Plan summer garden/ Purchase seeds
B	Attend concert series with friends	Write aunts and uncle	Prepare for department seminar	Schedule annual physical	Find 4 hours weekly to read recommended novels
C	Plan vacation	Build college fund	Prepare schedule of committee meetings	Get more sleep	Take evening class in woodworking

SELF-ASSESSMENT ■

Identifying Goals

Now try identifying and ranking your own goals.

Rank	Relationships	Family	Work	Health	Leisure

Strengthening Willpower and Waypower

Having identified their goals, hopeful people take responsibility for moving toward their attainment. Their sense of agency and pathways are primarily rooted in the ways they think about themselves and their worlds.

As we noted earlier, hopeful people tend to view their goals as challenges and in so doing, focus on success rather than failure. Instead of appraising them as difficult, they think of them as opportunities. "Taking this class in Korean language offers the chance to stretch myself"; "It's satisfying to help these mentally challenged kids master a vocational skill they can use." And when obstacles do come, hopeful people continue the positive internal dialogue with "I can," "I'll make it," and "I won't give up."

To assess the content of your internal dialogue, you might keep a diary of your goal-related thoughts for one week. How many of your thoughts are put-downs in which you repeatedly tell yourself that you cannot do something or that bad things are going to happen to you? Such thought patterns undermine willpower. Don't feel deflated. Rather, recognize that this awareness is the first step toward change.

Visualizing Success

"Hold the image of yourself succeeding," recommends positive-thinking advocate Norman Vincent Peale (1982, p. 15). "Visualize it so vividly that when the desired outcome comes, it seems to be merely echoing a reality that has already existed in your mind."

Good advice? Early on, Earl Woods taught his son Tiger to concentrate, especially to focus on the goal before long putts, mentally picturing the ball rolling into the cup (Tolson, 2000). Sports psychologists now include such mental simulation as a standard part of training to improve performance. Many athletes report that they actually experience the muscle twinges associated with their performance as they imagine themselves diving, serving in tennis, or jumping in skating.

In some cases, such mental simulation fosters willpower. More important, however, mental simulation seems to work by fostering waypower. Rehearsing the *process* needed to reach a desired goal pays better dividends than simply imagining the *destination*.

About a week before their midterm exam in psychology, students received training in mental simulation (Pham & Taylor, 1997). Some were told to imagine themselves earning an A. "Imagine yourself," suggested the researchers, "standing in front of the glass case where the grades are posted, holding your breath, finding your score, beaming with joy, and feeling confident and proud." Other students were told to visualize themselves studying for the exam in a way that would lead them to obtain an A. They were told to visualize themselves at their desks, on their beds, or at the library studying the chapters, going over the lecture notes, eliminating distractions such as turning off the television or stereo, and declining a friend's invitation to go out.

Each group practiced this simulation five minutes each day until the exam. Thinking about the outcome produced little improvement, adding only two points to exam scores. However, those who reflected on the process began to study sooner, spent more time on it, and improved performance by eight points. Rehearsing the process needed to reach a goal, suggested the researchers, helps one to identify the steps necessary to get there by creating a plan.

Learning Optimism

Recalling previous successful goal pursuits, particularly as we face difficulties in the present, fosters perseverance. Not only do they remind us that "If I did it once, I can do it again," but they often provide insight into specific strategies that once worked and just might work again.

Although we sometimes think that obstacles to goals necessarily have negative consequences, psychologist Albert Ellis (1989) taught otherwise. People are predisposed to analyze the causes of disappointment, he argued, and the specific answers they give are a key element in understanding why two people respond so differently to the same event.

For example, Jake's failure to make the soccer team leads him to believe, "I'm a terrible athlete," and he never tries out for another sports team. Ricardo's failure to make the cut leads to the conclusion "I didn't try hard enough," and he is inspired to try harder for track. In short, Jake's failure is paralyzing, while Ricardo's is energizing. As we saw earlier, pessimists tend to explain adversity in terms of causes that are internal ("I'm not good at athletics"), permanent ("I have poor eye-hand coordination"), and pervasive ("I'm such a loser"). Optimists favor causes that are external ("The coach doesn't like sophomores"), temporary ("I didn't get enough sleep"), and specific ("I'm not good at soccer").

In learning optimism, Martin Seligman (1990) suggests that we first understand its underlying ABCs. When we experience <u>a</u>dversity, we react by attempting to understand it. That understanding congeals into <u>b</u>eliefs that have real <u>c</u>onsequences for our feelings and actions.

SELF-ASSESSMENT ■

Learning Optimism

To see how the ABCs of optimism work, try the following. In each case the adversity is identified along with either the belief or the consequence. You fill in the missing component. Note that some of these examples reflect an optimistic outlook and others do not.

1. A. Someone breaks into line ahead of you to buy concert tickets.
   B. You think _____.
   C. You get angry and shout at the other customer.

2. A. An acquaintance you made at a coffee shop hasn't returned your phone calls.

B. You think _____

_____

C. You are not perturbed by it and go about your day's work.

3. A. You lose the key to your apartment.

B. You think, "I never do anything right."

C. You feel (or do) _____

_____

4. A. Your employer complains that you arrived for work five minutes late.

B. You think, "He must really be having a bad day."

C. You feel (or do) _____

_____

As part of your week's diary of goal-related thoughts, you might record several ABCs from your own life. Try to analyze the connection you draw between adversity, no matter how small, and your consequent feelings and actions. For example, adversity might be discovering that you overslept, missed the bus, or forgot to pay the telephone bill. Your beliefs are how you interpret the adversity: "I can't do anything right." For consequences, record your feelings and what you did. Were you depressed, angry, or sad? Did you lose energy, perhaps even waste the day?

If successfully challenged, pessimistic beliefs are unlikely to recur when the same adversity repeats itself. Learning to counterargue, to offer alternative causes for the disappointment, to recognize that you are overreacting, and even to show that the belief is factually incorrect undermine the pessimistic explanation and enable you to cope with setbacks more effectively.

Communal Hope

Hope flourishes best in community. The personal accounts of hope in this chapter are not merely narratives of individual perseverance. They are stories of communal effort. Benny Latino's restoration of "Toe" Nash's big-league hopes suggests that hope's survival requires social support. *The Shawshank Redemption,* too, is a story as much of friendship as of freedom. Whether through the promise of a new trial based on Tommy's testimony, or by way of a rock hammer and wall-sized posters that only Red can smuggle in, Andy's pursuit of hope involves others.

Research confirms that high-hope people have a social support network that they rely on in both good and bad times (Snyder, 1994). The corollary also happens to be true. The less hopeful are characterized by loneliness. They seem unable to initiate and sustain relationships.

Thus, a social environment that undermines the need to belong not only feeds loneliness, it may also fuel hopelessness. In analyzing the epidemic depression rate among Westerners, Seligman (1990) concludes that our society's message that we are masters of our own fate and thus should do our own thing comes with a cost. Such individualism has led to a decline of commitment to family, religious groups, and community. Thus, when disappointment comes, it's weathered alone. The self-focused individual assumes personal responsibility for problems and has no one to turn to for support. In more collectivist societies, where close-knit relationships and cooperation are the norm, depression is less common and less linked to self-blame over personal failure.

But Seligman's analysis penetrates more deeply. He raises fundamental questions about the very targets of our hope. Our best dreams will always include hopes for health, hopes for success at work and play, and even hopes for qualities of character and of what we can become. Our most fundamental hope is probably for our own well-being and happiness. But do our hopes also reach beyond ourselves? Do we have hope that others will experience the best that life offers? To what extent are we global hopers? Do we keep hope alive for our physical environment, for hungry and lonely people, for those suffering oppression and injustice?

Optimism is just a tool, suggests Seligman, to help people achieve the goals they have set for themselves. It is in the selection of goals that meaning or emptiness resides, and finding meaning requires commitment to something larger than yourself. "When learned optimism is coupled with a renewed commitment to the commons," concludes Seligman (1990), "our epidemic of depression and meaninglessness may end" (p. 291).

Snyder agrees. Hope is ultimately counterproductive, he argues, to the extent that individuals pursue their goals to the detriment of others. What is needed are environments in which people living and working together can interact to support one another so that both individual and collective goals can be met (Snyder & Feldman, 2000). Hope is for the many, not just the few.

Interestingly, research with the Hope Scale you completed earlier reports that hopeful people can and do think about communal or shared goals (Snyder, 1994). They have learned that while people gain satisfaction from individual goals, they gain even greater meaning in joining with others in pursuing goals aimed at a greater good. Those who have realized their own dreams want to make the hopes of others real as well.

So it is finally with Andy Dufresne. As much a giver as a receiver of help, he repeatedly renews despondent spirits at Shawshank. From his unorthodox winning of three beers apiece for his roofing coworkers to dissolving prison walls with an unauthorized broadcast of an Italian opera over the PA system, Andy instills hope in others. Most of all, he convinces his best friend Red that he, too, "can make it on the outside." By story's end, Red has internalized Andy's words: "One must either get busy living or get busy dying."

IN REVIEW

Fostering hope begins with identifying and prioritizing goals. Positive self-talk from the outset strengthens motivation and the search for appropriate pathways. Rehearsing the process, not simply the destination, promotes goal attainment. And interpreting disappointments in terms of causes that are external, temporary, and specific serves to maintain will power.

Hope survives best in community. Hopeful people have a strong support network and join with others in the pursuit of collective well-being.

friendship

Without friendship, life is not worth living.
—CICERO, *106–43 B.C.*

How we live shapes how we feel when we die. In their final years, observed psychologist Erik Erikson (1963), the elderly ask, "Did my life have purpose or was it a failure?" Answers lead to either *integrity*—the feeling that one's life has been meaningful—or *despair*—the conclusion that the time has been wasted. To set life's priorities, we might anticipate Erikson's end-of-life question (Suzuki, 2000). The deathbed test helps us identify the human strengths and thus what's really worth pursuing in life (Peterson & Seligman, in press). Try it for yourself.

CRITICAL THINKING ■

The Deathbed Test

Imagine that you have lived a rich, meaningful life and now are on your deathbed. As you reflect back, what memories fill you with happiness, pride, and satisfaction? Verbalize at least one before reading on.

Your answer is probably not designer clothing, an expensive house, a sport utility vehicle, or a yacht. It may not be your greatest educational or career achievement. Most people say that the best things in life have been close, satisfying relationships, especially bonds with family and friends (Reis & Gable, 2003; Suzuki, 2000). In late-life reminiscences, even those who have enjoyed exceptional career success attach greater meaning to their close relationships than to their stellar accomplishments (Sears, 1977).

■

Functions of Friendship

How does friendship foster human flourishing? What specific needs do friends meet? Let's begin by considering what friends do for each other as well as what it means to be rejected.

Life Satisfaction

Social connections predict life satisfaction across time and place. From childhood through old age, those with friends experience greater psychological well-being than those without friends (Hartup & Stevens, 1997). An extensive cross-cultural review found only one common predictor of happiness across all countries studied: social relationships (Diener, 2001).

Time spent with friends seems to be particularly satisfying (Larson & Bradney, 1988). In one study, adults and teens were paged every two hours and asked what they were doing, who, if anyone, was with them, and how they felt. About 65 percent of the time the volunteers were in the presence of others. The most striking result was that participants of all ages reported higher levels of enjoyment and excitement when they were with friends than when they were alone or with casual acquaintances, coworkers, or family. Even married adults were happier with friends than when they were alone with their spouses. These adults' happiest times, however, were when they and their spouses were together with friends. Summarizing their results, the investigators concluded:

> With friends our attention becomes focused, distractions lessen, awareness of time disappears: We emerge into a world in which the intimacy and joy shared with others is the fundamental reality, and for a time the world becomes a different place. (p. 124)

Social Support

But friends do much more than make for a fun-filled life. "My friends have made the story of my life," observed Helen Keller. "In a thousand ways they have turned my limitations into beautiful privileges, and enabled me to walk serene and happy in the shadow cast by my deprivation." Classic rock radio regulars James Taylor and Carole King remind us: "When you're down and troubled and you need a helping hand, you're in luck *if* . . . you've got a friend."

Three-time cancer survivor Kathlyn Conway knows. Friends provided an anchor during her most difficult times (Steiner, 2001, pp. 69–70). They gave *emotional support*—a listening ear for confiding painful feelings. "I had friends I could talk to at any time," she reports. "If I was upset, it was easy for me to call someone and expect them to listen no matter what." At other times they provided *instrumental assistance*—tangible goods and services. "One friend went to the hospital after my mastectomy and helped me wash my hair. Later, another friend left her very busy job in the middle of the week to go shopping with me for a wig." Friends also offered *informational support*—expert counsel and advice: "Another, who had had breast cancer herself, visited and stealthily, humorously, kindly opened her blouse to show me her implanted breast in order to reassure me."

How strong is your social support? Complete the following scale to find out.

Your Social Support

Decide whether each of the following statements is true or false for you.

T   F   **1.** If I needed an emergency loan of $100, there is someone I could get it from.

T   F   **2.** There is someone who takes pride in my accomplishments.

T   F   **3.** I often meet or talk with family or friends.

T   F   **4.** Most people I know think highly of me.

T   F   **5.** If I needed an early-morning ride to the airport, there's no one I would feel comfortable asking to take me.

T   F   **6.** I feel there is no one with whom I can share my most private worries and fears.

T   F   **7.** Most of my friends are more successful making changes in their lives than I am.

T   F   **8.** I would have a hard time finding someone to go with me on a day trip to the beach or country.

Source: Insel & Roth, 2002, p. 43. Quiz source: Adapted from Japenga, 1995, p. 94. Copyright © 1995 *Health*.

Add up the number of true answers to questions 1–4 together with the number of false answers to questions 5–8. If your score is 4 or more, your support network may be adequate. If your score is 3 or less, you should probably work on strengthening your social ties (Insel & Roth, 2002).

Why develop social ties? Having a social network with a variety of relationships predicts overall wellness—physical as well as psychological. "Good friends," concludes psychologist Irwin Sarason, "are good for your health."

A social network affects both the likelihood of contracting an illness and the course of recovery from an illness. People who enjoy strong support consistently are shown to have a lower risk of early death (see Straub, 2002, for a review). Here are some examples:

- A survey of 7,000 adults in Alameda County, California, revealed that having a large number of social contacts enabled women to live an average of 2.8 years longer and men an average of 2.3 years longer. This greater longevity remained even when rates of smoking, alcohol use, physical activity, and obesity were taken into account.

- A 7-year study of 50-year-old men in Sweden found that social support was inversely related to mortality. Those with the highest levels of support had the lowest mortality rates. Low levels of social support had an impact on mortality equivalent to that of cigarette smoking.

- Over a 17-year period, cancer patients with the fewest daily social contacts were more than twice as likely to die than those with greater social support. And over a 9-year period, heart disease patients with low social support had a 50 percent survival rate compared with an 82 percent rate for those with a strong social network.

- Both men and women with strong social ties are less likely to suffer heart attacks or even to contract colds. Social support has been linked with either better adjustment to, or faster recovery from, coronary artery surgery, rheumatoid arthritis, childhood leukemia, and stroke.

How does social support convey its health benefits? Some researchers suggest that it provides a buffer against the effects of stress. By providing important resources, others help us cope more effectively. Friends may see that we receive medical attention more quickly. In addition to providing tangible support, they help us to evaluate and overcome the stressful events, perhaps by giving us reassurance or by bolstering our self-esteem. Psychologists suggest that social support is always beneficial whether we are experiencing stress or not. For example, others may help us eat, smoke, and drink less.

Social support comes from a variety of sources, including family, neighbors, co-workers, and social, community, and religious organizations. Perhaps most significantly, though, it comes from friends. For example, in studying senior citizens' social networks, psychologist Laura Christensen reports that "it is the *quality* of their relationships that matters—not the *quantity*. In our work we find that three is the critical friend number. If you have three people in your life that you can really count on, then you are doing as well as someone who has ten friends. Or twenty, for that matter. If you have fewer than three friends, then you could be a little precarious" (Steiner, 2001).

So take out a piece of paper and begin listing your friends. Do you have three people you really get excited about seeing and are certain you can trust (Steiner, 2001)?

Lessons of Social Rejection

We've learned plenty about the functions of social bonds by studying social rejection. Cut off from family and friends, we suffer.

At one time or another each of us has experienced the discomfort of being unwelcome or left out. We feel deviant, defective, or just "different." As the next-to-smallest eighth grader, I found physical education class to be painful. Basketball was not my game. When my two tallest classmates—both of whom I considered friends—picked teams, I was often the last one left standing in the middle of the gym floor.

At times, individuals and groups deliberately exclude or ignore others. As Kipling Williams and Lisa Zadro (2001) observe, *ostracism* ranges from complete removal of an individual or group from the community (solitary confinement, exile, banishment) to giving another the "silent treatment." By adulthood everyone has been both a victim and a perpetrator of some form of ostracism. Consider those feelings more closely in the following exercise.

SELF-ASSESSMENT ■

Feeling Excluded

Reflect on a time when you felt excluded or ignored. Perhaps it was a time when you were the target of the "silent treatment." What led to your being excluded or ignored? What feelings did the ostracism elicit and how did you attempt to deal with it?

_____

_____

_____

_____

_____

_____

_____

_____

_____

_____

A full 67 percent of a representative U.S. sample admitted using the silent treatment (deliberately not speaking to a person in their presence) on a loved one, and 75 percent indicated that they had been a target of the silent treatment (Williams & Zadro, 2001).

Structured interviews reveal the pain of being ignored. Consider the following (Williams & Zadro, 2001):

> In high school, the other students thought me weird and never spoke to me. I tell you in all honesty that at one stage they refused to speak to me for 153 days, not one word at all. That was a very low point for me in my life and on the 153rd day I swallowed 29 Valium pills. My brother found me and called an ambulance. When I returned to school, the kids had heard the whole story and for a few days they were falling over themselves to be my friend. Sadly, it didn't last. They stopped talking to me again and I was devastated. I stopped talking myself. I figured that it was useless to have a voice if no one listened. (pp. 41–42)

Another interviewee explained a familial tendency to use the silent treatment:

At the present time, my sister, aged 58, in the U.S. won't talk to either my father or myself—for supposedly differing reasons. My father's sister has not spoken to him for over 30 years. My mother's brother once refused to talk to his wife for 6 months. My mother regularly refused to talk to me or my sister for days at a time. It seems like ostracism is a congenital condition in my family. (p. 42)

One source of ostracism described not only the devastating consequences of ostracism but how, once started, it is difficult to stop:

After two weeks, I woke up one morning with a blinding flash of insight: "What are you doing to your relationship with your son?" In that short period of time my son had already become intimidated by this treatment—he did exactly what his mother said at all times and whenever he spoke, it was in a quiet whisper. I am ashamed to say that I was sort of pleased with the effects of my ostracism but, as I say, one day I realized that it was making him weak and submissive and that it was eroding the future quality of our relationship.

To terminate the ostracism, however, was an extremely difficult process. I could only begin with grudging monosyllabic responses to his indirect overtures. I was only able to expand on these responses with the passing of time and it is only now, about six weeks since the ostracism ceased, that our relationship appears to be getting back to pre-row normality . . . if it had lasted much longer, I might not have been able to stop and not only would our relationship have been destroyed but also my son himself might have been permanently emotionally and psychologically disfigured. Further . . . it may have led to illness and perhaps, ultimately, to his premature death . . . ostracism can be like a whirlpool or quicksand. If you, the user, don't extract yourself from it as soon as possible, it is likely to become impossible to terminate regardless of any subsequent will to do so. (p. 43)

From their interviews, Williams and Zadro (2001) conclude that ostracism undermines our need for *belonging* ("You didn't belong. You thought, 'I'm a mistake, I shouldn't be here, I'm not wanted here'"), our need for *self-esteem* ("I'm just no good at anything . . . failure, failure, failure"), our need for *control* ("I felt helpless in so many areas of my life"), and our need for *meaning* ("[The silent treatment] made me question 'What's it all for? Why am I still here?' whereas before I never questioned that. I knew why I was there and I knew what it was all for").

Social rejection also impacts behavior. It can undermine self-regulation. Roy Baumeister (2002) explains:

A great deal of psychological functioning is predicated on belonging to the group and enjoying the benefits, both direct and indirect, of that belongingness. Social exclusion undermines the basis for these sacrifices—it ceases to be worth it. The whole purpose of controlling yourself, behaving appropriately and making sacrifices is defeated. And so behavior may become impulsive, chaotic, selfish, disorganized and even destructive.

In one laboratory study, Baumeister (2002) asked research participants in small groups to name privately one fellow participant with whom they would like to continue working. Some participants were then told that all the other participants had chosen them; others were told that no one had chosen them. In another manipulation, participants took a personality test and then were informed that people with their profiles tended to be surrounded by friends as they grew older. Others were told that people with their profile tended to become increasingly isolated.

Results of the studies indicated that being excluded increases antisocial and self-defeating behaviors. Compared to their well-liked counterparts, people who felt excluded were more aggressive, more likely to cheat, less likely to help others, more likely to procrastinate, less likely to choose healthy behaviors, and less able to delay self-gratification. In short, they exercised less self-control.

The study of social rejection suggests that communities provide a lot more than a sense of belonging. Social connections, especially our friends, reassure us of our *worth* (Duck, 1983). They do this not only directly by admiring and supporting us but also by listening to us, seeking our advice, and by generally indicating that they value our perspective. By giving us the chance to help them, friends also foster our sense of *personal control* and *responsibility*. Finally, friends meet our need for *meaning* by providing necessary anchor points for opinions, beliefs, and emotional responses. They suggest how we should react and guide our actions in subtle ways. Friends help us to see where we are right and where we are wrong.

Of course social influence is not always beneficial. Friends, suggested author Alexander Lockhart, are like the buttons on an elevator—they can take you up or take you down. For example, peer influence is among the most powerful predictors of drug use. If an adolescent's friends use drugs, chances are good that he or she will too. If friends do not, the opportunity to do drugs may never present itself. Recognizing that social influence can work both ways, Cicero aptly noted, "Friendship was given by nature to be an assistant to virtue, not a companion to vice." The lesson? Select friends carefully and wisely.

IN REVIEW

Many people recall bonds with family and friends as life's greatest satisfaction. Research indicates that social support predicts both psychological and physical well-being. Ostracism not only undermines our need to belong but also weakens our sense of self-esteem, personal control, and meaning. Social rejection may also interfere with the important human capacity for self-regulation. Friends foster our sense of self-worth and responsibility. They also help us evaluate our beliefs and guide our behavior. Recognizing that social influence can be either constructive or destructive, wise people choose friends carefully.

Features of Friendship

Our friends may be unique, but as we will see, there are a number of features most of us expect in someone we call "friend."

Defining Friendship

Let's first focus on how we define a friend. Reflect carefully before answering the following question for yourself.

CRITICAL THINKING ■

What Is a Friend?

What do you think are the important characteristics of friendship? Complete the sentence "A friend is someone . . . " in five different ways.

1. _____
2. _____
3. _____
4. _____
5. _____

Answers from professional men and women in several large urban centers fell into the following eight categories, from most to least frequent (Sapadin, 1988). A friend is someone

- with whom we are intimate.
- whom we trust.
- on whom we can depend.
- who shares.
- who is accepting.
- who is caring.
- with whom we are close.
- whom we enjoy.

On her popular Web site, the Friendship Page, Bronwyn Polson devotes over two hundred pages to friendship. Visitors are asked to indicate what things mean most to them in a friendship. In 2003, honesty, fun, understanding, and loyalty (in descending order) headed the list.

Do you have a *best* friend? Complete the following exercise to give that relationship some thought.

Intimate Friendship Scale

This scale suggests that our closest friendships reflect eight dimensions. Thinking of your best friend, how many items are true?

T   F   **1.** I feel free to talk with him/her about almost anything.

T   F   **2.** I know what kinds of books, games, and activities he/she likes.

T   F   **3.** When he/she is not around, I miss him/her.

T   F   **4.** The most exciting things happen when I am with him/her and nobody else is around.

T   F   **5.** Whenever he/she wants to tell me about a problem I stop what I am doing and listen for as long as he/she wants.

T   F   **6.** I can be sure he/she will help me whenever I ask for it.

T   F   **7.** I like to do things with him/her.

T   F   **8.** I know that whatever I tell him/her is kept secret between us.

Source: Selected items from Sharabany, 1994, p. 454.

Each of the statements in the Intimate Friendship Scale assesses a different dimension of close friendship:

1. **Frankness and spontaneity.** Your relationship includes honest self-disclosure of strengths and weaknesses as well as frank feedback about the other's actions.

2. **Sensitivity and knowing.** Understanding and empathy counterbalance frankness.

3. **Attachment.** Closeness and liking produce feelings of connection to the friend.

4. **Exclusiveness.** Unique qualities in the relationship lead to its elevation over other relationships.

5. **Giving.** You and your friend provide one another with material goods as well as social support.

6. **Imposition.** You and your friend stand ready to seek and accept each other's help.

7. **Common activities.** You enjoy time spent together in joint activities.

8. **Trust and loyalty.** You can hold each other's disclosures in confidence and will defend one another from outside attack.

Beverly Fehr (1996) summarizes the survey literature on friendship with a helpful definition. Friendship, she suggests, is a "voluntary, personal relationship, typically providing intimacy and assistance, in which the two parties like one another and seek each other's company (p. 20)." Sharing (intimacy) and caring (assistance) seem to be the central, perhaps even the defining, features of friendship.

Sharing

"A friend is a person with whom I may be sincere," wrote Ralph Waldo Emerson. "Before him I may think aloud." And the result of such honesty? "Your friend," observed nineteenth-century physician and author Elbert Hubbard, "is the person who knows all about you and still likes you."

SELF-ASSESSMENT ■

Self-Concealment Scale

Respond to each of the following statements using a scale from 1 = strongly disagree to 5 = strongly agree.

_____ **1.** I have an important secret that I haven't shared with anyone.

_____ **2.** If I shared all my secrets with my friends, they'd like me less.

_____ **3.** There are lots of things about me that I keep to myself.

_____ **4.** Some of my secrets have really tormented me.

_____ **5.** When something bad happens to me, I tend to keep it to myself.

_____ **6.** I'm often afraid I'll reveal something I don't want to.

_____ **7.** Telling a secret often backfires and I wish I hadn't told it.

_____ **8.** I have a secret that is so private I would lie if anybody asked me about it.

_____ **9.** My secrets are too embarrassing to share with others.

_____ **10.** I have negative thoughts about myself that I would never share with anyone.

Source: Larson & Chastain 1990.

The Self-Concealment Scale was designed to measure the extent to which people typically share or disclose personal information that they perceive as distressing or negative. Total scores, which can range from 10 to 50, are obtained by summing the numbers placed before all the items. In this case, higher scores reflect a greater tendency toward self-concealment and lower scores reflect greater sharing. The mean score obtained from 306 respondents who included human service workers and graduate students in counseling psychology was 25.92.

Higher scores on the Self-Concealment Scale predict anxiety, depression, and a variety of physical symptoms. Sharing mends both body and soul. Disclosing to a friend stressful events and problems that threaten our self-esteem can be liberating. Those who write about personal trauma in a diary enjoy better physical health than those who don't, but talking to a friend is even more beneficial. As we have already seen, benefits from our friends include everything from medical assistance to the bolstering of our self-esteem. Sometimes the benefit may be simply in knowing that our situation is not unique, that others experience the same distress. "We are so fond of one another," confessed Jonathan Swift, "because our ailments are the same." The act of *not* discussing or confiding a stressful event may be more damaging than the event itself (Pennebaker, 1985).

Caring

Given human interdependence, it is not surprising that we may come to think of interpersonal relationships in terms of social economics, or an exchange of favors. A "tit-for-tat" exchange of favors is in fact one important way casual acquaintances maintain their relationships. From coworkers in a carpool taking turns driving to students exchanging lecture notes for the class days they missed, people trade similar benefits. Is this how you operate? Consider the following questions.

SELF-ASSESSMENT ■

Exchange Orientation Scale

Do you tend to agree or disagree with the following statements?

1. When I give something to another person, I generally expect something in return.
   _____ Agree _____ Disagree

2. When someone buys me a gift, I try to buy that person as comparable a gift as possible.
   _____ Agree _____ Disagree

3. When people receive benefits from others, they ought to repay those others right away.

_____ Agree _____ Disagree

4. It's best to make sure that things are always kept "even" between two people in a relationship.

_____ Agree _____ Disagree

Source: Mills & Clark, 1994, p. 36.

Agreement with the statements reflects a stronger exchange orientation—seeing interpersonal relationships as structured on the giving and receiving of favors.

Research findings indicate that those with a strong exchange orientation

- are motivated by a desire to have "fair" relationships.

- expect benefits given or received to be repaid immediately.

- monitor individual inputs into tasks for which there will be a joint reward.

- keep track of another person's needs only when they expect the person to have an opportunity in the near future to reciprocate in taking care of their own needs.

- show little change in mood or self-evaluation when they help another person.

This orientation seems to work well with strangers, casual acquaintances, and business partners. As friendships develop, however, we should be less concerned with instant repayment. True friends show a communal orientation—they respond to each others' needs without expecting immediate repayment.

People vary in the strength of their communal orientation. How about you? Consider the following.

SELF-ASSESSMENT ■

Communal Orientation Scale

Do you tend to agree or disagree with the following statements?

1. It bothers me when other people neglect my needs.

_____ Agree _____ Disagree

2. When making a decision, I take other people's needs and feelings into account.

_____ Agree _____ Disagree

3. When I have a need, I turn to others I know for help.
_____ Agree _____ Disagree

4. I often go out of my way to help another person.
_____ Agree _____ Disagree

Source: Mills & Clark 1994, p. 36.

Agreement with the statements reflects a tendency to watch out for others' welfare as well as the expectation that others will watch out for you.

Research indicates that those with a strong communal orientation

- are motivated by a desire to please others.

- dislike immediate repayment for favors.

- do not monitor individual contributions to a relationship.

- keep track of another person's needs even when that person is unlikely to have an opportunity in the near future to reciprocate.

- are more cheerful and show a heightened self-evaluation when they help another person.

"Friendship is based on what it gives, not what it gets. It is motivated by love, not debt, and is willing to sacrifice without seeing or expecting a return," explain John Maxwell and Dan Reiland (1999, p. 73). Friendship is a *communal* relationship in which partners are oriented toward each other's needs (Mills & Clark, 1994). Only when the benefits are voluntary, when partners freely give and receive, do we tend to view a relationship as true friendship or love. In fact, while tit-for-tat exchanges increase people's liking when the relationship is relatively formal, the same social economics decreases liking when two people seek true friendship (Clark & Mills, 1993).

Gender Differences in Friendship

Women show a stronger tendency than men to think of themselves in terms of their close relationships. They are more likely to define themselves in terms of their social connections rather than their independence. Indeed, when asked to provide photos that reflect who they are, women, more than men, include pictures of themselves with others.

Consider this fascinating dilemma: Suppose you had to spend the rest of your life on a small island with only one other human being. Further suppose that you couldn't choose the specific individual with whom you'd be sharing the island but that you could specify what this person's sex would be. What sex would your island-mate be?

The response of most men and women is "Female!" (Weber, 1994). Why?

Early in life, females more than males give priority to relationships (see Myers, 2000, for a review). Boys strive for independence. Girls embrace their interdependence. Although both sexes enjoy group activity, girls play in smaller groups involving more intimate sharing and less aggression. As teens, girls tend to spend more time with friends and less time alone than do boys. And in college, women more than men say it is very important to "help others who are in difficulty."

Humorist Dave Barry (1995) characterizes gender differences in friendship in the following account:

> It seems that some winters ago, Mark and Bob were sitting around a gas station with not much to do. If Mark and Bob had been women, they probably would have passed the time in some nonproductive matter, such as nurturing their friendship, exploring their innermost feelings or helping each other gain significant insights into the important relationships in their lives. But fortunately for humanity, Mark and Bob are not women. Mark and Bob are guys and what they did is invent snowplow hockey. (p. C4)

Putting the tongue-in-cheek value judgment of "productivity" aside, do you think Barry's portrayal of gender differences, at least in same-sex friendships, is accurate?

Several studies (for a review, see Brehm et al., 2002) suggest that women's friendships are more often characterized by *emotional sharing,* whereas men's friendships are more likely to revolve around *common activities.* In comparison to men, women

- demonstrate greater self-disclosure.
- show stronger social support, especially emotional support.
- are more likely to express feelings of love and affection.
- tend to have closer friendships.
- are more likely to talk about relationships and personal issues.
- are more likely to have "all-purpose" friendships covering many areas of experience (men are more likely to have different friends for different activities).

Researchers do not all agree on the size of gender differences. Some see them as pervasive, others as small and perhaps due to factors other than gender. Thus, the research continues. One research analysis (Wright, 1998) suggests that gender differences in *agency* (for example, activities) are relatively small whereas differences in *communion* (for example, intimacy, expressiveness, and self-disclosure) are larger.

People regard trust, honesty, and understanding as important features in their closest relationships. One popular definition of friendship regards intimacy and assistance as its core ingredients. Disclosing stressful events to a close friend can be liberating. Friends share a communal relationship in which they are mutually responsive to each other's needs. Research on gender differences suggests that male and female friendships may differ more in terms of affect than in terms of activity.

■

Forming Friendships

In his best-selling book *The Friendship Factor*, Alan Loy McGinnis (1979) explains the importance of friendship:

> In research at our clinic, my colleagues and I have discovered that friendship is the springboard to every other love. Friendships spill over onto the other important relationships of life. People with no friends usually have a diminished capacity for sustaining any kind of love. They tend to go through a succession of marriages, be estranged from various family members, and have trouble getting along at work. On the other hand, those who learn how to love their friends tend to make long and fulfilling marriages, get along well with the people at work, and enjoy their children. (p. 9)

However, making friends is not a high priority for many of us. "We take care of our health," noted Ralph Waldo Emerson, "we lay up money, we make our rooms tight, and our clothing sufficient; but who provides wisely that he shall not be wanting in the best property of all—friends?" The seventeenth-century French writer François de La Rochefoucauld agreed. "A true friend," he lamented, "is the most precious of possessions and the one we take least thought about acquiring."

Perhaps we think that friendship, unlike other strengths such as commitment, compassion, and self-control, "just happens." Those who enjoy close social connections are simply luckier than others. Or maybe we assume that the ability to form friendships is an inherent strength: "Others are extraverts but I'm an introvert—always have been, always will be."

However, friendship *can* be cultivated just as much as the other strengths. It's not a matter of suddenly becoming the life of the party. Rather, friendship involves the challenge of developing meaningful, intimate relationships with a few other people. "True happiness," suggested seventeenth-century playwright Ben Jonson, "consists not in the multitude of friends but in their worth and choice."

History provides some famous models. Both Abraham Lincoln and Benjamin Franklin were, at one time, dismal flops at forming close relationships. But they worked at it. After Mary Owens turned down his proposal, young Lincoln wrote, "I have now come to the conclusion never again to think of marrying, and for this reason—I can never be satisfied with anyone who would be blockhead enough to have me." Eventually, of course, he became a master at building relationships. Early on, Franklin was insufferable. "Ben," warned an old Quaker friend, "you are impossible. Your opinions have a slap in them for everyone who differs with you. Your friends find they enjoy themselves better when you are not around." Taking those harsh words to heart, Franklin worked at strengthening his social connections.

So how do we foster friendship? Both the wisdom of the ages and the advice of contemporary students of friendship, such as McGinnis (1979), help us. Guidelines for deepening relationships and for cultivating intimacy include the following.

1. **Assign priority to close relationships.** Friendship doesn't merely happen. It unfolds when we recognize its importance and commit our lives to it.

   Friendship is a basic source of happiness, and it is worth developing a lifestyle that allows time for close relationships. In making connections, look for a few people who interest you, begin to communicate care to them in small ways, and invest in their lives. Friendship often begins with a simple show of interest or word of encouragement. You make more friends in two months, observed popular author and speaker Dale Carnegie, by becoming more interested in other people than you can in two years by trying to get people interested in you. The secret to being interesting is to be interested (McGinnis, 1979).

   Once a relationship is established, make getting together with your friends a priority along with work, school, family, and recreation. If necessary, schedule a regular get-together such as a weekly lunch, a movie night, or a book club. If you are really pressed for time, combine what you must do with meeting each other. For example, you might exercise together, share a vacation, or jointly enroll in an evening class. With a schedule, friends won't fall by the wayside. Ritual, anthropologists remind us, is one of the most important ingredients in good relationships.

2. **Practice transparency.** Allow people to see what is in your heart. We form friendships with windows, not walls. Such honesty does not come easily. We long to be known, but also to remain hidden. When we are transparent, we risk rejection. However, only honesty promotes intimacy, a central feature of friendship.

   Like affection itself, self-disclosure tends to be reciprocated. If you take the initiative in revealing yourself to a friend, the friend is more likely to disclose secrets to you. There are, of course, important caveats. Intimacy does not occur instantaneously. It is a process, not an event. People who empty their hearts and let it all hang out in the first hour of acquaintance will surely be viewed as indiscreet and unstable. Rather, intimacy, observes David Myers (2002), "progresses like a dance: I reveal a little, you reveal a little—but not too much. You then reveal more, and I reciprocate" (p. 458).

Such disclosure pays an unexpected dividend, suggests McGinnis (1979). Expanding the familiar counsel "Know yourself," he writes, "Make yourself known, and you will then know yourself." By revealing ourselves to others, we come to know ourselves better.

3. **Learn to listen.** Listening is the other half of intimacy—the corollary to making oneself known. It's an important route to forming as well as strengthening friendship. "The road to the heart," observed Voltaire, "is the ear."

Our whole body conveys the intensity of our interest. In Western cultures, eye contact is one of the surest signs of a good listener. Looking others directly in the eye, allowing nothing to distract, conveys strong interest and is a powerful social magnet. Listening attentively pays the highest compliment.

Sympathetic listeners, adds McGinnis, dispense advice sparingly. Merely acknowledging another's statement is enough to complete the communication loop. Often troubled friends are not seeking advice. They simply want to unburden themselves and thank you for being there. Once they have expressed themselves, they often see their problem more clearly and are able to arrive at their own solution. Merely expressing gratitude that another trusted you enough to divulge a secret builds intimacy.

4. **Communicate warmth.** Dare to talk about your affection and express your admiration. "Many a friendship," observes English theologian Frederick Faber, "long, loyal, and self-sacrificing, rests on no thicker a foundation than a kind word."

Communicating affection does not come easily. Sometimes fear of sentimentality gets in the way. Other times we may be afraid that our warmth will not be reciprocated. Perhaps we even worry that we'll be ridiculed. The words "I care about you" may be especially difficult. A good alternative is to tell your friend you missed seeing him or that it means a lot to get together or that your friendship is a wonderful thing.

Be as liberal with praise as you are cautious with criticism. We have enormous ability to motivate people with our admiration. "The deepest principle in human nature," noted early psychologist William James, "is the craving to be appreciated." Some of the best ways to feed friendship include a heartfelt note or just calling to say how much you care.

The expression of admiration affects both the admirer and the recipient. In spite of our fears of rejection, liking is usually mutual. Experiments show that people who are told that certain others like or admire them usually feel a reciprocal affection (Berscheid & Walster, 1978). Emerson was right: "To have a friend one must be a friend."

Of course, it's not empty flattery that marks friendship. Rather, "The more we love our friends," argued playwright Jean-Baptiste Molière, "the less we flatter them; it is by excusing nothing that pure love shows itself." True friends are honest with each other, but even when they reveal foibles, it's against the backdrop of unconditional acceptance. There is tremendous relief in being known and still accepted. In telling the truth, friends spur us to growth. Most important, true friends bring out the best in us. They bring to light strengths that no one else looked hard enough to find.

5. **Create space in your friendships.** Intimacy is important, but it is equally important to recognize the role of freedom in friendship. "There can be no friendship," observed American statesman William Penn, "where there is no freedom." Lasting friendships combine the need to belong with the need for space.

Consider relationships you've had that never became friendships. Were the relationships you dropped with people who were controlling, manipulative, and/or judgmental? Here are some more painful questions (McGinnis, 1979): Do you have a tendency to want to control others? Do you usually go to the restaurant or movie you prefer? Do you enjoying correcting factual errors in other people's conversation? Do you use humor to put down friends? Do you have to know more about a topic than others to feel comfortable discussing it?

In true friendship, no one has the upper hand. Most important, in helping friends to realize their dreams, we will permit, even encourage, them to develop other relationships, and we will always leave room for solitude.

6. **Be loyal.** "Loyalty" and "devotion" are among the qualities we admire most in friends. They suffer alongside us even when many others find us insufferable.

In long-term relationships there will be times when friends are not functioning well. They give nothing to the friendship and test our staying power (McGinnis, 1979). Friendship is not founded on reciprocity but instead on genuine caring. Demanding a return on our investment can undermine the friendship. Perseverance keeps us connected through tough times.

Although we may imagine that the greatest strain comes when our friends are "down and troubled, and they need a helping hand," this may actually be one of the easier times (Langer, 2002). Listening to another's woes can make us feel superior. This makes it easy to find a sympathetic ear. It may actually be more challenging to maintain friendship in times of triumph.

In one study, research participants were asked to provide clues to help others complete a task (Langer, 2002). When described as a game, participants were more helpful to their friends than they were to strangers. However, when the task was presented as serious, participants were more helpful to strangers than they were to their friends.

Unfortunately, we can feel threatened by our friends' successes. English statesman Lord Chesterfield declared, "Most people enjoy the inferiority of their best friends." Think about it: Would you prefer that a stranger or a friend wins the lottery? Would the friend still need you? Would he or she still want you as a friend? Although it may be easy to say, "I'm happy for you," can we really listen to the details of another's success?

True friends are loyal in good times as well as bad. Friendship aims to transcend envy. "A real friend," concludes Langer, "can be happy for someone independent of his or her own life experiences . . . Sharing someone's happiness can be its own positive experience and enable us to enjoy and relive it together. Attention to this mutual, positive need will likely be noticed, and in the long run, better serve the friendship" (p. 74).

Finally, being loyal means never breaking confidence. Perhaps nothing shakes relationships more than learning that a friend has revealed a secret.

7. Follow the universal rules of friendship. Are there universal norms to follow in maintaining friendships? Adults in various countries indicated which of 43 possible friendship rules they would endorse (Argyle & Henderson, 1984). Interestingly, Japanese participants endorsed the fewest, participants from Britain and Hong Kong the most. Overall, the researchers found the following rules to be strongest:

1. Volunteer help in time of need.

2. Respect the friend's privacy.

3. Keep confidences.

4. Trust and confide in each other.

5. Stand up for the person in their absence.

6. Don't criticize each other in public.

7. Show emotional support.

8. Strive to make him/her happy while in each other's company.

9. Don't be jealous or critical of a friend's other relationships.

10. Be tolerant of each other's friends.

11. Share news of success with the other.

12. Don't nag.

13. Seek to repay debts and favors and compliments.

When people compare their current and former friendships, they remember following the rules of friendship less regularly in the latter than the former (Argyle & Henderson, 1984).

In pursuing close relationships, we quickly discover how fundamental friendship is to flourishing. As the people closest to us meet our basic needs for belonging, meaning, and self-worth, we probably echo Helen Keller's grateful lament, "With the death of every friend I love, a part of me has been buried, . . . but their contribution to my being of happiness, strength, and understanding remains to sustain me in my altered world."

IN REVIEW

The ability to form and maintain friendship may predict success in other interpersonal relationships. Like the other strengths, friendship can be cultivated. Assigning priority to close relationships, practicing transparency, and developing good listening skills are important first steps. Daring to express one's affection and admiration strengthens bonds. The road to friendship is paved with small kindnesses. True friends allow space for the development of other relationships as well as simple solitude. They are loyal in times of triumph as well as trial and follow what seem to be universal rules of friendship.

References

Adams, J. M., & Jones, W. H. (1997). The conceptualization of marital commitment: An integrative analysis. *Journal of Personality and Social Psychology, 72,* 1177–1196.

Albrecht, M. (2001, November). Advantage of a Harvard MBA. Retrieved October 22, 2003, from http://www.degreeinfo.com.

Allison, M. T., & Duncan, M. C. (1988). Women, work, and flow. In M. Csikszentmihalyi & I. Csikszentmihalyi (Eds.), *Optimal experience: Psychological studies of flow in consciousness* (pp. 118–137). New York: Cambridge University Press.

Andersen, S. M. (1998). *Service learning: A national strategy for youth development.* Position paper issued by the Task Force on Education Policy. Washington, DC: Institute for Communitarian Policy Studies, George Washington University.

Andrews, F. M., & Withey, S. B. (1976). *Social indicators of well-being: Americans' perception of life quality.* New York: Plenum.

Argyle, M., & Henderson, M. (1984). The rules of friendships. *Journal of Social and Personal Relationships, 1,* 211–237.

Aron, A., Aron, E. N., & Smollan, D. (1992). Inclusion of other in the Self Scale and the structure of interpersonal closeness. *Journal of Personality and Social Psychology, 63,* 596–612.

Aron, A., Norman, C. C., & Aron, E. N. (2001). Shared self-enhancing activities as a means of maintaining and enhancing close romantic relationships. In J. H. Harvey & A. Wenzel (Eds.), *Close romantic relationships: Maintenance and enhancement* (pp. 47–66). Mahwah, NJ: Erlbaum.

Aron, A., & Westbay, L. (1996). Dimensions of the prototype of love. *Journal of Personality and Social Psychology, 70,* 53–55.

Aronson, E., & Bridgeman, D. (1979). Jigsaw groups and the desegregated classroom: In pursuit of common goals. *Personality and Social Psychology Bulletin, 5,* 438–446.

Aspinwall, L. G., & Brunhart, S. M. (1996). Distinguishing optimism from denial: Optimistic beliefs predict attention to health threats. *Personality and Social Psychology Bulletin, 22,* 993–1003.

Aspinwall, L. G., & Taylor, S. E. (1992). Modeling cognitive adaptation: A longitudinal investigation of the impact of individual differences and coping on college adjustment and performance. *Journal of Personality and Social Psychology, 63,* 989–1003.

Baltes, P. B., Gluck, J., & Kunzmann, U. M. (2002). Wisdom: Its structure and function in regulating successful life span development. In C. R. Snyder & S. J. Lopez (Eds.), *Handbook of positive psychology* (pp. 327–347). New York: Oxford University Press.

Baltes, P. B., & Smith, J. (1990). The psychology of wisdom and its ontogenesis. In R. J. Sternberg (Ed.), *Wisdom: Its nature, origins, and development* (pp. 87–120). New York: Cambridge University Press.

Baltes, P. B., & Staudinger, U. M. (2000). Wisdom: A metaheuristic (pragmatic) to orchestrate mind and virtue toward excellence. *American Psychologist, 55,* 122–135.

Barry, D. (1995, January 9). Hockey like you've never seen. *Winnipeg Free Press,* p. C4.

Batson, C. D. (1991). *The altruism question: Toward a social-psychological answer.* Hillsdale, NJ: Erlbaum.

Batson, C. D. (2002). Empathy and altruism. In C. R. Snyder & S. J. Lopez (Eds.), *Handbook of positive psychology* (pp. 485–498). New York: Oxford University Press.

Batson, C. D., Duncan, B. D., Ackerman, P., Buckley, T., & Birch, K. (1981). Is empathic emotion a source of altruistic motivation? *Journal of Personality and Social Psychology, 40,* 290–302.

Baumeister, R. F. (1996). Should schools try to boost self-esteem? Beware the dark side. *American Educator, 20,* 14–19, 43.

Baumeister, R. F. (1998). The self. In D. T. Gilbert, S. T. Fiske, & G. Lindzey (Eds.), *The handbook of social psychology* (Vol. 1, 4th ed., pp. 680–740). New York: McGraw-Hill.

Baumeister, R. F. (1999). The nature and structure of the self: An overview. In R. F. Baumeister (Ed.), *The self in social psychology* (pp. 1–20). Philadelphia: Psychology Press.

Baumeister, R. F. (2002, August). *Psychology of evil and violence.* Paper presented at the 110th Annual Convention of the American Psychological Association, Chicago, IL.

Baumeister, R. F., Campbell, J. D., Krueger, J. I., & Vohs, K. D. (2003). Does high self-esteem cause better performance, interpersonal success, happiness, or healthier lifestyles? *Psychological Science in the Public Interest, 4,* 1–44.

Baumeister, R. F., & Exline, J. J. (1999). Virtue, personality, and social relations: Self-control as the moral muscle. *Journal of Personality, 67,* 1165-1194.

Baumeister, R. F., Heatherton, T. F., & Tice, D. M. (1994). *Losing control: How and why people fail at self-regulation.* San Diego, CA: Academic Press.

Baumeister, R. F., & Ilko, S. A. (1995). Shallow gratitude: Public and private acknowledgement of external help in accounts of success. *Basic and Applied Social Psychology, 16,* 191–209.

Baumeister, R. F., Smart, L., & Boden, J. M. (1996). Relation of threatened egotism to violence and aggression: The dark side of high self-esteem. *Psychological Review, 103,* 5–33.

Baumeister, R. F., Tice, D. M., & Hutton, D. G. (1989). Self-presentational motivations and personality differences in self-esteem. *Journal of Personality, 57,* 547–579.

Beaton, R. (2001, January 15). Youth a real-life version of "The Natural." *USA Today,* pp. 1A–2A.

Berg, M. B., Janoff-Bulman, R., & Cotter, J. (2001). Perceiving value in obligations and goals: Wanting to do what should be done. *Personality and Social Psychology Bulletin, 27,* 982–995.

Berry, J. W., Worthington, E. L., Jr., Parrott, L., III, O'Connor L. E., & Wade, N. G. (2001). Dispositional forgiveness: Development and construct validity of the Transgression Narrative Test of Forgivingness (TNTF). *Personality and Social Psychology Bulletin, 27,* 1277–1290,

Berscheid, E. (2003). The human's greatest strength: Other humans. In L. A. Aspinwall & U. M. Staudinger (Eds.), *A psychology of human strengths: Fundamental questions and future directions for a positive psychology* (pp. 37–48). Washington DC: American Psychological Association.

Berscheid, E., & Meyers, S. A. (1996). A social categorical approach to a question about love. *Personal Relationships 3,* 19–43.

Berscheid, E., & Walster, E. H. (1978). *Interpersonal attraction* (2nd ed.). Reading, MA: Addison-Wesley.

Bettelheim, B. (1960). *The informed heart.* New York: Free Press.

Black, A. L., & McCafferty, D. (1998, July 3–5). The age of contentment. *USA Weekend,* pp. 4–6.

Blanchard, F. A., & Cook, S. W. (1976). Effects of helping a less competent member of a cooperating interracial group on the development of interpersonal attraction. *Journal of Personality and Social Psychology, 34,* 1245–1255.

Block, J. R., & Yuker, H. (1989). *Can you believe your eyes?* New York: Gardner Press.

Blum, D. (2002). *Love at Goon Park: Harry Harlow and the science of affection.* Cambridge, MA: Perseus.

Bolt, R. (1960). *A man for all seasons: A play in two acts.* New York: Random House.

Borba, M. (2001). *Building moral intelligence: The seven essential virtues that teach kids to do the right thing.* San Francisco: Jossey-Bass.

Bowlby, J. (1988). *A secure base: Parent-child attachment and healthy human development.* New York: Basic Books.

Breathnach, S. B. (1995). *Simple abundance: A daybook of comfort and joy.* New York: Warner Books.

Brehm, S. S., Miller, R. S., Perlman, D., & Campbell, S. M. (2002). *Intimate relations* (3rd ed.). New York: McGraw-Hill.

Brehony, K. A. (1999). *Ordinary grace: An examination of the roots of compassion, altruism, and empathy, and the ordinary individuals who help others in extraordinary ways.* New York: Penguin.

Breslau, N., Peterson, E., Schultz, L., Andreski, P., & Chilcoat, H. (1996). Are smokers with alcohol disorders less likely to quit? *American Journal of Public Health, 86,* 985–990.

Brickman, P. (1987). *Commitment, conflict, and caring.* Englewood Cliffs, NJ: Prentice Hall.

Brown, J. D. (1998). *The self.* New York: McGraw-Hill.

Brown, K. W., & Ryan, R. M. (2003). The benefits of being present: Mindfulness and its role in psychological well-being. *Journal of Personality and Social Psychology, 84,* 822–848.

Brown, S. L., Nesse, R. M., Vinokur, A. D., & Smith, D. M. (2003). Providing social support may be more beneficial than receiving it: Results from a prospective study of mortality. *Psychological Science, 14,* 320–327.

Bryant, F. (1989) A four-factor model of perceived control: Avoiding, coping, obtaining, and savoring. *Journal of Personality, 57,* 773–797.

Burger, J. M. (2004). *Personality* (6th ed.). Belmont, CA: Wadsworth/Thomson.

Burger, J. M., & Burns, L. (1988). The illusion of unique invulnerability and the use of effective contraception. *Personality and Social Psychology Bulletin, 14,* 264–270.

Buss, D. M. (1989). Sex differences in human mate preferences: Evolutionary hypotheses tested in 37 cultures. *Behavioral and Brain Sciences, 12,* 1–49

California Task Force to Promote Self-Esteem and Personal and Social Responsibility (1990). *Toward a state of self-esteem.* Sacramento, CA: California State Department of Education.

Campbell, A. (1981). *The sense of well-being in America.* New York: McGraw-Hill.

Campbell, J. D., & Lavallee, L. F. (1993). Who am I? The role of self-concept confusion in understanding the behavior of people with low self-esteem. In R. F. Baumeister (Ed.), *Self-esteem: The puzzle of low self-regard* (pp. 3–20). New York: Plenum.

Carvajal, S. C., Clair, S. D., Nash, S. G., & Evans, R. I. (1998). Relating optimism, hope, and self-esteem to social influences in deterring substance use in adolescents. *Journal of Social and Clinical Psychology, 17,* 443–465.

Carver, C. S., & Gaines, J. G. (1987). Optimism, pessimism, and postpartum depression. *Cognitive Therapy and Research, 11,* 449–462.

Carver, C. S., Pozo, C., Harris, S. D., Noriega, V., Scheier, M. F., Robinson, D. S., et al. (1993). How coping mediates the effect of optimism on distress: A study of women with early-stage breast cancer. *Journal of Personality and Social Psychology, 65,* 375–390.

Carver, C. S., & Scheier, M. F. (1981). *Attention and self-regulation: A control theory approach to human behavior.* New York: Springer-Verlag.

Carver, C. S., & Scheier, M. F. (1999). Optimism. In C. R. Snyder (Ed.), *Coping: The psychology of what works* (pp. 182–204). New York: Oxford University Press.

Cialdini, R. B. (2001). *Influence: Science and practice* (4th ed.). Boston: Allyn and Bacon.

Clark, M. S., & Mills, J. (1993). The difference between communal and exchange relationships: What it is and is not. *Personality and Social Psychology Bulletin, 19,* 684–691.

Coats, E. J., Janoff-Bulman, R., & Alpert, N. (1996). Approach versus avoidance goals: Differences in self-evaluation and well-being. *Personality and Social Psychology Bulletin, 22,* 1057–1067.

Collins, J. (2001). *Good to great: Why some companies make the leap . . . and others don't.* New York: Harper-Collins.

Crocker, J., Luhtanen, R., & Bouvrette, S. (2001). Contingencies of self-worth in college students: Predicting freshman year activities. Unpublished manuscript, University of Michigan, Ann Arbor.

Crocker, J., Luhtanen, R., Cooper, M. L., & Bouvrette, S. (2003). Contingencies of self-worth in college students: Theory and measurement. *Journal of Personality and Social Psychology, 85,* 894–908.

Crocker, J., & Wolfe, C. T. (2001). Contingencies of self-worth. *Psychological Review, 108,* 593–623.

Csikszentmihalyi, M. (1990). *Flow: The psychology of optimal experience.* New York: Harper and Row.

Csikszentmihalyi, M. (1997). *Finding flow.* New York: Basic Books.

Csikszentmihalyi, M. (1999). If we are so rich, why aren't we happy? *American Psychologist, 54,* 821–827.

Csikszentmihalyi, M. (2003). *Good business: Leadership, flow, and the making of meaning.* New York: Viking.

Csikszentmihalyi, M., Rathunde, K., & Whalen, S. (1993). *Talented teenagers: The roots of success and failure.* New York: Cambridge University Press.

Cytowic, R. E. (1993). *The man who tasted shapes.* New York: Plenum.

Daloz, L. A., Keen, C. H., Keen, J. P. & Parks, S. D. (1997). *Common fire: Lives of commitment in a complex world.* New York: Beacon Press.

Danner, D. D., & Snowdon, D. A. (2001). Positive emotions in early life and longevity: Findings from the Nun Study. *Journal of Personality and Social Psychology, 80,* 804–873.

Davis, M. H. (1980) A multidimensional approach to individual differences in empathy. *Catalog of Selected Documents in Psychology, 10,* 85.

Deci, E. L. (1995). *Why we do what we do: The dynamics of personal autonomy.* New York: Putnam.

Deci, E. L., Eghrari, H., Patrick, B. C., & Leone, D. R. (1994). Facilitating internalization: The self-determination theory perspective. *Journal of Personality, 62,* 119–142.

Deci, E. L., & Ryan, R. M. (1995). Human autonomy: The basis for true self-esteem. In M. H. Kemis (Ed.), *Efficacy, agency, and self-esteem* (pp. 31–49). New York: Plenum.

DeNeve, K. M. (1999). Happy as an extraverted clam? The role of personality for subjective well-being. *Current Directions in Psychological Science, 8,* 141–144.

DeNeve, K. M., & Cooper, H. (1998). The happy personality: A meta-analysis of 137 personality traits and subjective well-being. *Psychological Bulletin, 124,* 197–229.

Dermer, M., Cohen, S. J., Jacobsen, E., & Anderson, E. A. (1979). Evaluative judgments of aspects of life as a function of vicarious exposure to hedonic extremes. *Journal of Personality and Social Psychology, 37,* 247–260.

Diener, E. (2000). Subjective well-being: The science of happiness and a proposal for a national index. *American Psychologist, 55,* 34-43.

Diener, E. (2001, February). *Subjective well-being.* Address presented at the annual meeting of the Society for Personality and Social Psychology, San Antonio, TX.

Diener, E., Emmons, R. A., Larsen, R. J., & Griffen, S. (1985a). The Satisfaction with Life Scale. *Journal of Personality Assessment, 49,* 71–75.

Diener, E., Horwitz, J., & Emmons, R. A. (1985b). Happiness of the very wealthy. *Social Indicators, 16,* 263–274.

Diener, E., & Seligman, M. E. P. (2002). Very happy people. *Psychological Science, 13,* 81–84.

Dittes, J. E. (1959). Justification by faith and the experimental psychologist. *Religion in Life, 28,* 567–576.

Drigotas, S. M. (2002). The Michelangelo phenomenon and personal well-being. *Journal of Personality, 70,* 58–77.

Duck, S. (1983). *Friends, for life: The psychology of close relationships.* New York: St. Martin's Press.

Dutton, D. G., & Aron, A. P. (1974). Some evidence for heightened sexual attraction under conditions of high anxiety. *Journal of Personality and Social Psychology, 30,* 510–517.

Dweck, C. S. (1999). *Self-theories: Their role in motivation, personality and development.* Philadelphia: Psychology Press.

Dweck, C. S. (2002). Beliefs that make smart people dumb. In R. J. Sternberg (Ed.), *Why smart people can be so stupid* (pp. 24–41). New Haven, CT: Yale University Press.

Elias, M. (2002, November 11). A generous spirit may yield generous life span. *USA Today,* p. 4A.

Elias, M. (2002, December 9). Ask "Dr. Happiness." *USA Today,* p. 11D.

Elliot, A. J., & Sheldon, K. M. (1998). Avoidance, personal goals, and the personality-illness relationship. *Journal of Personality and Social Psychology, 75,* 1282–1299.

Elliot, A. J., Sheldon, K. M., & Church, M. (1997). Avoidance, personal goals, and subjective well-being. *Personality and Social Psychology Bulletin, 23,* 915–927.

Ellis, A. (1989). Rational-emotive therapy. In R. J. Corsini (Ed.), *Current psychotherapies* (4th ed.). Itasca, IL: Peacock.

Emmons, R. A. (1999). *The psychology of ultimate concerns.* New York: Guilford.

Emmons, R. A., & Kaiser, H. (1996). Goal orientation and emotional well-being: Linking goals and affect through the self. In A. Tesser & L. Martin (Eds.), *Striving and feeling: Interactions among goals, affect, and self-regulation* (pp. 79–98). New York: Plenum.

Emmons, R. A., & McCullough, M. E. (2003). Counting blessings versus burdens: An experimental investigation of gratitude and subjective well-being in daily life. *Journal of Personality and Social Psychology, 84,* 377–389.

Enright, R. D. (2001). *Forgiveness is a choice: A step-by-step process for resolving anger and restoring hope.* Washington, DC: American Psychological Association.

Epstein, R. (2002, June). Editor as guinea pig. *Psychology Today,* p. 5.

Erikson, E. (1963). *Childhood and society.* New York: Norton.

Exline, J. J., Campbell, W. K., Baumeister, R. F., Joiner, T. E., & Krueger, J. I. (in press). Humility and modesty. In C. Peterson & M. E. P. Seligman (Eds.), *The values in action classification of strengths.* Washington, DC: American Psychological Association.

Exline, J. J., & Geyer, A. L. (in press). Perceptions of humility: A preliminary study. *Self and Identity.*

Fehr, B. (1988). Prototype analysis of the concepts of love and commitment. *Journal of Personality and Social Psychology, 55,* 557–579.

Fehr, B. (1996). *Friendship processes.* Thousand Oaks, CA: Sage.

Fitzgerald, T. E., Tennen, H., Affleck, G., & Pransky, G. S. (1993). The relative importance of dispositional optimism and control appraisals in quality of life after coronary artery bypass surgery. *Journal of Behavioral Medicine, 16,* 25–43.

Fordyce, M. W. (1977). Development of a program to increase personal happiness. *Journal of Counseling Psychology, 24,* 511–521.

Frantz, S. (2003, June 5). Rap essay. Message posted to http://www.frostburg.edu/dept/psyc/southerly/tips.

Frederickson, B. L. (2001). The role of positive emotions in positive psychology: The broaden-and-build theory of positive emotions. *American Psychologist, 56,* 218–226.

Freedman, J. (1978). *Happy people.* New York: Harcourt, Brace, Jovanovich.

Freedman, J. S. (1965). Long-term behavioral effects of cognitive dissonance. *Journal of Experimental Social Psychology, 1,* 145–155.

Friedrich, J. (1996). On seeing oneself as less self-serving than others: The ultimate self-serving bias? *Teaching of Psychology, 23,* 107–109.

Gallup, G. H., Jr. (1998). *Thankfulness: America's saving grace.* Paper presented at the National Day of Prayer Breakfast, Thanks-Giving Square, Dallas, TX.

Gibbons, F. X., Eggleston, T. J., & Benthin, A. C. (1997). Cognitive reactions to smoking relapse: The reciprocal relation between dissonance and self-esteem. *Journal of Personality and Social Psychology, 72,* 184–195.

Gilbert, D. T., & Ebert, J. E. J. (2002). Decisions and revisions: The affective forecasting of changeable outcomes. *Journal of Personality and Social Psychology, 82,* 503–514.

Given, C. W., Stommel, M., Given, B., Osuch, J., Kurtz, M. E., & Kurtz, J. C. (1993). The influence of cancer patients' symptoms and functional states on patients' depression and family caregivers' reaction and depression. *Health Psychology, 12,* 277–285.

Glass, J. (2001, June–July). Nurturing empathy. *Parenting,* p. 72

Goldman, J. L., & Sparks, A. N. (Eds.). (1996). Webster's new world student's dictionary (Rev. ed.). Cleveland, OH: Wiley.

Goleman, D. (1995). *Emotional intelligence.* New York: Bantam Books.

Goleman, D. (1998). *Working with emotional intelligence.* New York: Bantam Books.

Goleman, D. (2002, June 16). Could you be a leader? *Parade Magazine,* pp. 4–5.

Gollwitzer, P. M. (1999). Implementation intentions. *American Psychologist, 54,* 493–503.

Gollwitzer, P. M., & Brandstätter, V. (1997). Implementation intentions and effective goal pursuit. *Journal of Personality and Social Psychology, 73,* 186–199.

Gottfredson, M. R., & Hirschi, T. (1990). *A general theory of crime.* Stanford, CA: Stanford University Press.

Gottman, J. (1994). *Why marriages succeed or fail.* New York: Fireside.

Gottman, J., & Silver, N. (1999). *The seven principles for making marriage work.* New York: Three Rivers.

Greenwald, A. G., Carnot, C. G., Beach, R., & Young, B. (1987). Increasing voting behavior by asking people if they expect to vote. *Journal of Applied Psychology, 72,* 315–318.

Hamilton, T. F. (2001, December 2). The right stuff. *Grand Rapids Press,* p. J1.

Harter, J. K., Schmidt, F. L., & Keyes, C. L. M. (2003). Well-being in the workplace and its relationship to business outcomes: A review of the Gallup studies. In C. L. M. Keyes & J. Haidt (Eds.), *Flourishing: Positive psychology and the life well-lived* (pp. 205–224). Washington, DC: American Psychological Association.

Harter, S. (2002). Authenticity. In C. R. Snyder & S. J. Lopez (Eds.), *Handbook of positive psychology* (pp. 382–394). New York: Oxford University Press.

Hartup, W. W., & Stevens, N. (1997). Friendships and adaptation in the life course. *Psychological Bulletin, 121,* 355–370

Harvey, J. H., & Omarzu, J. (1997). Minding the close relationship. *Personality and Social Psychology Review, 1,* 223–239.

Harvey, J. H., & Omarzu, J. (1999). *Minding the close relationship: A theory of relationship enhancement.* New York: Cambridge University Press.

Hashtroudian, J. (2003). Teaching stories: The Mullah Narudin. Retrieved November 3, 2003, from http://www.lifefocuscenter.com/teach.htm.

Hatfield, E. (1988). Passionate and companionate love. In R. J. Sternberg & M. L. Barnes (Eds.), *The psychology of love* (pp. 191–217). New Haven, CT: Yale University Press.

Hazan, C., & Shaver, P. (1986). *Parental caregiving style questionnaire.* Unpublished manuscript.

Hazan, C., & Shaver, P. (1990). Love and work: An attachment-theoretical perspective. *Journal of Personality and Social Psychology, 59,* 270–280.

Hazan, C., & Shaver, P. (1994). Attachment as an organizational framework for research on close relationships. *Psychological Inquiry, 5,* 1–22,

Heider, F. (1958). *The psychology of interpersonal relations.* New York: Wiley.

Heilman, M. (1976). Oppositional behavior as a function of influence attempt intensity and retaliation threat. *Journal of Personality and Social Psychology, 33,* 574–578.

Heine, S. J., Lehman, D. R., Markus, H. R., & Kitiyama, S. (1999). Is there a universal need for positive self-regard? *Psychological Review, 106,* 766–795.

Herzog, A. R., Franks, X., Markus, H. R., & Holmberg, X. (1995). *The American self in its sociocultural variations.* Unpublished manuscript.

Hill, T., Smith, N. D., & Lewicki, P. (1989). The development of self-image bias: A real-world demonstration. *Personality and Social Psychology Bulletin, 15,* 205–211.

Hodges, B. H. (2000). Remapping psychology: A new look at values in scientific ontology. *Christian Scholar's Review, 29,* 471–497.

Holahan, C., & Moos, R. (1987). Personal and contextual determinants of coping strategies. *Journal of Personality and Social Psychology, 52,* 946–955.

Inglehart, R. (1990). *Culture shift in advanced industrial society.* Princeton, NJ: Princeton University Press.

Insel, P. M., & Roth, W. T. (2002). *Core concepts in health* (9th ed.). New York: McGraw-Hill.

Isaacson, W. (2003, July 7). Citizen Ben's 7 great virtues. *Time,* pp. 40–53.

Jackson, S. A., & Marsh, H. W. (1996). Development and validation of a scale to measure optimal experience: The flow state scale. *Journal of Sport and Exercise Psychology, 18,* 17–35.

Japenga, A. (1995, November/December). A family of friends. *Health,* p. 94.

Jourard, S. M. (1964). *The transparent self.* Princeton, NJ: Van Nostrand.

Jurors prefer lawyers who are well-prepared—and not arrogant (1993, February 22). *National Law Journal, 15,* 10.

Kasser, T., & Ryan, R. M. (1993). A dark side of the American dream: Correlates of financial success as a central life aspiration. *Journal of Personality and Social Psychology, 65,* 410–422.

Kasser, T., & Ryan, R. M. (1996). Further examining the American dream: Differential correlates of intrinsic and extrinsic goals. *Personality and Social Psychology Bulletin, 22,* 280–286.

Katz, J., & Joiner, T. E. (2002). Being known, intimate, and valued: Global self-verification and dyadic adjustment in couples and roommates. *Journal of Personality, 70,* 33–58.

Keltner, D., & Haidt, J. (2003). Approaching awe, a moral, spiritual, and aesthetic emotion. *Cognition and Emotion, 17,* 297–314.

Kenrick, D. T., Neuberg, S. L., & Cialdini, R. B. (2002). *Social psychology: Unraveling the mystery* (2nd ed.). Boston: Allyn and Bacon.

Kim, Y., Butzel, J. S., & Ryan, R. M. (1998, June). *Interdependence and well-being: A function of culture and relatedness needs.* Paper presented at the annual meeting of the International Society for the Study of Personal Relationships, Saratoga Springs, NY.

King, L. A., & Emmons, R. A. (1991). Psychological, physical, and interpersonal correlates of emotional expressiveness, conflict, and control. *European Journal of Personality, 5,* 131–150.

Kohn, A. (1990). *The brighter side of human nature.* New York: Basic Books.

Kotler, T. (1985). Security and autonomy within marriage. *Human Relations, 38,* 299–321.

Kramer, D. A. (2000). Wisdom as a classical source of human strength: Conceptualization and empirical inquiry. *Journal of Social and Clinical Psychology, 19,* 83–101.

Landers, A. (1990, March 14). Ann Answers. *Detroit Free Press,* p. 2C.

Langer, E. J. (1977). The psychology of chance. *Journal for the Theory of Social Behavior, 7,* 185–208.

Langer, E. J. (2002, July/August). I'll be there. *Psychology Today,* p. 74.

Larson, D. G., & Chastain, R. L. (1990). Self-concealment: Conceptualization, measurement, and health implications. *Journal of Social and Clinical Psychology, 9,* 439–455.

Larson, R. (2000). Toward a psychology of positive youth development. *American Psychologist, 55,* 170–183.

Larsen, R. J., & Buss, D. M. (2002). *Personality psychology: Domains of knowledge about human nature.* New York: McGraw-Hill.

Larsen, R. J., & Ketelaar, T. (1991). Personality and susceptibility to positive and negative emotional states. *Journal of Personality and Social Psychology, 61,* 132–140.

Larson, R. W., & Bradney, N. (1988). Precious moments with family members and friends. In R. M. Milardo (Ed.), *Families and social networks* (pp. 107–126). Newbury Park, CA: Sage.

Lerner, M. J. (1980). *The belief in a just world.* New York: Plenum.

Levenson, H. (1981). Differentiating among internality, powerful others, and chance. In H. M. Lefcourt (Ed.), *Research with the locus of control construct* (Vol. 1, pp. 1–63). New York: Academic Press.

Levy, B. R., Slade, M. D., Kunkel, S. R., & Kasl, S. V. (2002). Longevity increased by positive self-perceptions of aging. *Journal of Personality and Social Psychology, 83,* 261–270.

Lewis, C. S. (1949). *The weight of glory and other addresses.* New York: Macmillan.

Lewis, C. S. (1960). *Mere Christianity.* New York: Macmillan.

Logue, A. W. (1995). *Self-control: Waiting until tomorrow for what you want today.* Englewood Cliffs, NJ: Prentice Hall.

Lombardo, M. M., Ruderman, M. N., & McCauley, C. D. (1988). Explanations of success and derailment in upper-level management positions. *Journal of Business and Psychology, 2,* 199–216.

Lykken, D. (1999). *Happiness: The nature and nurture of joy and contentment.* New York: St. Martin's Press.

Lyubomirsky, S. (2001). Why are some people happier than others? *American Psychologist, 56,* 239–249.

Markus, H. R., & Kitayama, S. (1998). The cultural psychology of personality. *Journal of Cross-Cultural Psychology, 29,* 63–87.

Martin, A. J., & Debus, R. L. (1999). Alternative factor structure for the Revised Self-Consciousness Scale. *Journal of Personality Assessment, 72,* 266–282.

Maruta, T., Colligan, R.C., Malinchoc, M., & Offord, K. P. (2000). Optimism versus pessimism: Survival rate among medical patients over a 30-year period. *Mayo Clinic Proceedings, 75,* 140-143.

Marvin, N. (Producer), & Darabont, F. (Director). (1994). *The Shawshank redemption* [Motion picture]. United States: Warner Bros.

Maslow, B. G. (1972). *Abraham H. Maslow: A memorial volume.* Monterey, CA: Brooks/Cole.

Maxwell, J. C., & Reiland, D. (1999). *The treasure of a friend.* Nashville, TN: Nelson.

McCrae, R. R., & Costa, P. T. (1990). *Personality in adulthood.* New York: Guilford.

McCullough, M. E. (2001). Forgiving. In C. R. Snyder (Ed.), *Coping with stress: Effective people and processes* (pp. 93–113). New York: Oxford University Press.

McCullough, M. E., Emmons, R. A., Tsang, J. (2002). The grateful disposition: A conceptual and empirical topography. *Journal of Personality and Social Psychology, 82,* 112–127.

McCullough, M. E., Pargament, K. I., & Thoresen, C. T. (2000). The psychology of forgiveness: History, conceptual issues, and overview. In M. E. McCullough, K. I. Pargament, & C. E. Thoresen (Eds.), *Forgiveness: Theory, research, and practice* (pp. 1–14). New York: Guilford.

McDermott, C., & Snyder, C. R. (1999). *Making hope happen: A workbook for turning possibilities into reality.* Oakland, CA: New Harbinger.

McGinnis, A. L. (1979). *The friendship factor.* Minneapolis, MN: Augsburg.

McQuaid, C. (Ed.). *Gambler's digest.* Chicago: Digest Books, 1971.

Metcalfe, J., & Mischel, W. (1999). A hot/cool system analysis of delay of gratification: Dynamics of willpower. *Psychological Review, 106,* 3–19.

Middlebrook, P. N. (1974). *Social psychology and life.* New York: Knopf.

Miller, L. C., Berg, J. H., & Archer, R. L. (1983). Openers: Individuals who elicit intimate self-disclosure. *Journal of Personality and Social Psychology, 44,* 1234–1244.

Miller, T. (1995). *How to want what you have.* New York: Henry Holt.

Mills, J., & Clark, M. S. (1994). Communal and exchange relationships: Controversies and research. In R. Erber & R. Gilmour (Eds.), *Theoretical frameworks for personal relationships* (pp. 29–42). Hillsdale, NJ: Erlbaum.

Mischel, W. (1974). Processes in delay of gratification. In L. Berkowitz (Ed.), *Advances in experimental social psychology* (Vol. 7, pp. 249–292). New York: Academic Press.

Mischel, W., Ebbesen, E. B., & Zeiss, A. R. (1972). Cognitive and attentional mechanisms in delay of gratification. *Journal of Personality and Social Psychology, 21*, 204–218.

Monks of New Skete. (1999). *In the spirit of happiness*. Boston: Little, Brown.

Morris, H. J. (2001, September 3). New science shows how to inject real joy into your life. *U.S. News and World Report*, pp. 46–54.

Mother Teresa. (1995). *A simple path*. New York: Ballantine Books.

Mueller, C. M., & Dweck, C. S. (1997). *Implicit theories of intelligence: Malleability beliefs, definitions, and judgments of intelligence.* Unpublished manuscript.

Muraven, M. (1998). *Mechanisms of self-control failure: Motivation and limited resources.* Doctoral dissertation, Case Western Reserve University, Cleveland, OH.

Muraven, M., & Baumeister, R. F. (2000). Self-regulation and depletion of limited resources: Does self-control resemble a muscle? *Psychological Bulletin, 126*, 247–259.

Muraven, M., Baumeister, R. F., & Tice, D. M. (1999). Longitudinal improvement of self-regulation through practice: Building self-control strength through repeated exercise. *Journal of Social Psychology, 139*, 446–457.

Muraven, M., Tice, D. M., & Baumeister, R. F. (1998). Self-control as a limited resource: Regulatory depletion patterns. *Journal of Personality and Social Psychology, 74*, 774–789.

Myers, D. G. (1992). *The pursuit of happiness: Who is happy—and why.* New York: William Morrow.

Myers, D. G. (2000). *The American paradox: Spiritual hunger in an age of plenty.* New Haven: Yale University Press.

Myers, D. G. (2000). The funds, friends, and faith of happy people. *American Psychologist, 55*, 56–67.

Myers, D. G. (2001). *Psychology* (6th ed.). New York: Worth.

Myers, D. G. (2002). *Social psychology* (7th ed.). New York: McGraw-Hill.

Myers, D. G. (2004). *Psychology* (7th ed.). New York: Worth.

National Wellness Institute. (1992). *Making wellness work for you.* Stevens Point, WI: National Wellness Institute.

Neff, K. (2003). Self-compassion: An alternative conceptualization of a healthy attitude toward oneself. *Self and Identity, 2*, 85–101.

Niven, D. (2001). *The 100 simple secrets of happy people.* San Francisco: HarperCollins.

Notarius, C., & Markman, H. (1993). *We can work it out: Making sense of marital conflict.* New York: Putnam.

Oliner, P., & Oliner, S. (1988). *The altruistic personality: Rescuers of Jews in Nazi Europe.* New York: Free Press.

Omarzu, J., Whalen, J., & Harvey, J. H. (2001). How well do you mind your relationship? A preliminary scale to test the minding theory of relating. In J. H. Harvey & A. Wenzel (Eds.), *Close romantic relationships: Maintenance and enhancement* (pp. 345–356). Mahwah, NJ: Erlbaum.

Palant, J. F. (2000). Development and validation of a scale to measure perceived control of internal states. *Journal of Personality Assessment, 75*, 308–337.

Parke, R. D. (1974). Rules, roles, and resistance to deviation: Recent advances in punishment, discipline, and self-control. In A. Pick (Ed.), *Minnesota symposia of child psychology, Vol. 8* (pp. 111–143). Minneapolis, MN: University of Minnesota Press.

Paulhus, D. (1983). Sphere-specific measures of perceived control. *Journal of Personality and Social Psychology, 44*, 1253–1265.

Paulus, D. L., Wehr, P., Harms, P. D., & Strasser, D. I. (2002). Use of exemplar surveys to reveal implicit types of intelligence. *Personality and Social Psychology Bulletin, 28*, 1051–1062.

Peale, N. V. (1982). *Positive imaging: The powerful way to change your life.* New York: Fawcett Crest.

Peele, S. (1989). *The diseasing of America.* Boston: Houghton Mifflin.

Pennebaker, J. W. (1985). Traumatic experience and psychosomatic disease: Exploring the roles of behavioral inhibition, obsession, and confiding. *Canadian Psychology, 26*, 82–95.

Peterson, C., & Bossio, L. M. (2001). Optimism and physical well-being. In E. C. Chang (Ed.), *Optimism* and pessimism: Implications for theory, research, and practice* (pp. 127–145). Washington, DC: American Psychological Association.

Peterson, C., & Seligman, M. E. P. (in press). *The values in action classification of strengths*. Washington, DC: American Psychological Association.

Peterson, C., Seligman, M. E. P., Yurko, K. H., Martin, L. R., & Friedman, H. S. (1998). Catastrophizing and untimely death. *Psychological Science, 9*, 49–52.

Peterson, K. S. (1992, December). Guiding kids with a curriculum of compassion. *USA Today*, p. 10D.

Peterson, K. S. (2003, June 26). Falling in love by design. *USA Today*, p. 8D.

Pham, L. B., & Taylor, S. E. (1997). *The effects of mental stimulation on exam performance*. Unpublished manuscript.

Piechowski, M. M., & Tyska, C. (1982). Self-actualization profile of Eleanor Roosevelt—A presumed nontranscender. *Genetic Psychology Monographs, 105*, 95–153.

Pinker, S. (2002). *The blank slate: The modern denial of human nature*. New York: Penguin.

Plantinga, N. (1987, October 19). Christian compassion: Obstacles. *The Banner*, p. 17.

Pliner, P., Hart, H., Kohl, J., & Saari, D. (1974). Compliance without pressure: Some further data on the foot-in-the-door technique. *Journal of Experimental Social Psychology, 10*, 17–22.

Putnam, R. (2000). *Bowling alone*. New York: Simon & Schuster.

Reed, R. W. (2000). Toward a psychology of positive youth development. *American Psychologist, 55*, 175–183.

Regan, P. C., Kocan, E. R., & Whitlock, T. (1998). Ain't love grand! A prototype analysis of the concept of romantic love. *Journal of Social and Personal Relationships, 15*, 411–420.

Reilly, S., & Simmons, K. (2003, June 9). How satisfied are Americans with life? *USA Today*, p. 1A.

Reis, H. T., & Gable, S. L. (2003). Toward a positive psychology of relationships. In C. L. M. Keyes & J. Haidt (Eds.), *Flourishing: Positive psychology and the life well-lived* (pp. 129–159). Washington, DC: American Psychological Association.

Rimland, B. (1982). The altruism paradox. *The Southern Psychologist, 2*(1), 8–9.

Roberts, R. (1982). *Spirituality and human emotion*. Grand Rapids, MI: Eerdmans.

Robitschek, C. (1998). Personal growth initiative: The construct and its measure. *Measurement and Evaluation in Counseling and Development, 30*, 183–198.

Robitschek, C., & Cook, S. W. (1999). The influence of personal growth initiative and coping styles on career exploration and vocational identity. *Journal of Vocational Behavior, 54*, 127–141.

Rodin, J. (1986). Aging and health: Effects of the sense of control. *Science, 233*, 1271–1276.

Rogers, C. R. (1951). *Client-centered therapy*. Boston: Houghton Mifflin.

Rogers, C. R. (1980). *A way of being*. Boston: Houghton Mifflin.

Rosenberg, M. (1989). *Society and the adolescent self-image* (Rev. ed.). Hanover, NH: University Press of New England.

Rowling, J. K. (2003). *Harry Potter and the order of the phoenix*. New York: Scholastic.

Rubin, Z., & Peplau, L. A. (1975). Who believes in a just world? *Journal of Social Issues, 31*, 65–89.

Ryan, R. M., & Deci, E. L. (2000). Self-determination theory and the facilitation of intrinsic motivation, social development, and well-being. *American Psychologist, 55*, 68–78.

Ryan, R. M., Stiller, J., & Lynch, J. H. (1994). Representations of relationships to teachers, parents, and friends as predictors of academic motivation and self-esteem. *Journal of Early Adolescence, 14*, 226–249.

Sabini, J., & Silver, M. (1982). *Moralities of everyday life*. New York: Oxford University Press.

Salovey, P., Mayer, J. D., & Caruso, D. (2002). The positive psychology of emotional intelligence. In C. R. Snyder & S. J. Lopez (Eds.), *Handbook of positive psychology* (pp. 159–171). New York: Oxford University Press.

Sapadin, L. A. (1988). Friendship and gender: Perspectives of professional men and women. *Journal of Social and Personal Relationships, 5*, 387–403.

Scheier, M. F., & Carver, C. S. (1985). Optimism, coping, and health: Assessment and implications of generalized outcome expectancies. *Health Psychology, 4*, 219–247.

Scheier, M. F., Carver, C. S., & Bridges, M. W. (1994). Distinguishing optimism from neuroticism (and trait anxiety, self-mastery, and self-esteem): A reevaluation of the Life Orientation Test. *Journal of Personality and Social Psychology, 67,* 1063–1078.

Scheier, M. F., Mathews, J. F., Owens, G. J., Magovern, G. R., Lefebvre, R., Abbott, R. C., & Carver, J. S. (1989). Dispositional optimism and recovery from coronary artery bypass surgery: The beneficial effects of optimism on physical and psychological well-being. *Journal of Personality and Social Psychology, 57,* 1024–1040.

Schelling, T. C. (1992). Self-command: A new discipline. In G. F. Loewenstein & J. Elster (Eds.), *Choice over time.* New York: Russell Sage Foundation.

Schimmack, U., & Diener, E. (2003). Predictive validity of explicit and implicit self-esteem for subjective well-being. *Journal of Research in Personality, 37,* 100–106.

Schneider, S. L. (2001). In search of realistic optimism: Meaning, knowledge, and warm fuzziness. *American Psychologist, 56,* 250–263.

Schroeder, D. A., Penner, L. A., Dovidio, J. F., & Piliavin, J. A. (1995). *The psychology of helping and altruism.* New York: McGraw-Hill.

Schutte, N. S., Malouff, J. M., Hall, L. E., Haggerty, D. J., Cooper, J. T., Golden, C. J., & Dornheim, L. (1998). Development and validation of a measure of emotional intelligence. *Personality and Individual Differences, 25,* 167–177.

Schwartz, B. (2000). Self-determination: The tyranny of freedom. *American Psychologist, 55,* 79–88.

Schwartz, B., Ward, A., Monterosso, J., Lyubomirsky, S., White, K., & Lehman, D. R. (2002). Maximizing versus satisficing: Happiness is a matter of choice. *Journal of Personality and Social Psychology, 83,* 1178–1197.

Schwarz, N. (1990). Feelings as information: Informational and motivational functions of affective states. In E. T. Higgins & R. M. Sorrentino (Eds.), *Handbook of motivation and emotion, Vol. 2* (pp. 527–561). New York: Guilford Press.

Sears, R. R. (1977). Sources of life satisfaction of the Terman gifted men. *American Psychologist, 32,* 119–128.

Seckel, A. (2002). *More optical illusions.* New York: Carlton Books.

Seligman, M. E. P. (1990). *Learned optimism.* New York: Knopf.

Seligman, M. E. P. (1994). *What you can change and what you can't.* New York: Knopf.

Seligman, M. E. P. (2002). *Authentic happiness: Using the new positive psychology to realize your potential for lasting fulfillment.* New York: Free Press.

Seligman, M. E. P., & Schulman, P. (1986). Explanatory style as a predictor of productivity and quitting among life insurance sales agents. *Journal of Personality and Social Psychology, 50,* 832–838.

Sentyrz, S. M., & Bushman, B. J. (1999). Mirror, mirror on the wall, who's the thinnest one of all? Effects of self-awareness on consumption of full-fat, reduced-fat, and no-fat products. *Journal of Applied Psychology, 83,* 944–949.

Sharabany, R. (1994). Intimate Friendship Scale: Conceptual underpinnings, psychometric properties, and construct validity. *Journal of Social and Personal Relationships, 11,* 449–469.

Sheldon, K. M., Elliot, A. J., Kim, Y., & Kasser, T. (2001). What is satisfying about satisfying events? 10 candidate psychological needs. *Journal of Personality and Social Psychology, 80,* 325–339.

Shepell, W. (2000, June). Building and maintaining a healthy relationship. *UM EAP Newsletter,* pp. 1–2.

Shepperd, J. A., Maroto, J. J., & Pbert, L. A. (1996). Dispositional optimism as a predictor of health changes among cardiac patients. *Journal of Research in Personality, 30,* 517-534.

Simpson, J. A., Campbell, B., & Berscheid, E. (1986). The association between romantic love and marriage: Kephart (1967) twice revisited. *Personality and Social Psychology Bulletin, 12,* 363–372.

Slater, L. (2003). The trouble with self-esteem. In K. G. Duffy (Ed.), *Personal growth and behavior* (23rd ed., pp. 4–7). Guilford, CT: McGraw-Hill/Duskin.

Slevin, C. (2003, May 9). Hiker describes cutting off arm. *Wisconsin State Journal,* pp. A1, A11.

Smedes, L. B. (1982). *How can it be all right when everything is all wrong?* San Francisco: Harper & Row.

Smedes, L. B. (1987). *The making and keeping of commitments.* Grand Rapids, MI: Calvin College.

Smedes, L. B. (2003). *My God and I: A spiritual memoir.* Grand Rapids, MI: Eerdmans.

Snapper, J. (2003, June 14). Minister's tractor trek honors dad. *Grand Rapids Press,* pp. A1, A6.

Snyder, C. R. (1994). *The psychology of hope: You can get there from here.* New York: Free Press.

Snyder, C. R. (1995). Conceptualizing, measuring, and nurturing hope. *Journal of Counseling and Development, 73,* 355–360.

Snyder, C. R., & Feldman, D. B. (2000). Hope for the many: An empowering social agenda. In C. R. Snyder (Ed.), *Handbook of hope: Theory, measures, and applications* (pp. 389–412). San Diego: Academic Press.

Snyder, C. R., Harris, C., Anderson, J. R., Holleran, S. A., Irving, L. M., Sigmon, S. T., et al. (1991). The will and the ways: Development and validation of an individual-differences measure of hope. *Journal of Personality and Social Psychology, 60,* 575–585.

Snyder, C. R., LaPointe, A. B., Crowson, J. J., Jr., & Early, S. (1998). Preferences of high- and low-hope people for self-referential feedback. *Cognition and Emotion, 12,* 807–823.

Snyder, C. R., & Lopez, S. J. (2002). The future of positive psychology: A declaration of independence. In C. R. Snyder & S. J. Lopez (Eds.), *Handbook of positive psychology* (pp. 751–767). New York: Oxford University Press.

Star of "Camelot," "Potter" films. (2002, October 26). *Grand Rapids Press,* p. D9.

Starr, M. (2003, March 24). Michelle Kwan. *Newsweek,* p. 67.

Staub, E. (1999). Aggression and self-esteem. *APA Monitor, 30,* 4.

Staw, B. M., Bell, N. E., & Clausen, J. A. (1986). The dispositional approach to job attitudes. *Administrative Science Quarterly, 31,* 56–77.

Steele, C. M. (1997). A threat in the air: How stereotypes shape intellectual identity and performance. *American Psychologist, 52,* 613–629.

Steiner, A. (2001, September/October). Got time for friends? *Utne Reader,* pp. 67–71.

Sternberg, R. J. (1985). Implicit theories of intelligence, creativity, and wisdom. *Journal of Personality and Social Psychology, 49,* 607–627.

Sternberg, R. J. (1986). *Intelligence applied: Understanding and increasing your intellectual skills.* San Diego, CA: Harcourt Brace Jovanovich.

Sternberg, R. J. (1988). Triangulating love. In R. J. Sternberg & M. L. Barnes (Eds.), *The psychology of love* (pp. 119–138). New Haven, CT: Yale University Press.

Sternberg, R. J. (1996). *Successful intelligence: How practical and creative intelligence determine success in life.* New York: Simon & Schuster.

Sternberg, R. J. (2001). Why schools should teach for wisdom: The balance theory of wisdom in educational settings. *Educational Psychologist, 36,* 227–245.

Sternberg, R. J. (2002a, August). *Wisdom, schooling, and society.* Paper presented at the annual convention of the American Psychological Association, Chicago, IL.

Sternberg, R. J. (Ed.). (2002b). *Why smart people can be so stupid.* New Haven, CT: Yale University Press.

Sternberg, R. J. (2003, March). Responsibility: One of the other three Rs. *Monitor on Psychology,* p. 5.

Sternberg, R. J., & Horvath, J. A. (Eds.). (1999). *Tacit knowledge in professional practice: Researcher and practitioner perspectives.* Mahwah, NJ: Erlbaum.

Sternberg, R. J., & Whitney, C. (1991). *Love the way you want it: Using your head in matters of the heart.* New York: Bantam Books.

Stotland, E. (1969). Exploratory investigations of empathy. In L. Berkowitz (Ed.), *Advances in experimental social psychology* (Vol. 4, pp. 271–314). New York: Academic Press.

Strathman, A., Gleicher, F., Boninger, D. S., & Edwards, C. S. (1994). The consideration of future consequences: Weighing immediate and distant outcomes of behavior. *Journal of Personality and Social Psychology, 66,* 742–752.

Straub, R. O. (2002). *Health psychology.* New York: Worth.

Suh, E., Diener, E., & Fujita, F. (1996). Events and subjective well-being: Only recent events matter. *Journal of Personality and Social Psychology, 70,* 1091–1102.

Suzuki, D. (2000, February 22). A death-bed test for life's priorities. *Sydney Morning Herald.* Retrieved August 22, 2003, from http://old.smh.com.au/news/literarylunches/suzuki.html.

Tangney, J. P. (2000). Humility: Theoretical perspectives, empirical findings and directions for future research. *Journal of Social and Clinical Psychology, 19,* 70–82.

Tangney, J. P., & Baumeister, R. F. (2000). *High self-control predicts good adjustment, less pathology, better grades, and interpersonal success.* Unpublished manuscript, George Mason University, Fairfax, VA.

Tice, D. M., & Baumeister, R. F. (1997). Longitudinal study of procrastination, performance, stress, and health: The costs and benefits of dawdling. *Psychological Science, 8,* 454–458.

Tice, D. M., & Bratslavsky, E. (2000). Giving in to feel good: The place of emotion regulation in the context of general self-control. *Psychological Inquiry, 11,* 149–159.

Titchener, E. B. (1909). *Elementary psychology of the thought processes*. New York: Macmillan.

Tolson, J. (2000, July 3). Into the zone. *U.S. News and World Report*, pp. 38–45.

Triandis, H. C. (1994). *Culture and social behavior*. New York: McGraw-Hill.

Tucker, J. S., & Anders, S. L. (1999). Attachment style, interpersonal perception accuracy, and relationship satisfaction in dating couples. *Personality and Social Psychology Bulletin, 25,* 403–412.

Tuckman, B. W. (1991). The development and concurrent validity of the procrastination scale. *Educational and Psychological Measurement, 51,* 473–480.

Twenge, J. M., & Baumeister, R. F. (2002). Self-control: A limited but renewable resource. In Y. Kashima, M. Foddy, & M. J. Platow (Eds.), *Self and identity: Personal, social, and symbolic* (pp. 57–70). Mahwah, NJ: Erlbaum.

Unger, L., & Thumuluri, L. (1997). Trait empathy and continuous helping. *Journal of Social Behavior and Personality, 12,* 785–800.

Veroff, J., Douvan, E., & Kulka, R. A. (1981). *Mental health in America: Patterns of help-seeking from 1957 to 1976*. New York: Basic Books.

Weber, A. (1984). Teaching social psychology. *Contemporary Social Psychology, 10*(3), 9–10.

Weinstein, N. D. (1980). Unrealistic optimism about future life events. *Journal of Personality and Social Psychology, 39,* 806–820.

Weinstein, N. D. (1982). Unrealistic optimism about susceptibility to health problems. *Journal of Behavioral Medicine, 5,* 441–460.

Williams, K. D., & Zadro, L. (2001). Ostracism: On being ignored, excluded, and rejection. In M. R. Leary (Ed.), *Interpersonal rejection*. New York: Oxford University Press.

Wilson, C. (2003, February 5). A mere 10 seconds can stretch a smile for a lifetime. *USA Today*, p. 1D.

Witvliet, C. V. O., Ludwig, T., & Vander Laan, K. (2001). Granting forgiveness or harboring grudges: Implications for emotion, physiology, and health. *Psychological Science, 121,* 117–123.

Wright, P. H. (1998). Toward an expanded orientation to the study of sex differences in friendship. In D. J. Canary & K. Dindia (Eds.), *Sex differences and similarities in communication: Critical essays and empirical investigations of sex and gender in interaction* (pp. 41–63). Mahwah, NJ: Erlbaum.

Wrzesniewski, A., McCauley, C., Rozin, P., & Schwartz, B. (1997). Jobs, careers, and callings: People's relations to their work. *Journal of Research in Personality, 31,* 21–33.

Wrzesniewski, A., Rozin, P., & Bennett, G. (2003). Working, playing, and eating: Making the most of most moments. In C. L. M. Keyes & J. Haidt (Eds.), *Flourishing: Positive psychology and the life well-lived* (pp. 185–204). Washington, DC: American Psychological Association.

Wu, P. (1988). *Goal structures of materialists versus nonmaterialists*. Unpublished doctoral dissertation. University of Michigan, Ann Arbor.

Yancey, P. (1989). *I was just wondering*. Nashville, TN: Word.

Yoshinobu, L. R. (1989). *Construct validation of the Hope Scale: Agency and pathways components*. Unpublished master's thesis. University of Kansas, Lawrence.

Index